ACCENTS ON SHAKESPEARE

General editor: TERENCE HAWKES

Shakespeare and Modern Theatre

Shakespeare's works are now performed for an increasingly diverse cultural market. At the start of the twenty-first century film, video and live performance have overtaken the printed book as the main ways in which people are introduced to Shakespeare. Therefore, is there any reason to ask people to read Shakespeare's plays any more?

The essays in this volume explore this question and the institutional practices that shape contemporary performances of Shakespeare's plays. The book gathers together a particularly strong line-up of contributors from across the literary–performative divide to examine the relationship between Shakespeare, the 'culture industries', modernism and live performance.

Contributors: Hugh Grady, Paul Yachnin, Catherine Graham, Jean-Michel Déprats, Sarah Werner, W. B. Worthen, Irena R. Makaryk, Maarten van Dijk.

Michael Bristol is Greenshields Professor of English at McGill University in Montreal. **Kathleen McLuskie** teaches in the English Department at the University of Southampton. **Christopher Holmes** is a Ph.D. student at McGill University in Montreal.

ACCENTS ON SHAKESPEARE
General editor: TERENCE HAWKES

It is more than twenty years since the New Accents series helped to establish 'theory' as a fundamental and continuing feature of the study of literature at the undergraduate level. Since then, the need for short, powerful 'cutting edge' accounts of and comments on new developments has increased sharply. In the case of Shakespeare, books with this sort of focus have not been readily available. **Accents on Shakespeare** aims to supply them.

Accents on Shakespeare volumes will either 'apply' theory, or broaden and adapt it in order to connect with concrete teaching concerns. In the process, they will also reflect and engage with the major developments in Shakespeare studies of the last ten years.

The series will lead as well as follow. In pursuit of this goal it will be a two-tiered series. In addition to affordable, 'adoptable' titles aimed at modular undergraduate courses, it will include a number of research-based books. Spirited and committed, these second-tier volumes advocate radical change rather than stolidly reinforcing the status quo.

IN THE SAME SERIES

Shakespeare and Appropriation
Edited by Christy Desmet and Robert Sawyer

Shakespeare without Women
Dympna Callaghan

Philosophical Shakespeares
Edited by John J. Joughin

Shakespeare and Modernity: Early Modern to Millennium
Edited by Hugh Grady

Marxist Shakespeares
Edited by Jean E. Howard and Scott Cutler Shershow

Shakespeare in Psychoanalysis
Philip Armstrong

Shakespeare and Modern Theatre: The Performance of Modernity
Edited by Michael Bristol, Kathleen McLuskie and Christopher Holmes

Shakespeare and Feminist Performance: Ideology on Stage
Sarah Werner

Shakespeare and Modern Theatre

The performance of modernity

Edited by
MICHAEL BRISTOL and
KATHLEEN McLUSKIE, with
CHRISTOPHER HOLMES

London and New York

First published 2001
by Routledge
11 New Fetter Lane,
London EC4P 4EE

Simultaneously published in
the USA and Canada
by Routledge
29 West 35th Street,
New York, NY 10001

Routledge is an imprint of the Taylor
& Francis Group

Selection and editorial matter
© 2001 Michael Bristol and
Kathleen McLuskie; individual
chapters © the contributors

Typeset in Baskerville by Keystroke,
Jacaranda Lodge, Wolverhampton
Printed and bound in Great Britain
by TJ International Ltd, Padstow,
Cornwall

British Library Cataloguing in
Publication Data

A catalogue record for this book is
available from the British Library

Library of Congress Cataloging in
Publication Data

Shakespeare and modern theatre: the
performance of modernity / [edited by]
Michael Bristol and Kathleen
McLuskie.
p. cm. — (Accents on Shakespeare)
Includes bibliographical references
(p.) and index.
1. Shakespeare, William,
1564–1616—Stage history—1950–
2. Theater—Production and
direction—History—20th century.
3. Shakespeare, William,
1564–1616—Dramatic production.
4. Postmodernism (Literature)
5. Modernism (Literature)
I. Bristol, Michael D., 1940–
II. McLuskie, Kathleen. III. Series.

PR31000 .S52 2001
792.9′5—dc21   00–065307

ISBN 0–415–21984–1 (hbk)
ISBN 0–415–21985–X (pbk)

Contents

Contributors

Michael Bristol is Greenshields Professor of English Literature at McGill University. He is the author of *Big Time Shakespeare, Shakespeare's America / America's Shakespeare,* and *Carnival and Theatre.*

Jean-Michel Déprats is Senior Lecturer in English Literature and Theatre Studies at the University of Nanterre (Paris X). He has written many articles in the field of Shakespeare studies, in particular on Shakespearean theatre productions and on problems of translation. He has done more than twenty translations of Shakespeare's plays for the principal theatre companies in France, including la Comédie Française, le Theâtre de l'Odéon, le TNP de Villeurbanne. His translations extend beyond Shakespeare to include J. M. Synge's *The Playboy of the Western World,* an adaptation of Virginia Woolf's *Orlando,* Oscar Wilde's *The Importance of Being Earnest* and John Ford's *'Tis Pity She's a Whore.* He is now completing a bilingual edition of *Shakespeare's Complete Works* for Gallimard.

Hugh Grady is Professor of English at Beaver College and author of *The Modernist Shakespeare: Critical Texts in a Material World* (1991) and *Shakespeare's Universal Wolf: Studies in Early Modern Reification* (1996). He has also published numerous articles in *Modern Language Review, Comparative Literature, Shakespeare Quarterly, Textual Practice* and elsewhere.

Catherine Graham is an Assistant Professor of Drama in the School of Art, Drama and Music at McMaster University. Her research interests include the study of dramatic performance as a form of social thought, issues in cross-cultural performance, and the theoretical and practical problems posed by interdisciplinary approaches to performance. She has published on Irish, English-Canadian, Québecois and First Nations' popular theatre and is currently working on a book-length study on community-based theatre in Canada, the USA, the United Kingdom and France.

Christopher Holmes is completing his Ph.D. dissertation on 'Calendars, Customs, and Early Modern Literature' at McGill University. His article 'Why Brutus Can't Tell Time: Interpretive Fashion and *Julius Caesar*' will appear in *Early Modern Literary Studies*.

Kathleen McLuskie is Professor of English at the University of Southampton. In 1999 she became Deputy Vice-Chancellor at the University of Southampton. Her research centres on early modern theatre with a special interest in feminist criticism and theory, the commercialization of theatre and post-colonial cultural production. She is currently editing *Macbeth* for Arden III and working on a book on the commercialization of early modern theatre. Her publications include: *Renaissance Dramatists* (1989), *Dekker and Heywood: Professional Dramatists* (1994), and, with Jennifer Uglow, an edition of *The Duchess of Malfi*, by John Webster (1989).

Irena R. Makaryk is Professor of English at the University of Ottawa. Her teaching and research interests embrace Shakespeare, Renaissance, comparative, and Slavic drama. She is the author of numerous articles, editor or co-editor of eight books, including *The Encyclopedia of Contemporary Literary Theory* and (with Diana Brydon) co-editor of '*A world elsewhere*': *Shakespeare in Canada*, the first book to examine the reception and history of Shakespeare in Canada. She is currently at work on a major project on Les' Kurbas, Shakespeare and the early Soviet period.

Maarten van Dijk teaches drama at the University of Waterloo. He has performed, directed, and written on Brecht and Shakespeare. Since 1994 he has been managing editor of *The Brecht Yearbook*.

Sarah Werner has taught Shakespeare and theatre classes at the University of Pennsylvania, McGill University and George Washington University. Her book *Shakespeare and Feminist Performance: Ideology on Stage* is forthcoming from Routledge.

W. B. Worthen, Professor and Chair of the Department of Dramatic Art at the University of California, Berkeley, is the author of *The Idea of the Actor: Drama and the Ethics of Performance*; *Modern Drama and the Rhetoric of Theater*; and *Shakespeare and the Authority of Performance*. He has written widely on drama and performance theory, and is currently completing a book entitled *Shakespearean Performativity*.

Paul Yachnin is Professor of English at the University of British Columbia. His first book is *Stage-Wrights: Shakespeare, Jonson, Middleton, and the Making of Theatrical Value* (1996); his second, co-authored with Anthony Dawson, is *The Culture of Playgoing in Shakespeare's England: A Collaborative Debate* (Cambridge, forthcoming). He is an editor of the forthcoming Oxford edition of *The Works of Thomas Middleton*, and editor of *Richard II*, also under contract with Oxford. His book-in-progress, *Shakespeare and the Dimension of Literature*, argues that literature's political importance is an effect of the long rather than the short term.

General editor's preface

In our century, the field of literary studies has rarely been a settled, tranquil place. Indeed, for over two decades, the clash of opposed theories, prejudices and points of view has made it more of a battlefield. Echoing across its most beleaguered terrain, the student's weary complaint 'Why can't I just pick up Shakespeare's plays and read them?' seems to demand a sympathetic response.

Nevertheless, we know that modern spectacles will always impose their own particular characteristics on the vision of those who unthinkingly don them. This must mean, at the very least, that an apparently simple confrontation with, or pious contemplation of, the text of a 400-year-old play can scarcely supply the grounding for an adequate response to its complex demands. For this reason, a transfer of emphasis from 'text' towards 'context' has increasingly been the concern of critics and scholars since the Second World War: a tendency that has perhaps reached its climax in more recent movements such as New Historicism or Cultural Materialism.

A consideration of the conditions, social, political or economic within which the play came to exist, from which its derives, and to which it speaks will certainly make legitimate demands on the attention of any well-prepared student nowadays. Of course, the serious pursuit of those interests will also inevitably start to undermine ancient and inherited prejudices, such as the supposed distinction between 'foreground' and 'background' in literary studies. And even the slightest awareness of the pressures of gender or of race, or the most cursory glance at the role played by that strange creature 'Shakespeare' in our cultural politics, will reinforce a similar turn towards questions that sometimes appear scandalously 'non-literary'. It seems clear that very different and unsettling notions of the ways in which literature might be addressed can hardly be avoided. The worrying truth is that nobody can just pick up Shakespeare's plays and read them. Perhaps – even more worrying – they never could.

The aim of *Accents on Shakespeare* is to encourage students and teachers to explore the implications of this situation by means of an engagement with the major developments in Shakespeare studies over recent years. It will offer a continuing and challenging reflection on those ideas through a series of multi- and single-author books which will also supply the basis for adapting or augmenting them in the light of changing concerns.

Accents on Shakespeare also intends to lead as well as follow. In pursuit of this goal, the series will operate on more than one level. In addition to titles aimed at modular undergraduate courses, it will include a number of books embodying polemical, strongly argued cases aimed at expanding the horizons of a specific aspect of the subject and at challenging the preconceptions on which it is based. These volumes will not be learned 'monographs' in any traditional sense. They will, it is hoped, offer a platform for the work of the liveliest younger scholars and teachers at their most outspoken and provocative. Committed and contentious, they will be reporting from the forefront of current critical activity and will have something new to say. The fact that each book in the series promises a Shakespeare inflected in terms of a specific urgency should ensure that, in the present as in the recent past, the accent will be on change.

Terence Hawkes

Acknowledgements

This volume of essays originally grew out of a conference on 'Shakespeare and Theatrical Modernism' that took place at McGill University in October 1997. The editors want to express their thanks to the members of the Shakespeare in Performance Research Team who organized that conference, Catherine Graham, Leanore Lieblein, Patrick Neilson, Ed Pechter, Keith Richards, John Ripley, Denis Salter, and Catherine Shaw. We also wish to acknowledge the work done by the team's graduate research assistants, Brad Clissold, Felicity Enayat, Wes Folkerth, Shellee Hendricks, and Christopher Holmes. Financial support for the team's research and for the conference was provided through the generosity of the Fonds pour la Formation de Chercheurs et l'Aide à la Recherche of the Québec Ministry of Education. Additional support for the conference came from Dr John Harrod, McGill University Faculty of Graduate Studies and Research, Faculty of Arts, The Department of English, The British Council, the Consulat Général de France à Québec, and the Zeller Family Foundation. Terry Hawkes has supported the project from its inception and we are particularly grateful for his work in helping us to bring the Introduction into better focus. Finally, we want to express our very special thanks to our Assistant Editor, Christopher Holmes. His hard work and his critical intelligence have made it possible for this volume to exist in the real world.

Introduction

MICHAEL BRISTOL and
KATHLEEN McLUSKIE

The essays in this volume explore the institutional practices that shape contemporary performances of Shakespeare's plays. At the start of the twenty-first century, film, video, and to a more limited extent, live performance have overtaken the printed book as the primary means of access to cultural experience for a significant fraction of the population. Many students have their defining encounter with Shakespeare by way of Baz Luhrmann's *Romeo + Juliet* or Kenneth Branagh's *Henry V*, films that have been widely praised for their accessibility. The current preoccupation with the accessibility of performances has apparently been achieved at the expense of those traditional notions of authority that had such tremendous urgency for Shakespeare and his contemporaries. There's a whole lot of Shakespeare going on and modern performances often take outlandish liberties with these valued works. But performance is not well understood as a derivative form that owes its social dignity to the originary force of a text. The stage has a constitutive power or authority in its own right (Weimann 2000: 1–17). The common aim in these essays is to take the notion of performance seriously in both a theoretical and a historical sense. But the contributors here understand that it doesn't help to replace reified notions of textual authority with a vague, diffuse and poorly delineated notion of 'performativity'.

Given the widespread availability and the convenient packaging of Shakespeare in performance, is there any reason to expect people to read the plays any more? After all, whatever Shakespeare wrote was intended as the script for staged performance, not for study in a printed book. And even the notion of an authoritative text has been discredited by recent developments in editorial scholarship. The diminished authority of the printed text has been accompanied by accelerating change, instability, and a relentless demand for innovation in the performance of Shakespeare's plays. The changing institutions of modern cultural production, in particular the development of new technologies and the advance of commercial mass culture, have fundamentally transformed the ways in which theatre artists struggle to realize their artistic vision. Theatrical producers, actors, designers, as well as cultural consumers have to find ways to cope with the exigencies of global markets, universal diaspora, and instantaneous mass communication.

Coleridge thought it would be better if Shakespeare's plays were never staged at all. The only way to experience the real pleasures of the verbal imagination, he claimed, is through the silent encounter between the written text and the isolated reader. And it remains a commonplace, at least among the reading public, that the movie is never as good as the book. But for much of the twentieth century it has seemed possible for serious readers to enjoy Shakespeare on stage without giving up the more difficult pleasures of traditional literary experience. This sense of a reasonable accommodation between printed text and theatrical performance is the guiding intuition in Helen Gardner's essay on 'The Directors Theatre' (1982). Gardner was an editor of early modern texts with a profound commitment to the idea of authorial intention and meaning. Still, she clearly enjoyed the way his plays were staged, at least in 'the years from the early nineteen-twenties to 1960, when Shakespeare in the study and Shakespeare in the theatre came together' (Gardner 1982: 67). The 'straightforward playing' of actors in this tradition provided vivid emotional experience without challenging the authority of the text as it was understood by meticulously trained readers.

Gardner's work as a textual editor was undoubtedly central to her experience as a theatre-goer. The reconciliation of text with performance during the 'classic age' was fully achieved when theatrical producers demonstrated their willingness to rely on professional redactions of early modern quarto and folio editions. The costly theatrical spectacles of the Restoration and Victorian stage disappeared as much closer attention was paid to the forms of poetic language transcribed in the early texts. Even Coleridge might have been able to enjoy these productions. Although Gardner herself doesn't make the connection, her account of the 'classic age' of Shakespearean performance corresponds roughly to the great period of the high modernism in theatre and in the arts more generally. It would be easy to show what high modernist aesthetics looked like since its visual contours are clearly evident in architecture, painting and industrial design. But it is far less easy to say exactly what the scenic environment of early-twentieth-century modernism was really all about or even to identify its most definitive forms of expression.

Hugh Grady, in his *Modernist Shakespeare* (1991), has argued that Shakespeare gave to modernism an unusually powerful resource for articulating its own contradictions. Shakespeare's themes of power, self-fashioning, and social transformation express the pathos of Western modernity with extraordinary vividness. At the same time his works represent a powerful desire for social coherence and meaning. For the modernist theatre, Shakespeare represents the possibility for the celebration of modernity's themes of emancipation and for resistance to modernity's chronic dislocations. Richard Halpern's *Shakespeare Among the Moderns* argues that 'high modernism' dominated reception of Shakespeare during the first half of the twentieth century and continues to exert a decisive influence right up to the present (Halpern 1997: 2). Halpern believes that the success of modernism in 'securing a base' in universities is an important reason for its continuing influence. More important however, is 'the fact that the modernist reading responded to a novel set of social, cultural, economic and political developments which have evolved, but not disappeared. The modernists' reading of Shakespeare has not vanished, because the world that gave birth to it has not' (Halpern 1997: 2).

In her essay on 'The Directors Theatre' Helen Gardner chronicles the waning of this paradigm, not only for theatre but for literature as well. The theatre she enjoyed so much during the 'classic age' of the repertory companies was a reader's theatre, a theatre oriented to the rewards and the pleasures of the printed text. This theatrical regime came to an abrupt end for her with Peter Brook's landmark production of *A Midsummer Night's Dream*. Helen Gardner liked and trusted actors. She acknowledges that

she enjoyed the exuberance and playfulness of their work in
Brook's *Dream*. But when she learned of the intellectual collab-
oration linking Brook's production with Jan Kott's *Shakespeare
Our Contemporary* (1964) she felt somehow violated.

> I had no idea that I was witnessing a sex-orgy, that Oberon
> was punishing his wife Titania by making her commit bestiality,
> or that in the persons of Oberon and Titania, Theseus and
> Hippolyta were working out their own sexual problems, or any
> of the dreary absurdities and solemn nonsense with which Kott
> has smeared the play.
>
> (Gardner 1982: 71)

The significance of Gardner's grievance is easy to misunderstand.
It's not just the sex. What ended for Gardner with Brook's *Dream*
was her belief that Shakespeare's plays could actually be performed without compromising the experience of literature as a
practice of disciplined and careful reading. It suddenly became
apparent that performance could succeed perfectly well without
the support of a large, well-informed reading public and even
without literature itself.

Gardner's feelings should not be dismissed as feckless nostalgia; her sense of loss has been reiterated many times (Kermode
1999). It has been central to the contest over Shakespeare that
has recurred throughout the twentieth century. For although
a pleasurable relationship between text and reader is still available, it has no unique purchase on the cultural production of
public discourse about Shakespeare. The experience of reading
Shakespeare can only be shared through other institutions of
culture – the theatre, the education system, the literary journals
– institutions that compromise the intense personal connection
between text and reader. In any case, it is of the essence of live
theatre that its moments of pleasure cannot be reproduced
or repeated; they leave, as Prospero puts it, not a wrack behind.
What is left is the endless echoing discussion *in language* of their
aesthetic and their meaning. So Gardner enjoyed the Brook
production but hated the explanatory critical gloss.

Perhaps because of her recoil from a new, sexualized, discourse
of theatre criticism, Gardner did not dwell on the important
continuities between Brook's production and the work of the
theatre practitioners of the early twentieth century: the extent

to which both articulated the intellectual crisis of modernism. Peter Brook's restless, eclectic search for new theatrical styles has always been in the service of a theatrical experience whose satisfying sense of authenticity will transcend the language of Shakespeare's plays, allowing an almost mystical communication between performance and audience, a union of past and present unmediated by institutions or the material circumstances of particular performance events:

> The Shakespearean theatre speaks simultaneously in performance to everyone, it is 'all things to all men', not in general, but at the moment when it's being played, in actual performance. It does so by reconciling a mystery, because it is simultaneously the most esoteric theatre that we know in a living language, and the most popular theatre.
> (Quoted in Williams 1988: 144)

These words could be echoed in numerous statements made about theatre since the early twentieth century and they would be endorsed by many theatre practitioners working today. However they elide a number of key concepts which are much harder to reconcile in material practice. The real 'mystery' at the heart of theatre is in the gap between the commercial realities of play production and the aspiration to communicate with a coherent, inclusive audience.

Every performance of a play by Shakespeare requires complicated negotiation between the demands of the play-text and the exigencies of the moment of its performance. The thought and feeling of the author continues to resonate even in historically distant contexts. At the same time, an actor's performance can reveal a semantic intonation that would not have been intelligible to the author's own public. The straightforward playing that Helen Gardner enjoyed so much in the repertory theatres of the classic age seemed to her to make genuine dialogue between these terms possible for the first time. This is the great achievement of the modernist theatre, for which Gardner credited William Poel's pioneering use of the platform stage, Gordon Craig's minimal, non-representational scene designs, and Harley Granville-Barker's work with 'virtually uncut' quarto and folio texts (Gardner 1982: 65). The governing impulse in these artistic initiatives is frankly and very boldly experimental, rejecting the lavishly overblown style of the Victorian stage with its lumbering machinery in favour of the stripped-down immediacy of the actor reading 'the words Shakespeare had written for them to speak' (1982: 65). In the theatre of the 'classic age' as Helen Gardner conceives it, experimentation is welcome and indeed necessary. But the aim of theatrical innovation is discovery of what is in the text's expressive structure.

One way to discover what's in a Shakespeare play is to reconstruct its historical context, a course of action recommended by Brecht: 'What really matters is to play these old works historically, which means setting them in powerful contrast to our own time' (1965: 63). William Poel, Harley Granville-Barker, William Bridges Adams and Nugent Monck all worked from the premise that historical fidelity to Elizabethan staging practices would permit the essence of the play to reveal itself. The success of these Elizabethan reconstructions enabled theatre artists to discover and to work with the underlying performance structure of the Shakespearean script. Modernist productions of Shakespeare gradually began to move away from the historicist preoccupation with literal fidelity to early modern forms of theatrical representation. Directors and designers began to focus on the formal qualities of Shakespearean works – space, structure, language, and above all visual style.

These concerns were expressed in a trend towards abstraction, especially marked in Edward Gordon Craig's scenography. Though his scenic devices of flats and screens were often comically impractical – he suggested vaguely that they needed no more than 'three girls, three pairs of scissors & innumerable pieces of paper' for their realisations (quoted in Flannery 1976: 270) – his overall aim, like Brook's, was to substitute abstract mood for the specificities of historical reproduction and pictorial scenery. The use of masks and the dominance of the scenic architecture subordinated character and narrative to a more abstract evocation of Beauty. As he put it in the first issue of *The Mask*, his manifesto journal of the new theatre movement:

> Once let the meaning of this word 'Beauty' begin to be thoroughly felt once more in the theatre, and we may say that the awakening day of the theatre is near.
>
> (Quoted in Flannery 1976: 246)

The problem of Shakespearean production as Craig understands it is to discover the durable meanings sedimented in the archaic language of his plays and to make that meaning transparent using the visual arts of costume and scene design. His desire, in effect, is to rewrite Shakespeare in a modernist style, to articulate the complex textuality of the play as an ensemble of abstract visual images.

Unfortunately for Craig his projects were repeatedly thwarted by the material and economic constraints of a theatre that worked in the real world as a commercial enterprise. His entire theatrical career was dogged by conflict with producers whose crass philistinism, as Craig saw it, deformed his scenic designs in the interests of successful commerce. The opposition between artistic vision and the practical realities of theatre was summed up when Craig exhibited his designs for *Macbeth* to coincide with the opening of Beerbohm Tree's 1911 production of the play. Tree had been persuaded to reject Craig's designs by his chief scene painter, Joseph Harker, on the grounds that they would not be realizable on stage. They could excite the imagination as free standing works of art but could not survive the material demands of performance. When Craig's designs for *Macbeth* were commissioned by the Broadway producer George C. Tyler, he refused to co-operate with the production team. He sent over sketches, ironically signed C.p.b (Craig's pot-boiler).

Craig's efforts to find a production worthy of his designs for *Macbeth* show him grappling with the gap between text and meaning. His vision of the play emphasized its insubstantial mystery, described in terms that seem to deny the possibility of precise theatrical realizations.

> It is just those figures which seldom shape themselves more definitely than a cloud's shadow, that give the play its mysterious beauty, its splendour, its depth and immensity, and in which lies its primary tragic element.
>
> (Quoted in Sheren 1971: 45)

Craig was enough of a theatre practitioner to know that something must appear on the stage but the examples he chose did not refer to the language or narrative of Shakespeare's play. They offer, instead, iconic theatrical moments. In some cases these iconic moments have no part in the text. For example, in his discussion of the witches, he suggests:

> We should see them . . . offering the woman a crown for her
> husband, flattering her beyond measure, whispering to her of
> her superior force, of her superior intellect; whispering to him
> of his bravery.
>
> (Quoted in Sheren 1971: 45)

It's clear from this statement that Craig did not intend to rely
exclusively on the background knowledge of a well-read audience
to fill in gaps in the dramatic narrative. The role of the production
designer is to make the text's narrative meaning visible using the
existing technologies of theatre.

Modernist exploration of Shakespearean performance often
attempts to speak even more directly to the interests of a contemporary audience through the self-conscious application of
specifically modern psychological or social paradigms. Les'
Kurbas's 1924 Soviet Ukrainian modernist production of *Macbeth*
called for a rejection of the didactic 'pathos' of earlier literature,
as well as the erasure of the boundaries between art forms and
genres, between high and low. For Kurbas, modernism meant
the rejection of a 'museum' Shakespeare in favour of a classic
reworked to fit the demands of the new times. The influence of
Freud was strongly apparent during the administration of Tyrone
Guthrie at the Old Vic in London. Guthrie admired Freud and
he consulted with Ernest Jones for his productions of *Hamlet*
and *Othello*. His *Othello* and *Coriolanus* explored the homo-erotic
and homosexual implications of these works in vivid and controversial ways. Orson Welles' productions in the mid-thirties of
Macbeth, Julius Caesar, and, again, *Coriolanus*, focused less on the
sexual psychology of characters and more on the contemporary
political resonances of the plays. Welles drew his inspiration for
interpretation and stage design from newsreels chronicling the
rise of Mussolini and Hitler, the fall of Ethiopia, and the burning
of the German Reichstag. More recent examples of this trend are
Michael Bogdanov's *Measure for Measure* at Stratford, Ontario
(1985) and Silviu Purcarete's *Titus Andronicus* at the Craiova
National Theatre in Rumania (1993).

Late Victorian actor-managers like Beerbohm Tree and Henry
Irving had seen their theatres as institutions for the edification
of a broad, inclusive public and the improvement of popular
morality. But the modernist impulse in Shakespearean production was often frankly élitist. Modernist directors like Poel focused
on formal content and structure without attempting to bring their

productions into line with public morality. Poel, like a number of modernist aestheticians, painters, and poets addressed his work to an intellectual élite. Lawrence Levine has argued that towards the end of the nineteenth century an emerging taste community of privileged élites adopts the preference for taking Shakespeare seriously, and that this preference entails a strong intolerance for the characteristic forms of popular art (Levine 1988: 11–83). It may well be that the rejection of a popularly accessible Shakespeare by cultural élites was on the whole nothing more than the snobbery of newly wealthy social groups. For modernist critics like Van Wyck Brooks, T. E. Hulme, and T. S. Eliot, however, the preference for élite and exclusive art forms was something more than just supercilious dismissal of popular taste (Bristol 1996: 88–9). Modernism was in some respects a movement to defend high culture against the threatening encroachment not of traditional popular culture, but of a commercialized mass culture of pulp fiction, film and other media.

The supposed antidote to the vitiated culture of commercial entertainment has been, for some artists in the tradition of modernist theatre, a culture of 'the people'. Peter Brook's invocation of a Shakespearean theatre which would be '"all things to all men"... simultaneously the most esoteric theatre that we know in a living language, and the most popular theatre' echoed Edward Gordon Craig's more categorical assertion that 'The theatre was for the people, and always should be for the people' (quoted in Flannery 1976: 246). As so often in Craig's writing, 'the people' for whom he wished to create a new theatre were an abstraction rather than a specifically defined segment of the larger population. His sentimental view of popular theatre invoked a continuity with a mythologized past and drew on ideas about the supposed coherent populism of Shakespeare's original audience. Nevertheless, this ideal of popular support, a return to the cohesive values of an inclusive society animated many of the most influential movements of the time, including W. B. Yeats's attempts to create a theatre based on peasant myth or Meyerhold's celebration of carnivalesque theatrical forms.

The division between 'the people' and 'a select company of dilettanti' marks an important shift in the discourse of theatre and one which was central to modernism. That shift was further elaborated in Meyer Schapiro's 1937 essay on 'The Nature of Abstract Art'. Writing on early impressionist painting, he described its appeal to 'those imaginative members of the middle class who accepted the norms of freedom, but lacked the economic means to attain them, and were spiritually torn by a sense of helpless isolation in an anonymous, indifferent mass' (quoted in Clark 1985: 1). Schapiro's description of this class does not correspond with the actual purchasers and champions of impressionist art. What's important in Schapiro's analysis, however, is the recognition of the extent to which controversies over abstract art embodied the negotiations of classes within a commercial culture. In the case of the theatre, the conditions of its production inflected the terms slightly differently. The fraction of the middle class with aesthetic aspirations is not ordinarily in a position to acquire expensive private art collections, but can usually budget for at least occasional nights out at the theatre. But the resistant materiality of theatre itself blurs the opposition between art and commerce. Theatre is, practically speaking, identical with show business and it can only sustain itself through some kind of accommodation to the demands of mass culture.

T. S. Eliot, perhaps the most influential of literary modernists, recognizes the complexity of the fractious relationship between show business and serious art. Much of his best-known poetry seems motivated by a powerful aversion to popular culture. But his essay on 'Marie Lloyd' in fact reveals a more positive attitude, applauding the popular art of the music-hall. And in *The Waste Land* he makes a deliberate effort to incorporate the rhythms and the intonations of vernacular speech. One of the more striking ironies of the High Modernist discomfort with mass culture may well be that T. S. Eliot's poetry has now reached a huge audience through the musical comedy version of *Cats* precisely at a moment when hardly anybody can see the point of reading *The Waste Land*. Eliot's 'serious' poetry represents the forms of close engagement with the printed book that have declined in both saliency and authority with the growth of mass media. The example of *Cats*, however, suggests the possibility of a fundamental self-transformation of cultural experience, a kind of postmodern life after death for the great works of literature. Theatre no longer counts on an audience of well-educated readers with wide experience of literature. Instead it looks for ways to adapt to other, more restless habits of cultural consumption created by typically late modern institutions such as tourism, theme parks, and the shopping mall.

Shakespeare's 'works' are now 'performed' for an increasingly diversified cultural market. The postmodern aesthetics of irreverent quotation and pastiche are evident in derivative forms such as Tom Stoppard's *Rosencrantz and Guildenstern are Dead* (1967). This 'work' is perhaps more accurately described as a theatrical commentary on *Hamlet* that appeals to people who haven't actually read the play. The impulse to alter Shakespeare's works radically has been described by Alan Sinfield (following Jonathan Dollimore) as 'creative vandalism' (Sinfield 1992: 101). This radically original theatrical creativity is evident in Heiner Müller's *Hamletmaschine* (1983), Margaret Clarke's *Gertrude and Ophelia* (1987), Ann-Marie MacDonald's *Goodnight Desdemona, Good Morning Juliet* (1990), Normand Chaurette's *Les Reines* (1991), and Robert Lepage's *Elsineur* (1995). The same impulse is apparent in developments within contemporary popular culture. Franco Zeffirelli's recent *Hamlet* (1990) and Kenneth Branagh's *Henry V* (1989), *Much Ado About Nothing* (1993), and *Love's Labour's Lost* (2000), along with Disney's *The Lion King* (1994), represent what might be termed a 'new populism' in Shakespearean performance. Avant-gardiste and postmodern Shakespeare has also found a wide audience through films such as Gus Van Sant's *My Own Private Idaho* (1992), Peter Greenaway's *Prospero's Books* (1991), and André Fortier's *Une Histoire Inventée* (1990). None of these works exhibits any deference to Shakespeare's texts, or to the community of serious readers of the printed book. Just as Helen Gardner feared, the authority of literature no longer governs the world of Shakespearean performance.

Baz Luhrman's enormously successful film version of *Romeo + Juliet* (1996) mockingly pre-empts the traditional values of literary criticism by signalling the director's awareness of the play's theatrical origins and its many subsequent performances. The tattered posters for Shakespeare plays on the city walls, the empty shell of the 'Globe' theatre's proscenium arch on the beach, the Shakespearean costumes of the masked ball all defy the disapproval of critics by offering them the seductive pleasure of recognizing references assumed not to be available to the teenage audience. The fragmented nature of the postmodern audience is both acknowledged and then made whole by the sheer range of diverse pleasures which the film has to offer. The same defiance of academic criticism is also evident in Tom Stoppard's script for John Madden's *Shakespeare in Love* (1998). Because of superior technology and finance, the film can create a simulacrum of historical authenticity far more convincing than anything dreamed of by Poel or Monck. The images of the teeming muddy streets of Elizabethan London draw on familiar cinematic conventions but the carefully researched detail of costumes and props, together with the use of 'real' Elizabethan country houses for some settings provide a spectrum of pleasures which it seems churlish to deconstruct. Moreover, the project of deconstruction has been pre-empted by knowing references to Shakespeare's father's dunghill, the death of Christopher Marlowe, the youth of John Webster and even, in passing, to John Taylor the Water poet. The film is already wised-up about itself. By knowing as much as, if not more than the critic, the film leaves the discourse of analysis limping lamely behind it. The intellectual crises of modernism – over the role of the artist in commercial culture, over the relationship of contemporary culture to the past, over tensions between the professional and the amateur and the struggle against the institutions of the censoring state – are subsumed within the comic pleasures of the narrative. The collective pleasures of making and participating in theatre are presented as the alchemy which will unite the queen and the commoner, seducing even the hard-bitten entrepreneur with a bit part which will include him in the collective enterprise. The modernist anxiety over how to realize the fulfilling and socially cohering aims of theatre is turned into a joke. As the production of 'Romeo and Ethel the Pirate's Daughter' lurches from crisis to crisis and anxious actors and entrepreneurs ask how it will ever come off, the Henslowe character mischievously replies in the terms used by theatre people throughout the twentieth century, 'It's a mystery!'

In this collection of essays, Hugh Grady's 'Modernity, Modernism and Postmodernism in the Twentieth-Century's Shakespeare' agrees with Helen Gardner's intuition that response to Shakespeare has shifted radically since about 1980. Unlike Gardner, however, Grady is able to take a dispassionate view of these postmodern transformations of Shakespeare. Grady maintains that the modernist Shakespeare of the early twentieth century was already a deeply conflicted and contradictory phenomenon. The modernist paradigm now must coexist with an emerging postmodern Shakespeare who expresses the pathos of twentieth century society through a set of new aesthetic 'lenses' which enable us to discover new meaning in these classic texts.

Grady accounts for the coexistence of vastly different styles of production as a response to the differentiation of markets within a capitalist cultural economy. As Grady explains, 'the capitalist market, with its demands for the ever new, creates one kind of powerful stimulus for change' but as he also notes 'there is a desire for new kinds of dissent and rebellion as older forms age and become contained' (below, p. 27).

In 'To Kill a King: The Modern Politics of Bardicide', Paul Yachnin is concerned with the possibility of oppositional rewriting of Shakespeare in modern theatre, literature, and mass media. Bourdieu's ideas about 'position-takings' in cultural production are used here to reveal the institutional politics behind ideological critiques of Shakespeare in oppositional figures such as Charles Marowitz, Jane Smiley and even Arnold Schwarzenegger. The essay also builds on Mikhail Bakhtin's intuition that the great works of literature are shared as well as contested property. The theoretical work of Bourdieu and Bahktin has helped us to understand the extent to which commerce inflects a range of relations beyond those of buyers and sellers in the field of cultural production. Critics affiliated with the Frankfurt school had already analysed the tensions between commercial and high culture that troubled early-twentieth-century artists. For those artists, the significance of that struggle depended less on the accuracy of historical evidence than on their ability to marshal history in support of aesthetic values which could stand outside commercial relations of production. Yachnin describes the extent to which Shakespeare's company, as much as any other, was involved in complex negotiations between patronage and commerce and these negotiations were articulated in the numerous manipulations of audience response in prologues to early-modern plays.

Catherine Graham elaborates some of these themes in 'The Problem of Professionalism in Twentieth-Century Stagings of *Hamlet*'. 'Professionalism' is structured by two imperatives: the separation of manual from mental labour and the use of specialized skills to create effects inaccessible to the non-professional. Her account of modernist stagings of *Hamlet* reveals two contradictory approaches to the concept of the 'professional artist': Hamlet's reflections upon existing social reality from a position outside the world he studies and Gertrude's attempt to build new relationships from within the world the old traditions have defined. Stagings of these two characters by modernist directors help to articulate and also to problematize the social role of the professional theatre artist. This tension between physical experience and the discursive language of theatre was summed up in the actor John Gielgud's modest remark, 'I fear I am an inveterate ham, and shall never be the conscientious interpreter of Shakespeare that I should like to be.' Graham quotes this remark as the epigraph to her essay and then describes the aspirations of early twentieth-century theatre practitioners to reconcile these two arenas of activity – the performer and the interpreter. The 'professional' was distinguished both from the amateur and from the hireling hack. His performance skills superseded those of the amateur actor and the superior aesthetic aspiration involved in playing Shakespeare distanced him from the mere entertainer of commercial productions. The 'professional' actor could thus embody a fantasy of a relationship to artistic truth unencumbered by either patronage or commerce, a symbiosis between political beliefs and authentic performance unmediated by language, text or institutional structures.

Jean-Michel Déprats's 'Translation at the Intersections of History' locates theatrical performance at the intersection between the antiquity of a text and the actuality of a performer's body in contemporary social space. The problem of modern staging is created by the historical distance between the epoch of the text and the epoch of its representation. Translation has a position exactly similar to the practice of the *mise-en-scène*. The translator of classic texts must navigate between the imperatives of historical accuracy and the countervailing demand for contemporary accessibility in the market for cultural goods. Déprats quotes Antoine Berman's remarks about German translations of Shakespeare:

> A. W. Schlegel and Tieck, for example, translate Shakespeare faithfully but as Rodolf Pannwitz has said, without going far enough 'to render the majestic barbarism of Shakespearean verse'. This barbarism in Shakespeare that refers to things obscene, scatological, bloody, overblown . . . in short to a series of verbal abuses . . . are aspects that the classical romantic German translation attempts to attenuate. It backs down, so to speak, before the Gorgon's face that is hidden in every great work.
>
> (Below, p. 89)

This account of translation tells us more about modernism and modernity than it ever could about the linguistic dimensions of translation. As Déprats remarks, 'the quotation describes the phenomenon of a certain modernity (obscenity, scatology, gore, extravagance) and draws the lineaments of a Shakespeare *interpretation* which . . . defines the side of Shakespeare that speaks most closely to our own modernity' (below, p. 89). The modernity thus invoked is of a special kind. The image of the Gorgon suggests a mythic past, more ancient even than Shakespeare; the buried reference to Freud's use of the myth to speak of the horrific primal and universal confrontation with female sexuality, closes the loop which connects the present to eternity.

Sarah Werner explores the gendered aspects of spoken language in 'Women's Work and the Performance of Shakespeare at the Royal Shakespeare Company'. She analyses the ideological structures that work against feminist performances through a discussion of the RSC Women's Group. In the 1980s feminist theatre practitioners in the Royal Shakespeare Company contested the stable meaning that male directors assumed would link the Shakespeare plays to their audience's lives. What was at issue was the access women directors and theatre workers would have to provide their interpretation of the canon of Shakespearean drama. As Werner puts it, 'Theirs was a search for a theatrical form that would equal the power of Shakespeare without relying on the masculinist ideology surrounding his plays' (below, p. 105). The RSC Women's Group existed only from 1985–6, and did not end up doing any performances of Shakespeare for the company. But during this period they analysed their position within the company in terms both of a politics of equal opportunity and a sense that women should be allowed equal access to 'Shakespeare and other classics, which are also their heritage' (below, p. 97). The RSC's emphasis on voice training constructs a relationship between language and character that hides Shakespeare's more radical dramaturgical strategies. And the RSC's sense of itself as a corporate 'family' prevents actresses from being heard as legitimate voices.

William Worthen's 'Shakespearean Performativity' takes up the critical question of historicity in contemporary performance. Richard Schechner's discussion of 'restored behavior' is used here to analyse the reconstruction of Shakespeare's Globe on the

Bankside. Although the Globe has been widely discussed as a tourist site, a laboratory, a theme park, this essay is focused on the relationship between the Globe's investment in history and how that is constituted as an aspect of the performances the Globe sells to its audiences. The desire for historical authenticity has been a dominant concern in twentieth-century critical discourse, famously in Stephen Greenblatt's longing 'to speak with the dead'. It has also been the guiding concern of large-scale commercial enterprise as in the thirty-year-long project to rebuild Shakespeare's Globe at its original London location. However as Worthen also explains, the mere accoutrements of scenery and building do not and cannot determine the performativity of the text, the roots of the experience in the theatre. There are changes other than building styles which separate us or the audience of the 1920s from Shakespeare, and it is these changes, more than realizable historical detail, which inflect our sense of the authenticity of Shakespeare performed. Theatre constitutes itself at the moment of its performance as the embodied behaviour of actors. The presence of the actor as the vehicle for the fictive immediacy of character firmly insists on material reality as the only truth of theatre. This insight is matched by a distrust of language as the medium of communication from Shakespeare to the modern world. But it's very difficult to get this right. Theatrical performance will seem unsatisfactory when the behaviour represented on stage is either unrecognizable because over-intellectualized, or overly familiar and so clichéd. This kind of disappointment with Shakespeare on stage is evident in the vernacular discourse that surrounds theatrical performances. It is even more vividly apparent in the intense dissatisfaction, exemplified in Helen Gardner's complaints about 'the directors theatre', that fuels intellectual analysis of Shakespearean performance.

Irena Makaryk's 'Heresies of Style: Some Paradoxes of Soviet Ukrainian Modernism' uses a 1924 Soviet Ukrainian modernist production of *Macbeth* created by the charismatic Ukrainian director Les' Kurbas as a case study of the problematics of modernism in Eastern Europe. Kurbas's interrogation of all of the elements of theatre (the classic, plot, role, character, hero, time, space, acting, prop, costume, lighting) was aimed at reconceiving the institution of theatre. The production created a tremendous scandal, it launched a polemical debate in the press which lasted over two months, and it is still being spoken about in the 1990s. As Irena Makaryk explains, this director's use of Shakespeare allowed the playwright to be associated with the interests of national and cultural revival. As with his Western counterparts and contemporaries, Kurbas tried to create a Shakespearean theatre that would repudiate the museum version of the past and allow the plays to be refracted in the prism of a contemporary world view. Kurbas's artistic practice in pursuit of this ideal also echoed the practical solutions of modernist scenographers such as Gordon Craig. Working with the artistic director Vadym Meller, Kurbas developed an abstract, almost allegorical theatrical style for his 1924 production of *Macbeth*. Like Brecht and Meyerhold, Kurbas looked for a theatre which would remove the passivity of the audience, would remove the boundary between work and play, replacing passive consumption with the active critical engagement necessary for the long-term project of creating new forms of communal life. Ironically, in the intellectual ferment of post-revolutionary culture, Kurbas's innovations were denounced as taking the bourgeois aesthetic to its absurd conclusions for creating overly abstract forms that failed to reflect objective reality.

Maarten van Dijk's '"Lice in Fur": the Aesthetics of Cheek and Shakespearean Production Strategy' explores the rebellious, anti-authoritarian energy of theatrical modernism. He builds on the ideas of the German philosopher Peter Sloterdijk's *Critique of Cynical Reason* (1987) to argue that the oppositional spirit of modernist aesthetic is something more than compulsive transgression. Van Dijk's 'aesthetic of cheek' recalls Alan Sinfield's notion of 'creative vandalism'. But there is something more than angry defiance in this determination to free audiences from the morbid enchantment of dead masterpieces. Sloterdijk's philosophy entails a critique of the facile cynicism that figures as the dominant mode of modern culture. The remedy for this debilitating cynicism takes the form of 'low theory', a counter-tradition that continually resists and subverts the idealizing metaphysics of 'high theory' from Plato onwards. Brecht called this *plumpes denken*, crude thinking. In terms of theatre practice the idea is to deny audiences the token satisfactions and the routine consolations of the 'culinary theatre'. The cheeky 'vandalism' of Brecht's theatre was oddly conservative in its insistence that there was something urgently valuable that could be recovered from the historical past.

The possibility of such a redemption would depend, however, on the surrender of empathy and identification with the great works of dramatic literature.

Brecht construed theatre in a radically non-aesthetic way, as a social practice or a means of production. This entails the rejection of notions of the autonomy of art in favour of the recognition of theatrical art as a larger social activity, a type of propaganda in favour of critical thinking. But the larger point for Brecht, as van Dijk's essay shows, is that the theatre is supposed to be fun. Brecht's idea of 'spass' – fun – is actually a fairly complex notion. In English fun comes from a dialect word that means something like a hoax or a deception, and the word still has the sense of a fiction when we say we are doing something 'in fun'. The word also conveys a sense of ridicule and abuse, when we 'make fun' of someone. To do something 'just for fun' is to do it for its own sake, without any ulterior purpose or goal. Finally, fun implies conviviality. Van Dijk's discussion argues that the 'aesthetic of cheek' finds its larger meaning in the tradition of Carnival. The cheekiness of the modern theatre is a form of knowledge of the social world as it actually is and a wish for radical social transformation.

It's fun to have fun, but you have to know how. Modernist Shakespeare performance, in all its variants, articulates a desire for a link from the present to the past. That desire, like all desire, is constantly renewed by the fact that it cannot ever be fulfilled. This would suggest that the experience of modernity is in some sense an experience of loss, precisely the sort of feeling expressed in Helen Gardner's unhappiness with Peter Brook or in Stephen Greenblatt's odd desire to speak with the dead. To really understand this rather mournful wish requires attention to the commercial modes of theatrical production in the twentieth century. In a political economy based on market exchange and on individualistic social ideals, theatre continues to have an extremely ambiguous status as a social agency or institution. Theatre-goers have the status of consumers and contemporary business practice requires that they receive value for their entertainment dollar. But the satisfactions available in this relationship entails a real existential loss for the audience who are no longer directly engaged in expressive creativity and con-viviality. In presenting amateur productions – as did Poel and Monck – or by presenting theatre in newly socialist Russia – as did Craig – the first generation of theatrical modernists saw themselves as resisting what they regarded as the deadening effect of commercial culture. The contest over authentic Shakespeare production in the modernist theatre has not been merely over the ideological 'meaning' of the plays but over their larger social role as cultural saviours. Shakespeare is the elusive point of coherence which might unite 'the people' against the dangerous and narcotizing seduction of endlessly proliferating modes of commercial and technological cultural pleasures. What the various modes of theatrical modernism all share is a questing after modes of visual and auditory play that would allow theatre to regain its lived immediacy as popular art.

1
Modernity, modernism and postmodernism in the twentieth-century's Shakespeare
HUGH GRADY

> In every era the attempt must be made anew to wrest tradition away from a conformism that is about to overpower it.
>
> Walter Benjamin (1968: 255)

Shakespeare and modernism

The impulses which brought about the new aesthetic movement of modernism at the beginning of the twentieth century were often iconoclastic and violent. The 1910 Futurist Manifesto, for example, exhorted its readers as follows:

> Take up your pickaxes, your axes and hammers, and wreck, wreck the venerable cities, pitilessly. Come on, set fire to the library shelves. Turn aside the canals to flood the museums. . . . So let them come, the gay incendiaries with charred fingers. . . . Here we are! Here we are!
>
> (Quoted in Williams 1989: 51)

This militant anti-traditionalism was in evidence everywhere in the arts at the beginning of the century. Revolutions across the cultural sphere produced radical transformations in painting, music, and literature. At first this wave of radical aesthetic experimentation was called simply 'modern art', and it ramified into scores of sub-movements, trends, and new directions which today we group together as a complex modernism.

Given the modernist desire to overcome tradition and the past, it seems something of an anomaly, then, to realize that in both the theatre and in literary criticism – two cultural institutions experiencing the challenge and shock of modernism early in the twentieth century – Shakespeare was an important component of the modernist revolution. The appropriation of Shakespeare as a modernist meant a thorough revision of his nineteenth-century image as a Romantic and realist, celebrated for his life-like characters and poetic powers. Already, in the 1890s, George Bernard Shaw had campaigned against Shakespeare's high status in *fin-de-siècle* cultural life, arguing tirelessly that after Ibsen, Shakespeare's dramaturgy was obsolete and only the strength of traditionalism in antiquarian Britain prevented this from being generally acknowledged (Shaw 1961). In Shaw's caustic view of literary history, Shakespeare was an anti-modern ripe for the overthrow.

Of course, the overthrow never came. Instead Shakespeare was refunctioned as a modernist poet and playwright of multiple dimensions for the twentieth century, and it was Shaw and his version of literary history that came to seem dated and quaint. As Raymond Williams argued, realists like Shaw perhaps deserve more credit as harbingers of modernism than they have generally received, having much the same relationship to more radical innovators to come as the Impressionists had to the Cubists in painting (1989: 31–5). But it proved a much more successful strategy for emerging modernists to transform than to discard Shakespeare.

In the second half of the twentieth century, I believe, a similar if less dramatic aesthetic revolution has taken place, and it, too, has changed the way we perceive Shakespeare. Modernism itself, under the twentieth century's endemic pressures for constant renovation and renewal, has given way to a new aesthetic paradigm – that of postmodernism. In what follows, I want to try to trace the production of a modernist and then a postmodernist Shakespeare over the course of the twentieth century. This development has been complex, and describing it involves us in an array of confusing terms – modern, modernism, modernity, modernization (not to mention postmodern and its variations), which deserve explication and exploration. In addition, some argue that postmodernism is really a variant of modernism (e.g.

Halpern 1997: 2) – a position which has its logic but which, I will argue below, is less persuasive than its contrary. But as we will see, different aesthetic paradigms can coexist in the same period. And to be sure, modernism itself proved a highly contradictory development, with opposing directions and impulses, and Shakespeare was implicated in more than one of its tendencies.

One strand of modernism, epitomized by the Italian and Russian Futurists (and by occasional American poets like Hart Crane or Carl Sandburg), tried to celebrate and appropriate the unprecedented social and technical developments that were so rapidly transforming the world in the late nineteenth and early twentieth centuries, as electrification, automobiles, airplanes, telephones, cinema, and other technical innovations radically transformed – modernized, we say – daily life and its rhythms for millions.

After the mass slaughters of the First World War, however, the celebrations of violence of the Futurists began to seem disastrously misplaced, and a different departure for modernism developed, particularly in the anglophone world under the influence of a new postwar generation. T. S. Eliot was instrumental in establishing the theme that modernization had transformed the world into a vast waste land. Such writers of the 1920s and 1930s as Yeats, Hemingway, Faulkner, and O'Neill charted the new situation of spiritual crisis faced by all those who had come to believe that the modern world was devoid of meaning and beauty and could be redeemed only by art. Such ideas, in general, informed American and British modernist art in the first half of the twentieth century. Thus modernism, which had begun with a desire to overthrow all previous traditions and renovate the world in all its forms, began instead to reflect the idea that to be true to its deepest values, modernism had to refunction, rather than jettison, the masterpieces of the past.

Eliot did what he could to refunction Shakespeare, urging a de-emphasis of Hamlet and his problems (Eliot 1932) and embracing the new techniques for appreciating Shakespeare's poetic imagery developed by G. Wilson Knight and others associated with what came to be called the New Criticism (Eliot 1949). He took on Shaw indirectly but decisively and argued that it was Shakespeare's very 'primitiveness', his closeness to ancient, pre-modern rituals, that made him truly modern, while the realist theatre, by distancing itself from ritual, had become obsolete in the accelerating modernism of the twentieth century (Halpern 1997: 15–50).

The impact of Eliot's ideas on a developing twentieth-century academic criticism was deep; the resulting critical revolution wound its slow way through the institutions of criticism and established by mid-century a specifically Anglo-Saxon modernist Shakespeare, very much imprinted with concepts from Eliot, who participated in a multi-layered critique of modernity (Grady 1991). In this peculiarly Anglo-American strand of modernism, then, modernism functioned as a critique of the processes which had created the world of modernity over several centuries. Shakespeare could be appropriated in this version of modernism as a representative of the values which modernity had devastated. And a good deal of twentieth-century literary criticism made precisely that case.

But a modernist Shakespeare needed to be more than an updated Romantic: formal issues became crucial in the trans-formation. Shakespeare was reinvented as part of modernism's reorganization of time and space within art works, plastic and literary (Quinones 1985: 33–4; Frank 1945). In this aesthetic revolution, everything associated with what Quinones called the 'historical values' – narrative, character, teleology, and time as an orderly, linear experience – became re-coded as aesthetically passé; and painting and literature, via Picasso, Joyce, and numerous others, replaced history with myth, linear narrative with simultaneity, and linear time with forms more complex and multi-layered. As I wrote about this modernist moment earlier:

> The revolt against time in the arts was a deeply felt revolt against history – the Hegelianized sense of history that had become the West's mythology and self-justification: history as progress, the present as the desired outcome of all that had come before. When history revealed itself instead to have given birth to Yeats's slouching beast, to Joyce's nightmare, to Eliot's hollow men, then history, as it had been understood, history with a *telos*, had lost its *raison d'être* and in that sense no longer existed. Time was replaced by space, history by myth.
>
> (1991: 111–12)

I attempted to show through an analysis of critical history in *The Modernist Shakespeare* the extent to which Shakespeare's meaning became radically refashioned in the wake of this fundamental aesthetic shift, as Shakespeare's texts became 'spatialized', read in terms of symbols, myths, and images rather than as narratives. And of course theatrical and the new film productions of Shakespeare were just as affected.

However, the Shakespeare of the avant-garde theatre often had completely different, anti-traditionalist characteristics, as several of the essays of this volume illustrate. Shakespeare was an important figure in the radical, Futurist-inspired theatrical experiments in Moscow before the Revolution and afterwards in the pre-Stalinist phase of the Soviet Union (Carlson 1993: 354–5). The shock-value, say, of the Cubist set used in Edward Gordon Craig's 1912 production of *Hamlet* in the Moscow Art Theatre came in large measure from the presentation of traditional Shakespeare through radically new artistic media, but there were also aspects of Hamlet's scepticism and alienation that worked well with modernist themes and values. For similar reasons, Shakespeare was a major presence in early twentieth-century German expressionist experiments, fascinating Brecht, for example, throughout the several phases of his long career and serving as a precedent for the epic theatre and its celebrated a-effect (Brecht 1964b). In America, Orson Welles was probably the best known 'modernizer' of Shakespeare, especially through his 1936 production of *Macbeth* set in a voodoo-haunted Haiti and his use of Fascist uniforms for many of the characters of his 1937 *Julius Caesar*. These were appropriately political shock tactics aesthetically allied to earlier modernist experiments. Such examples are only a sample of a much larger number of modernist-influenced productions of Shakespeare in the twentieth century.

From modernism to postmodernism

By the 1950s, however, modernism started to become institution-alized, in new museums and in a newly expanded educational system and lost much of its shock-value. Partly this was a matter of familiarity and the passage of time. As the masterpieces of the teens and twenties aged, they were no longer 'modern', at least in chronology, and the term 'modern*ist* art' arose to indicate that this art had become a chapter in art and literary history that had come to a close; it could no longer simply be 'modern'.

However, the new forms that had arisen after the Second World War, which were perceived as no longer the same as what sometimes was called 'high modernism' (meaning the masterpieces of the early days, in literature the works of Joyce, Eliot, Pound, Yeats, Woolf, and Faulkner, for example), needed a name of their own, and slowly, unevenly, the term 'postmodern' arose to describe a highly eclectic group of art works no longer modernist, but lacking any obvious unifying features to suggest a more assertive name. By the 1980s postmodernism had become a common term, and a body of theory describing some of its main features had developed.[1] These developments initiated a debate over whether a second aesthetic revolution, related to but surpassing the earlier modernist revolt, had occurred in the twentieth century. Was modernism superseded by a new set of aesthetic practices which everyone seemed pleased to call by the name of postmodernism, whether they agreed it existed or not?

To help clarify such issues of periodization, I developed a concept I call the aesthetic paradigm, a term intended to merge the aesthetic theory of Theodor Adorno (and other Frankfurt School practitioners) with the pragmatic sociology of science of Thomas Kuhn (Grady 1991: 8–27, 74–86). Precisely because the Frankfurt School texts tend to speak of 'modern art' as a unitary practice from the Enlightenment to the twentieth century, without much regard for the traditional periodizations of cultural history, I thought it needed refinement to account for the shifts in aesthetic form from neoclassicism to the present. A distinction is especially important to make between long-term modernity (in force since at least the eighteenth century) and twentieth-century modernism, which acts, as we saw previously, both as the fulfilment of and as a fundamental challenge to modernization and modernity.

First, the Frankfurt School component: for Adorno and his colleagues, modern art emerged in a series of fundamental cultural dissociations enacted by the Enlightenment[2] and constituting long-term modernity (Adorno 1992 and 1997). Art had an antagonistic, or at least potentially critical, relation to the rest of modernity from its beginnings; it was a development marked by the epochal replacement of pre-modern cosmology and myth by Enlightenment rationality. Crucially for Frankfurt theory, however, modern rationality is 'split' or differentiated into separate, mutually independent spheres: the technical or instrumental, the ethical, and the aesthetic, as Habermas put it in summarizing and developing Horkheimer and Adorno's theory (Habermas 1979). In this scheme, then, aesthetics is a potential space of critical rationality in opposition to the dominant technical or instrumental reason of economics and politics.

For Horkheimer and Adorno, instrumental reason was the most dynamic and most problematic form of rationality within modernity; it denoted the shared, value-free rationality characteristic of modern scientific technology, positivist social science, Machiavellian and Leninist politics, and the profit-motivated decision-making of capitalism (1977: 3–42). In the absence of the constraints (religious, mythical, material, and social) which in pre-modern cultures had held all of these systems in check or prevented them from becoming self-subsisting, modernity emerged as that era of human history in which a whole new logic of human oppression had arisen. It was a new kind of social order dominated by impersonal systems and institutions which held sway over the societies which had created them.[3] The result was, as Marx put it, like the predicament of the sorcerer's apprentice: society had created forces it was unable to control (Marx and Engels 1974: 72).

As twentieth-century history developed, Horkheimer's and Adorno's earlier hopes for an emancipatory working-class revolution faded. Art, along with critical rationality more generally, became for them the chief remaining locus of resistance within modernity to what their successor Habermas has termed the colonization of daily life by the impersonal systems of modernity. Art – sensuous, passionate, complex, multivalent and polysemous, resistant to reduction and instrumentalization – was constituted in early modernity as a kind of reservoir of the meaning-giving, emotion-imbued rituals and practices of pre-modern culture. Thus, art in modernity is in many ways archaic and paradoxically anti-modern. But unlike pre-modern religious rituals or mythical artifacts, modern art is secular and autonomous from the surviving religious and political ideologies; it is a sphere of a fragmented modernized culture and thus capable of preserving and containing utopian counter-memories hostile to the dynamics of instrumental reason and capitalist economics – although it is equally capable of serving as an ideological justification of and/or harmless escape from the society which creates it (Adorno: 1992 and 1997).

This Frankfurt analysis is a powerful one, but, as I indicated previously, it needs to take into account the dynamics of art that have given it a history of constant change and development over the last four centuries. The Frankfurt theory, in short, needs to be differentiated to account for the differences as well as the similarities of the inter-related major post-Enlightenment art movements. Changing styles and forms in art, in fact, are a necessity within the dynamics of modernity. On the one hand the capitalist market, with its demands for the ever-new, creates one kind of powerful stimulus for change. On the other hand, there is the desire to assert new kinds of dissent and rebellion as older forms age and become contained. In short, Frankfurt aesthetic theory requires modification to do justice to the dynamics of change characteristic of aesthetic forms in the West *after* the Enlightenment. And it is in this connection that Thomas Kuhn can be of assistance.

Kuhn's idea of the scientific paradigm (1962) provides, at least in broad terms, a model for the dynamics of shared cultural activities that applies to all of the spheres of rationality of modernity, not just to science and technology. And it has advantages over related ideas like Foucault's *episteme*, Althusser's ideology, or *Annales* school *mentalité*, at least as I see it, in being open to renegotiation, modification, and criticism in ways that the other structuralist-influenced terms notoriously are not. Hence we can think about the changing forms and movements constituted by the well-mapped cultural periods of Western art and literature as a succession of aesthetic paradigms each of which renegotiates and reconstitutes the terms and forms of aesthetic rationality and practice in a complex intersubjective process shaping and shaped by individual practitioners.

To turn now to the issue I alluded to earlier, the question of whether in the twentieth century a new aesthetic paradigm of postmodernism has come into existence to succeed modernism,[4] one point to observe is that there is nothing in the theory of paradigms to preclude the simultaneous coexistence within one chronological 'period' of disparate aesthetic paradigms. An aesthetic literary movement like literary realism, which twists in and out of the eighteenth, nineteenth and twentieth centuries, coexisting with many determinedly anti-realistic practices, seems to me best understood as constituting a separate aesthetic paradigm from those of, say, Romanticism and its late variant *fin-de-siècle*

Symbolism. And doubtless in the present are artists who would be at home much earlier in the century, and in that sense there is no doubt that modernism continues to the present. And it is quite possible that the two aesthetics which we now divide at the end of the century coexisted in transitional forms at mid-century – even within the minds and works of individual playwrights. As Ihab Hassan has written:

> Modernism and postmodernism are not separated by an Iron Curtain or a Chinese Wall; for history is a palimpsest, and culture is permeable to time past, time present, and time future. We are all, I suspect, a little Victorian, Modern, and Postmodern, at once. And an author may, in his or her own lifetime, easily write both a modernist and postmodernist work.
> (Hassan 1993: 149)

The history of twentieth-century drama in particular, it seems to me, does not lend itself to a simple division into modernist and postmodernist segments. Its development was complicated by the persistence of the realist aesthetic associated with Ibsen and championed in Britain by George Bernard Shaw. Some of the boldest modernist experiments – plays by Artaud, Brecht, Beckett, or Ionesco and the other figures of the theatrical avant-garde – seem already to have something transitional or directly post-modernist about them, and distinctions could doubtless multiply within the corpus of each dramatist as well as between individual authors. Most accounts of postmodernist aesthetics rightly recognize an overlap with earlier modernist forms; Jameson argued that even if virtually each individual characteristic of postmodernism had a precedent in a previous modernist work, it is still essential to differentiate the two aesthetics since the socio-cultural contexts for them are now so different (1991: 4). That is, all contemporary cultural expressions are affected by new levels of commercialization, commodification, and globalism. And at the same time the 'shock' effects of early modernism have worn off, requiring a new sensibility and a new aesthetic ensemble to achieve a similar effect. In short, the same forms have different meanings in different environments.

At the level of what Jameson calls the 'cultural dominant' ('a conception which allows for the presence and coexistence of a range of very different, yet subordinate features') (1991: 3–4), however, I believe we have in fact witnessed the emergence in recent decades of new aesthetic forms and themes which, while they have an affinity with a now partially repressed older modernist paradigm, and while the cultural crisis that is inscribed in them is much more gradual and less dramatic than that of the modernist break, are still sufficiently distinct – and exist in a sufficiently different social and technological environment – so that we can meaningfully speak of a new postmodernist paradigm in contemporary cultural production. For many theorists it began to take shape in the years after the Second World War, in such forms as the French *nouveau roman*, American confessional poetry, the self-consuming novels of Pynchon, the pop art of Andy Warhol, and the various avant-garde theatrical experiments.

As readers will discover in the other essays of this volume, a similar but later shift can be detected within the world of recent Shakespearean productions – for example, in the numerous highly politicized versions of the plays – a *Measure for Measure* with a 'convent' that is a lesbian-separatist commune, an *As You Like It* with the Forest of Arden set in the urban wastelands of 1980s London, for example – which have been mounted in the last decade or so in a postmodernist anti-hierarchical impulse. Because of some specific features of Shakespeare's construction as a modernist dramatist in the twentieth century, it is perhaps easier, in fact, to see these distinctions at work in productions of Shakespearean plays than it is in the works of twentieth-century avant-garde drama itself.

The modernist Shakespeare, even in the more radical, tradition-defying productions I alluded to above, was generally seen as part of the imaginary refuge from industrial capitalism's commodification, regimentation, and routinization, not a part of Futurist and allied attempts at the aestheticizing of modernization itself. Shakespeare was for both Romanticism and modernism an idealized, unified, and autonomous repository for values and meanings seen as redemptive of life in a degraded modernity, whose beginnings he perhaps also announced – and denounced. It is this feature of modernism with which the postmodernist Shakespeare breaks most decisively. Again, Ihab Hassan is eloquent about how such sudden changes can occur:

We continually discover 'antecedents' of postmodernism. . . .What this really indicates is that we have created in our mind a model of postmodernism, a particular typology of culture and imagination, and have proceeded to 'rediscover' the affinities of various authors and different moments with that model. We have, that is, reinvented our ancestors – and always shall.

(1993: 150)

The postmodernist Shakespeare tends to be formed *within* the surface of the commodified reality of late modernity, as an instance of an 'art-effect' dispersed within what had been for Romanticism and high modernism the very opposite of the aesthetic. Warhol's soup cans are one example of this effect; J. S. G. Bogg's painted 'counterfeit' money, exchanged for services rendered in a kind of deconstruction of monetary value (Weschler 1999), is another. Both of these art works (if that is the word) incorporate what had been considered most antithetical to art in order to create a complex comment that is itself a new form of art – art not really immanent in the images but rather an 'art-effect' created through the interactions of artifact, context, and perception.[5]

We can see similar tactics in some recent Shakespearean productions. Because of their wide audience and recent proliferation, film versions of Shakespeare can serve as convenient examples of these trends. Like several regional productions of plays one could name (the *Measure for Measure* and *As You Like It* I referred to above), the 1996 film version of *Romeo and Juliet* directed by Baz Luhrmann is an excellent example. The play is reset in the highly commodified, media-saturated environs of the greater Los Angeles of today, becoming a study in the colonization of idealized sexuality by a reified commodity culture of random violence and alienated street gangs. The commodified culture forms part of a complex postmodernist effect.

Others of the recent spate of Shakespeare films are perhaps much less consistently postmodernist in their approach, but all of them have been affected by postmodernism in one way or another. In addition to the subversion of the old distinction between art and popular culture that all these films embody, there is a more formal feature of postmodernism to take into account: postmodernist works are by and large based on an aesthetics of disparateness and disunity,[6] in distinction to the assumptions of modernism – in particular, as Jameson, argued, replacing irony (with its unified hierarchical value judgements) with the disparate 'neutral practice' of pastiche (1991: 17).

Branagh's *Hamlet* flirts with a postmodernist ironyless pastiche effect through its several non-ironic allusions to previous films[7] and its set of cameo appearances by media icons like Charlton Heston, while its use of an 'inclusive' (conflated) text of the play, for me at least, produced a postmodernist effect of disparateness and disunity, in that all the powerfully performed individual scenes failed to cohere into some intelligible pattern, message or theme.

Al Pacino's *Looking for Richard* seems to assume a similar disunity and to thematize it, even though at moments the film explicitly celebrates the chimera of an authentic 'living theatrical tradition' in which the truth about the play supposedly resides. However, the film goes on completely to subvert any such faith through its own 'textualist' form, underlined by the film's title, which suggests that any final meaning of *Richard III* is unreachable. And beyond these recent films, postmodernist ideas, as this anthology illustrates, have certainly helped form today's contemporary avant-garde productions, particularly in non-English speaking countries.

They have also, of course, impacted on much recent academic Shakespeare criticism. As those who have read the last chapter of my book *The Modernist Shakespeare* know, I believe something fundamental happened to the enterprise of literary-critical readings of Shakespeare just around the year 1980 – a change connected with the influence of postmodernist aesthetics (1991: 210–46). Before that, there had been a decade of continued development of previous critical paradigms and tentative explorations of alternatives to them. Before *that* had been three decades dominated by just two critical paradigms, positivist historical criticism (epitomized by E. M. W. Tillyard) and the so-called New Criticism, in somewhat different British and American versions, both, however, committed to a manifestly modernist method of close readings of texts as aesthetic, history-transcending formal embodiments of a vanished organic society. By 1970 these two paradigms were experienced as depleted by just about everyone, and in Shakespeare studies muted versions of the much more exuberant explorations taking place in other fields of English studies, employing continental critical theories like structuralism, phenomenology, feminism, and Marxism, began to appear in a small number of articles and a few books,[8] while otherwise business went on as before. But in 1980 or so these trends suddenly reconfigured Shakespeare studies in the form of such paradigm-recasting books as Stephen Greenblatt's *Renaissance Self-Fashioning* and the feminist anthology *The Woman's Part* (Lenz *et al.* 1980).

In only a few more years we began to hear from more North Americans like Michael Bristol, Carol Neely, and Louis Montrose and British cultural materialists and British post-structuralist feminists like Lisa Jardine, Catherine Belsey, Kathleen McLuskie, Alan Sinfield, and Jonathan Dollimore – and haven't looked back. Well, of course, some people have looked back – and in fact the 1990s have been marked by an aging of this process and a few calls for a return to the good old days – but these trends seem to me much less significant than new interventions by African-American, Indian and so-called 'queer' studies that have further developed themes opened up in the 1980s.

All of these works of the 1980s and 1990s display typically postmodernist characteristics, first, by ending the former autonomy of the art work under modernism through strategies of recontextualizing Shakespeare – in history, in the cultural present, or in that bracing combination of the two known as new historicism; or through a postmodernist anti-hierarchical impulse inverting formerly hegemonic binary pairs such as art/popular culture, male/female, European/Third World, or heterosexual/homosexual.[9] And of course, under the influence of Derrida and Lacan, the former unity of the text has been placed under suspicion, seen not as intrinsic to the work but instead a result of decisions made in the act of interpretation. The academic Shakespeare – or at least important segments of him, there being of course a continuing presence of more traditional interpretations – is now an aesthetically postmodernist Shakespeare.

Postmodernism and modernity

If there is substantial agreement that we are now living in a postmodernist cultural period, however, it is less clear what the implications of this are for what has happened to the long-period modern era, from the Renaissance to the present, and for the larger system we can call 'modernity' formed by the interactions of power, capitalism, and scientific technology.[10] For the term postmodernism really has come to imply two quite distinct notions of the significance of the cultural, social and technical changes which have been linked by any number of theorists with the idea of the postmodern.[11] On the one hand – and this is the view I have stressed here, for it is one I share – postmodernism is a new aesthetic paradigm, a shift in the ways we produce and interpret art under the influence of changing collective experience.

On the other hand, as Jean-François Lyotard (1984) and those he has influenced have argued, these changes may signify nothing less than the end of modernity itself. Former dissident playwright and now Czech president Vaclav Havel declared as much in an address given before the World Economic Forum on 4 February 1992 in which he announced 'the end of the modern era' – the end, he explains, of an era 'beginning in the Renaissance and developing from the Enlightenment to socialism, from positivism to scientism, from the Industrial Revolution to the information revolution'; an era, he tells us 'dominated by the culminating belief, expressed in different forms, that the world – and Being as such – is a wholly knowable system governed by a finite number of universal laws that man can grasp and rationally direct for his own benefit' (1992: 15). In this view, then, in addition to a shift in aesthetic forms and contents, there is also a much more fundamental move away from that systemic combination of a reified economy, a nation-state system operating according to Machiavellian logic, a secular mentality linked to modern science and science-based technology, and the approaches to knowledge they produce.

On the contrary, I would argue, these rumors of the death of modernity have been greatly exaggerated. Despite the raft of recent books with titles beginning with the phrase 'The End of . . .' – titles which are certainly symptoms, but of desire, not of the real, in my opinion – I see no signs of the end of science, art, systemization, exploitation, or even class struggle (however one-sided it has been of late). If modernity began with the establishment of a secular, autonomous rationality, a capitalist economy, and a nation-state system in the small promontory of Asia called Europe which unaccountably dominated the world for three or four centuries, we can trace a steady expansion of modernity continuing to this very moment. If anything, we are living in an era in which modernity has consolidated and established itself more implacably than ever.

The twentieth century witnessed the greatest scientific discoveries and technological achievements in human history. And it suffered calamities – wars, massacres, economic dislocations – far larger in scope than any that had been previously known. Given the huge range of success and failure in this singular century, there is little wonder that its art developed new forms and techniques through which to capture, comprehend, and evaluate these experiences – or that the specific forms of the modernism of the beginning of the century were superseded in its second half by postmodernist aesthetic forms. Change was accelerating in its pace in almost every facet of life; the aesthetic could not long escape.

One of the crucial paradoxes of a continuing modernity, pointed out by many of its theorists, is its constitutive dynamic of constant development and change, and this applies emphatically to its cultural as well as its economic productions. It is this feature of modernity which allows us to say – indeed requires us to say – that at the close of the twentieth century we have entered into a new cultural-aesthetic phase of modernity for which we have no better term than 'postmodernist'.

At the end of one century and the beginning of the next, we are still entrapped in the dynamics of a modernity which has reorganized the world over the last four centuries. There are inchoate, polyvalent desires to alter modernity's dynamics, ranging from the revival of religious fundamentalism, the discrediting of almost all ideologies of progress and science (like the Marxism-Leninism of the all but defunct Communist movement), and the search for new sources of meaning and experience in everything from New Age to Soho postmodernism (which the *New York Times* declared to be dead several years ago). But the systems of modernity have continued to function and extend their reach in spite of all this talk. Those oppositional 'forces of culture', as Gramscians have called us, have had to regroup and re-strategize, the older high modernist practices having been depleted and outmoded, having become, in effect, our new classics. But if the shape of a new theatrical and critical postmodernist Shakespeare has now emerged, as I have tried to show here (and as this anthology further indicates), the significance of the changes is still uncertain.

Walter Benjamin warned in the passage I used as the epigraph of this essay that new conformisms always arise to endanger the renovations that are the inescapable labor of all those working with the past. We simply have to keep experimenting, to find those constellations of ideas that will blast Shakespeare out of his past into a new relationship with us and the emerging world of the twenty-first century.

Notes

1 See Foster (1983), Arac (1986), Huyssen (1986), Jameson (1991), and Docherty (1993)

2 See Grady (1996: 219–23) for an argument that the Renaissance, not the Enlightenment, inaugurates the differentiations of modernity

3 These concepts are quite similar as well to Foucault's notions of autonomous power within a post-Enlightenment disciplinary society. However, Foucault developed them independently, as he explained in an interview (Foucault 1983). I discuss the similarity in Grady (1996: 47–55).

4 There is a large literature on this question The most influential and convincing argument for seeing postmodernism as a separate aesthetic paradigm which has superseded modernism is Jameson (1991) – a work I am indebted to. Foster (1983) is an extremely helpful anthology representing a number of facets of the debate, predominantly on the side of seeing postmodernism as breaking with modernism. I have found Huyssen (1986) useful as well. Lyotard (1984) has been a central document, but his notion of the postmodern condition goes beyond the idea of an *aesthetic* period, arguing instead for a break with a more global *modernity* – a question I return to in the conclusion.

5 See Crowther (1993) and Huyssen (1986: 44–62) for further discussion of the postmodernist 'art-effect' and/or 'conceptual art'.

6 This new disparateness within postmodernism is described by Bürger (1984: 68–82), Lyotard (1984: 81), and Jameson (1991: 25–31).

7 Two striking examples: the camera work in Hamlet's soliloquy before the intermission eerily and jarringly mimics that of Scarlett O'Hara's 'I'll never be hungry again' scene in *Gone with the Wind*, and the gymnastics of Hamlet's leap from the balcony to finish off Claudius out- Oliviers Olivier.

8 Early works of Terence Hawkes and Howard Felperin come to mind; see Hawkes (1973) and Felperin (1972)

9 Owens (1983) and Huyssen (1986: 44–62) demonstrate the centrality to postmodernist aesthetics of inverting the hierarchies constituted by colonialism and sexism.

10 For useful overviews of the debate about whether we have now broken with long-period modernity, see Docherty (1993) and Lyons (1994).

11 Docherty (1993: 1–30) provides an informed and incisive discussion of these two trends.

2

'To kill a king'
The modern politics of bardicide

PAUL YACHNIN

I

'*The Taming of the Shrew*', wrote Charles Marowitz in 1991, 'is a play
that always left a nasty taste in my mouth. Women despised it,
because, no matter how much irony one got into that last speech
of Katherine's to the assembled wives, it always smacked of
male chauvinism. The play itself, shorn of the highjinks and
slapstick which usually embroider it, is a detestable story about
a woman who is brainwashed by a scheming adventurer as cruel
as he is avaricious' (1991: 21–2). Marowitz's response to *Taming
of the Shrew* received theatrical expression in his 1973 pastiche
of the play, where the penultimate scene closes on a spectacle of
Petruchio raping his disobedient wife (with the assistance of his
father-in-law!), and where the ending presents the audience with
an utterly broken Katherine: 'KATE is ushered in by BAPTISTA.
She is wearing a simple, shapeless institutional-like garment. She
stares straight ahead and gives the impression of being mesmer-
ized. Her face is white; her hair drawn back; her eyes wide and
blank (Marowitz 1975: 77). Designed to 'reveal' Shakespeare's
chauvinism – 'It is nothing more or less than a head-on confrontation with the intellectual sub-structure of the [play]' (23)
– Marowitz's *Shrew* is an extreme but exemplary instance of
bardicide within the field of modern cultural production.

I focus here on bardicide in the modern theatre, in Marowitz
and especially in Ann-Marie MacDonald's *Goodnight Desdemona*

(Good Morning Juliet), but the practice can be found in a number of forms – in the film *Last Action Hero*, where Arnold Schwarzenegger applies high explosives to the high culture of Olivier's *Hamlet*, or in Richard Curtis' closet mini-drama 'The Skinhead Hamlet', which also levels Shakespeare's élite art (reducing the entire 'To be or not to be' soliloquy to the one-liner, 'To fuck or be fucked'), or Margaret Atwood's closet monologue, 'Gertrude Talks Back', a revisiting of the tragedy from the Queen's point of view ('I am *not* wringing my hands. I'm drying my nails' [Atwood 1992: 15]), or the novel *A Thousand Acres*, by Jane Smiley, which rewrites *King Lear* as a story about the consequences of the sexual abuse of daughters and the agribiz desecration of Nature. In each case, with lesser or greater gravity, the revisionist artist prosecutes a brief against Shakespeare, who emerges as an author of and for the social élite or, more often, as an apologist for patriarchal or imperialist violence. In each case, the revisionist's implicit claim to value is founded on an artistic revolution against the politico-moral authority of Shakespeare – the poet-kingpin of the Western tradition.

It is unlikely that bardicides such as Marowitz, MacDonald, Schwarzenegger, Curtis, Atwood, or Smiley would take much comfort from the views of Pierre Bourdieu, who explains so-called revolutions within theatre, cinema, and literature as prescribed forms of competitive maneuvering in a system of mutually constitutive oppositions:

> Because position-takings [within the field of cultural production] arise quasi-mechanically – that is, almost independently of the agents' consciousness and wills – from the relationship between positions, they take relatively invariant forms, and being determined relationally, negatively, they may remain virtually empty, amounting to little more than a *parti pris* of refusal, difference, rupture.
>
> (Bourdieu 1993: 59)

Bourdieu's analysis provides an invaluable way of understanding what I am calling the politics of bardicide; indeed, the idea of a relatively autonomous field of cultural production with its own institutional politics is crucial to any account of revisionist and oppositional rewriting of Shakespeare in modern drama, film, or literature. It needs to be said at the outset that a focus on the

institutional politics of cultural production does not amount to a
rejection of politics *tout court*; rather, an approach at the level of
the institution allows for a much finer-grained analysis of the
social context and consequences of cultural products than one
finds in writers and critics who mistake the imaginary relationships
of fictional characters for the relations of power that influence the
identities and transactions of real-life people.[1]

Instead of thinking about cultural production in terms of an
imaginary world of wall-to-wall power, where a Shakespearean play
is supposed to have a political impact indistinguishable from that
of the social and legal system of marriage or the European project
of imperialist expansion, Bourdieu proposes a structured set of
connections among three fields: the field of art lies within the field
of power, and both lie within the encompassing field of class
relations:

> [T]he literary and artistic field . . . is contained within the
> field of power . . . while possessing a relative autonomy with
> respect to it especially as regards its economic and political
> principles of hierarchization. It occupies a *dominated position*
> (at the negative pole) in this field, which is itself situated at
> the dominant pole of the field of class relations . . . It is thus the
> site of a double hierarchy: the *heteronomous* principle of
> hierarchization, which would reign unchallenged if, losing all
> autonomy, the literary and artistic field were to disappear
> as such (so that writers and artists became subject to the ordin-
> ary laws prevailing in the field of power, and more generally
> in the economic field), is *success*, as measured by indices
> such as book sales, number of theatrical performances, etc.
> or honours, appointments, etc. The *autonomous* principle of
> hierarchization, which would reign unchallenged if the field
> of production were to achieve total autonomy with respect
> to the laws of the market, is *degree specific consecration* (literary or
> artistic prestige), i.e. the degree of recognition accorded by
> those who recognize no other criterion of legitimacy than
> recognition by those whom they recognize.
>
> (Bourdieu 1993: 37–8)

This model cannot be applied unaltered to Shakespeare's theatre
because the principle of autonomous hierarchization (i.e., 'art for
art's sake') was no more than nascent in his day and because the

social orientation of the stage is explained far better in relation to the system of rank than in terms of class relations. Shakespeare was one of the first producers of popular, inexpensive versions of deluxe forms of entertainment.[2] As the liveried servants of the Lord Chamberlain, and after 1603, of the King himself, Shakespeare and the players could pass as court insiders before their public audience; they brought with them into the common playhouse something of the glamour of their Whitehall performances. 'Populuxe' theatre thus inserted itself into the early modern system of rank and capitalized on the desirability of the language, conduct, and dress of the gentry and the court.[3] Shakespeare's proto-egalitarian readiness to retail social prestige to all paying customers can help explain how a theatre that grew further away from 'the nation' as it grew nearer to the court could nevertheless have been the bearer of a powerful critique of the 'naturalness' of social rank. Indeed, it is precisely his commercial relationship with the crown that helped to produce critical representations of the rulers of the nation: Shakespeare's cultivation and critique of a courtly ethos was motivated by his dependency on both aristocratic and public audiences and by his company's own vexed relationship with the court, since the players' *trade* in courtliness was antithetical to the deluxe goods they were trading in.[4]

While the principle of a double hierarchy illuminates the political situation of Shakespeare's theatre only in a general way, it provides a strikingly precise insight into the politics of modern revisions of Shakespeare. According to the model, cultural producers who are in many ways allied with the dominant class – after all, what kind of people typically make up the audience for plays by Marowitz or MacDonald? – nevertheless feel solidarity with the dominated class by virtue of their economically dominated position within the double hierarchy of the artistic field. This view is particularly valuable in that it disposes of the notion that modern bardicides are somehow operating in bad faith.

Bourdieu's model of the connection between the artistic field and the fields of power and class relations renders intelligible the politics of modern cultural production, but needs also to be supplemented by a historical view longer than the one Bourdieu normally takes (he tends to look back no further than the nineteenth century) and by an understanding of the political implications of language and literature, that is, by an account of the wider socio-political consequences of literature's formal organization of the languages of heteroglossia. Bourdieu explains the structure of relations in which the cultural field operates, but it remains important to emphasize the specificity of literary language since literature changes how people talk and how they conceive of themselves and therefore, in a diffuse but profound way, it influences the shape and direction of the political formation.

In order to supplement these dimensions of Bourdieu's analysis, I draw on Mikhail Bakhtin's thinking about the operations of literature within what he calls 'great time.' In specific terms, a longer view is necessary because there are strong lines of continuity between the early modern and modern theatre that need to be taken into account, especially when we consider the widespread emphasis in modern drama and literature on authorship, artistic property, and literary self-consciousness – all elements that received their first sustained articulation in the Renaissance. In general, Bakhtin emphasizes both the semantic richness of literary texts in great time and the embeddedness of those texts in the soil of language as it is spoken and written by living, intending subjects:

> The semantic treasures Shakespeare embedded in his works were created and collected through the centuries and even millennia: they lay hidden in the language, and not only in the literary language, but also in those strata of the popular language that before Shakespeare's time had not entered literature, in the diverse genres and forms of speech communication, in the forms of a mighty national culture . . . that were shaped through millennia, in theatre-spectacle genres . . . in plots whose roots go back to prehistoric antiquity, and, finally, in forms of thinking. Shakespeare, like any artist, constructed his works not out of inanimate elements, not out of bricks, but out of forms that were already heavily laden with meaning, filled with it.
>
> (Bakhtin 1986: 5)

Combining a Bakhtinian emphasis on the thoroughgoing historicity of literature with Bourdieu's model of the field of cultural production can suggest productive ways of understanding the social politics of drama and can help us grasp the degree to which the early modern theatre shaped its modern counterpart, including the modern tendency toward radical revision of Shakespeare himself. Ann-Marie MacDonald testifies to the force of these lines of filiation when she explains her play as an act of homage to Shakespeare: 'This play obviously takes a lot of wicked cracks at Shakespeare, but essentially it's a tribute. Because it's written with a Shakespearean attitude – which is licence, which is plundering sources, turning them inside out, making them your own, being completely profane or wild or wicked or sublime, all in one play' (quoted in Branswell 1990). Since the playful, literary self-consciousness evident in MacDonald's engagement with past works was also a central feature of the entertainment marketplace of early modern London and since the possibility of literary engagement with someone identified as the author Shakespeare is in part an effect of the marketing of the Folio in 1623, the place to begin is not with the moderns, but rather with Ben Jonson, Shakespeare's first eulogist and bardicide.

II

October 31, 1614. At the Hope playhouse on the Bankside, Jonson strikes a blow for the cultural authority of dramatists. The scene is the Induction of his new play, *Bartholomew Fair*. Players representing a stage-keeper, a book-holder, and a scrivener, lead the spectators into a contract with the 'master-poet' Jonson, who 'promiseth to present them, by us, with a new sufficient play called *Bartholomew Fair*' (Jonson 1960: Induction, lines 80–2). The contract belittles those playgoers 'that will swear *Jeronimo* or *Andronicus* are the best plays yet' and assures the more judicious audience members that 'there be never a servant-monster i' the Fair', since 'our author' 'is loth to make Nature afraid in his plays, like those that beget *Tales*, *Tempests*, and such like drolleries' (lines 107–8, 128–9, 130–2).

I will return to Jonson's attempt to establish himself as 'master-poet', a project that can help us understand the origins of Shakespeare's cultural authority as well. More immediately important are Jonson's allusions to the old plays, Thomas Kyd's *The Spanish Tragedy* (1587) and Shakespeare's *Titus Andronicus* (1593) as well as to two more recent plays by Shakespeare – *The Winter's Tale* (1610) and *The Tempest* (1611). Jonson associates the taste for Kyd's tragedy and for *Titus* with 'a virtuous and staid ignorance' and characterizes plays such as *The Tempest* as unnatural, frivolous, carnal, and vulgar. '[L]et the concupiscence of jigs and dances reign as strong as it will amongst you', says the Scrivener on Jonson's behalf, he (i.e., the playwright) is loth 'to mix his head with other men's heels.' The terms by which Jonson attempts to valorize his play – it is up-to-date, aligned with nature, well-informed rather than ignorant, highbrow rather than lowbrow, and observant of social and artistic hierarchies – carry so little weight today that they function for us merely as windows on to Jonson's quasi-mechanical position-taking within the early modern field of cultural production. But Jonson's project of oppositional legitimation seems inconsequential or empty to us only because we no longer associate fashionability with high social rank, because indeed we set no great store on social rank, and because we regard artistic claims of naturalness with skepticism. To allow the possibility that Jonson's terms might have had some force for the 1614 audience, however, is to begin to understand that modern rewritings of Shakespeare, which often enlist themselves under the banner of the cause of social justice, might more accurately be described as deploying a set of terms that possess currency for modern audiences in a bid to gain specific capital within the field of cultural production.

Again I do not mean to suggest that modern rewritings of Shakespeare – whether Marowitz's cut-ups, MacDonald's or Tom Stoppard's parodies, Schwarzenegger's critique of *Hamlet*, or Smiley's feminist rebuttal of *King Lear* – are without socio-political consequences. However, I do suggest that it is misguided to accept these works' implicit accounts of their own political consequentiality. They, like the Induction of *Bartholomew Fair*, are projecting an institutional agenda upon the wider screen of social and ideological struggle, deploying a variety of weighty discourses – weighty for us – within a competitive field in order to wrest their due share of cultural capital from the Bard. They tend to treat Shakespeare as Hal treats Hotspur – as a 'factor', who 'engross[es] up glorious deeds on [his] behalf' (*1 Henry 4*, 3.2.147–8) – or as Claudius deals with King Hamlet, the figure who has kept him but one regicide away from pocketing the precious diadem and the Queen.[5]

I might add that Ben Jonson was hardly the first to valorize a new play by appealing to the connection between fashionability and high social rank, nor indeed was he the first to mock *Spanish Tragedy*. More than twenty years before the opening of *Bartholomew Fair*, Shakespeare himself had done precisely the same thing in the Induction to *Taming of the Shrew*, when he had the drunken commoner Christophero Sly jumble a familiar line from Kyd's play: 'Go by, Saint Jeronimy! go to thy cold bed, and warm thee' (Induction 1. 9–10). Hieronimo, the hero of Kyd's play, had vaulted from the stage to the heights of fame no more than seven years before Sly, collapsing on the same stage, offered testimony to that fame. By putting the reminiscence of Hieronimo in Sly's mouth, Shakespeare suggested his play's cultural superiority over Kyd's, a superiority reiterated by Sly's preference for 'a pot of small ale' over 'a cup of sack' (Induction 2.1–3) and by his fondness for 'a comonty, a Christmas gambold, or a tumbling trick' (Induction 2. 139–40), instead of which, of course, the tinker is offered 'a kind of history', a modern Italianate drama which soon puts him back to sleep. Shakespeare's Induction, like Jonson's, thus valorizes the play that it introduces by implying its opposition to putatively lowbrow, old-fashioned, popular plays like *Spanish Tragedy*.

That Shakespeare used the very terms that Jonson was to use against him twenty years later tends to confirm Bourdieu's description of the systemic nature of quasi-mechanical position-takings in the cultural field. One important element, however, that this view underestimates is the high degree of playfulness in both dramatists. Of course, to think about the competitive artistic field as a form of game playing is to begin to recognize a higher degree of self-awareness and agency than Bourdieu's model tends to allow. In this view, Jonson, like Montaigne's cat, toys with the very system that appears to be toying with him. He aligns himself stridently with élite culture, but also alludes disparagingly to his own activity as the King's masque-maker (a writer of scripts for courtly dancers) when he says that he is loth 'to mix his head with other men's heels.' Beyond that, *Bartholomew Fair* is an ironizing juggernaut that leaves intact no would-be authoritative religious or political position. Shakespeare also undermines the élite cultural position that he seems to be taking by his mockery of *Spanish Tragedy*. Not only does the Induction subject the lordly practical joker to a sly form of ridicule, but the play itself privileges a lowbrow tale of shrew-taming over the highbrow 'history' plucked from Gascoigne's translation of Ariosto. One effect of this ironic mixing of high and low has been Shakespeare's long-term versatility as a 'cross-over artist' (Bristol 1996: 90). Equally important is how *Bartholomew Fair* and *Taming of the Shrew* are able to assimilate their conditions of production into their own metadramatic apparatus. These texts take up into their production of meaning the institutional conditions under which they are obliged to operate, so as to convey an impression of the self-consciousness that has been the hallmark of high literary art since the time of Montaigne, Cervantes, and Shakespeare himself.

Indeed the self-consciousness of Shakespeare's plays is in part an effect of the entertainment marketplace, since the audience demanded a steady supply of new plays and since metatheatricality was the primary means of renovating older texts and conventions. The playwrights scoured the modern and classical literary canons for raw material, not to mention the traditions of English playing and the sociolects of English life. The formal, literary organization of a range of languages tends by itself to produce a consciousness effect (consider how Montaigne's or Robert Burton's skeptical browsing among authoritative points of view produces an impression of a centered intelligence); in the commercial drama, the competition among points of view and sociolects going on among the characters is able to produce a similar effect of authorial consciousness – witness how Katherine's appeal for freedom of expression against Petruchio's advocacy of marital hierarchy or Falstaff's prosy catechism on honour against Hal's poetic tribute to the honourable dead is able to yield a sense of an overarching intentionality. Equally important is the practice of metatheatrical framing, which serves almost automatically to renovate theatrical conventions and well-worn literary and dramatic material, as when Shakespeare frames, as a play-within-the-play, a familiar and ancient tale of shrew-taming, or when he opens the play-within with a studied parody of old-fashioned scene-setting:

> Tranio, since for the great desire I had
> To see fair Padua, nursery of arts,
> I am arriv'd for fruitful Lombardy,
> The pleasant garden of great Italy,
> And by my father's love and leave am arm'd
> With his good will and thy good company,
> My trusty servant, well approv'd in all,
> Here let us breathe, and haply institute

A course of learning and ingenious studies.
Pisa, renowned for grave citizens,
Gave me my being and my father first,
A merchant of great traffic through the world,
Vincentio, come of the Bentivolii;
Vincentio's son, brought up in Florence . . .
                              (*Taming of the Shrew,* I.i.1–14)

Bakhtin would describe this as a process of 'orchestration', where
the intentionality of the text operates to objectify the intentionality of the languages and conventions that the text imports
into its literary domain, transforming them from closed systematic
ways of understanding the world into '*things,* limited in their
meaning and expression' (1981: 289, emphasis in original). He
quite properly takes for granted 'the creative consciousness of
people who write novels' (292) – real-life writers are indeed self-
aware and intending subjects – but the point to emphasize here
is that the practises of orchestration, objectification, and ironic
revision, which serve to make old material new again, are
themselves the primary means by which writers produce what
could be called textual consciousness.

III

Most of the modern artists mentioned so far are the legatees of the
early modern development of the techniques of metadrama and
metanarrative, so that their texts are able to convey a certain self-
consciousness as part of their internal workings. Constance
Ledbelly, the protagonist of MacDonald's *Goodnight Desdemona,*
pursues both her own true identity and the true Author of
Shakespeare's tragedies, which she believes must have been comic
plays in their original incarnation. While this conjunction of
personhood and authorship is the core value of the play, it is also
treated ironically as if it were an outmoded and slightly ridiculous
idea:

'You who possess the eyes to see
this strange and wondrous alchemy
where words transform to vision'ry
where one plus two makes one, not three;

open this book if you agree
to be illusion's refugee,
and of return no guarantee –
unless you find your true identity.
And discover who the Author be.'

$$(1.1, pp. 27–8)^6$$

As MacDonald's play demonstrates, modern rewritings of Shakespeare continue to be informed by the literary self-consciousness
crystallized by early modern literature and theatre; however,
they differ from their forebears in at least one important respect.
Shakespeare's *Taming of the Shrew* implies a criticism of the shop-
worn vulgarity of Kyd's play, but does not seem to care about Kyd
himself. Jonson similarly attacks the style of certain plays by
Kyd and Shakespeare, but seems indifferent toward both as
authors, and hence mentions neither of them by name. In
contrast, Marowitz, MacDonald, and others are involved in a cult
of personality around the figure of the Bard, a figure upon whom
they play out their most elaborate fantasies of mastery and
subjection, identification and rejection. The critic Diana Brydon
speaks of how modern postcolonial writers are able 'to talk back'
to Shakespeare (1993: 166–7). Marowitz names one chapter in
a recent book 'How to Rape Shakespeare' and another, 'Free
Shakespeare! Jail scholars!' (1991). Constance Ledbelly, like our
own coteries of Baconians and Oxfordians, pursues the true
identity of 'the Author' of Shakespeare's plays (Shakespeare himself figuring as evil demiurge), only to discover in the end, by
means of a proper interpretation of Shakespeare's gnomic text,
which is prompted by a ghost representing Yorick, King Hamlet,
and Shakespeare, that she herself is the Author:

> *Constance*: Do you know something of the Manuscript?!
> Do you know who the Author is?
> *Ghost*:   A lass.
> *Constance*: I know, 'alas, alas poor Yorick,' so?!
> Who wrote this thing?
> *Ghost*:   A beardless bard.
> *Constance*:   A boy?
> *Ghost*:   A lass!
> *Constance*:   Oh here we go again, 'alas'!
> Who is the Author?

Ghost:	A Fool, a Fool.
Constance:	The Fool and the Author are one in the same?
Ghost:	Ha, ha, ha, ha.
Constance:	What's his name?!
Ghost:	*Do not forget. This visitation*
	is but to whet thy almost blunted purpose.
	Beware of Tybalt.
	He hath not a sense of humour.
	Audieu, audieu [sic], *adieu. Remember me-e-e.*

[*Ghost begins to sink back down the trap*]

Constance:	No, wait! Don't go yet! Yorick!
Ghost:	Yo-o-u-u're it.

(3.6, pp. 73–4)

Constance has magically entered the world of Shakespearean tragedy in pursuit of evidence, specifically the previously in-decipherable 'Gustav manuscript', in order to substantiate her theory that *Othello* and *Romeo and Juliet* were originally naturalistic, proto-feminist comedies, both containing wise fools as central characters.[7] Shakespeare, the impostor who perverted the real author's intentions, 'plundered and made [these comedies] over into ersatz tragedies' (1.1, p. 21), expunged the fool's part from both texts, and filled up the space with an obsessive and invariably violent drive toward death-marked certainty. Vindicated at the end of the play, Constance unites with Desdemona and Juliet to form a redeemed and redemptive trinity of women who, coincidentally, share the same date of birth, and who also agree to put aside 'all the tragic tunnel vision around here' in exchange for 'real life' (3.9, p. 85). At the moment when she finally grasps the Ghost's 'Yorick/you're it' pun, Constance comes to embody a trinity in herself – Wise Fool, Author, and true self. Her intention is to restore the two tragedies to their supposed original comic form, a central feature of which is a renunciation of the male exploitative violence that is embodied in Shakespeare's appropriation of the original comic sources and Professor Claude Night's plagiarism of Constance's critical work. But the singularity of this intention is put in question by her rejoicing in Desdemona's Amazonian violence, the high point of which rejoicing is the war cry, 'Bullshit!!! Bullshit!!! Bullshit!!!' against male academics and their claim that Desdemona is 'a doomed and helpless victim'

(2.2, p. 41). Further aligning herself with the masculine tradition
that the play seems intent on dislodging, Constance chooses the
dangerous but rewarding public world of Shakespearean tragedy
over what she constructs as the comfortable, private world of
her cats and Charlotte Brontë's *Jane Eyre*: 'I want to see my cats.
I want to read / "Jane Eyre" again and never leave the house' (3.1,
p. 55). These ironic countercurrents tend to blunt the political
purposefulness of the play and hence to undermine its project
of self-legitimation in terms of ideological enlightenment. Even
Shakespeare the master impostor is recuperated as a ghostly
double to Constance the ghostwriter, and as the guiding spirit
of her quest for self-fulfillment. The crypt where she weds her
sisters Desdemona and Juliet, and recognizes herself as wise fool
and author is also Shakespeare's tomb, where Desdemona reads
the inscription: 'Blessed be the man that spares these stones.
And cursed be he that moves my bones' (3.9, p. 82). Like the
ghost of Hamlet's father, Shakespeare is *hic et ubique* – here and
everywhere – in MacDonald's play.

How did Shakespeare rise from his somewhat demeaning
labor in the Elizabethan commercial theatre to become a haunt-
ing presence in the *longue durée* of the Western canon? Perhaps
the most satisfactory answer to this complex and contested
question has been provided by Michael Bristol's recent book, *Big-
Time Shakespeare*. I will return to the question of Shakespearean
bardicide and literary politics in terms of 'big time' (Bristol's
translation of Bakhtin's phrase, *bolshoe vremja*, usually 'great time'
or 'macrotemporality' [1996: 10]); here I want to suggest something about the initiatory moment in the historical process by
which Shakespeare became a figure one could talk back to, the
particular maneuvers by which he was started down the road to
becoming the preferred target for modern bardicides. In this
matter, Ben Jonson is again a pivotal figure.

Jonson, who sought legitimation by mocking Shakespeare's
dramatic style, also attempted to recruit Shakespeare to his project
of literary self-promotion. He seems to have wanted to redescribe
Shakespeare's achievement in terms of a Jonsonian configura-
tion of dramatic meaning as authorial property. Seven years
after Shakespeare's death and seven years after publishing his
own plays in an up-market folio volume entitled *The Workes of
Beniamen Jonson*, he had a hand in the posthumous printing of
Shakespeare's plays, also in folio. In addition to both the short

commendatory poem that faces the title-page, and the longer
eulogistic poem, 'To the Memory of my Beloved', Jonson was
clearly involved in writing the dedicatory epistle, which appears in
the volume over the names of John Heminge and Henry Condell
(see Greg 1955: 18–21). That much is clear because the epistle
reprises key phrases from the Induction to *Bartholomew Fair*,
performed two years earlier. Just as the folio volume provided an
organizing frame for the physical texts of Shakespeare's plays, so
Jonson's idea of authorial property provided the organizing
principle for a set of texts peculiarly rich in the kind of literary self-
consciousness produced by the operations of irony and metadrama. In effect, Jonson unified and personalized the scattered
and impersonal moments of self-consciousness in Shakespeare's
plays by christening them with the playwright's name. The effect
of this imposition of an idea of authorship on Shakespeare's
multiform drama can be likened to a chemical reaction where
a catalyzing agent instantly creates a solid structure in a fluid.
Jonson's idea of authorship worked on Shakespeare's plays like
poison that 'swift as quicksilver . . . doth posset / And curd, like
eager droppings into milk, / The thin and wholesome blood'
(*Hamlet* I.v.66–70).

If Jonson was the first bardicide, then, he was also the first to
consecrate Shakespeare's authorship. The conjunction of these
two seemingly opposed operations has tended to characterize the
history of the revisionist, oppositional rewriting of Shakespeare, as
has the ironizing playfulness that helps to vitalize a text such
as *Goodnight Desdemona*. It seems clear, accordingly, that modern
bardicides are bound within a literary field that is neither of their
own creation nor within their power to alter. It is, as Bourdieu says,
a system of 'relatively invariant forms . . . determined relationally,
negatively.' But must we therefore conclude that modern rewritings of Shakespeare in terms of issues of social justice arise
quasi-mechanically, independently of the writers' consciousness
and wills, so that those positions 'may remain virtually empty,
amounting to little more than a *parti pris* of refusal, difference,
rupture'?

Bakhtin's theory of language as utterance (my words do not
belong to me, but neither am I merely spoken by language)
provides a powerful way of seeing social and institutional structures (such as the field of cultural production) as collective
and disputed property and as deeply historical contexts for living

and acting. Instead of struggling within the toils of what Jürgen Habermas calls 'the philosophy of the subject', Bakhtin proposes an intersubjective view in which language is shared, contested property – 'completely taken over, shot through with intentions and accents. . . . Each word tastes of the context and contexts in which it has lived its socially charged life; all words and forms are populated by intentions' (1981: 293). As such, language is historical through and through. We can extrapolate from this idea of the historicity of language in order to argue that the truly systemic nature of the field of cultural production does not preclude the fact that it belongs, as shared, contested property, to the writers who work within it, that the system is not indeed quasi-mechanical, but rather 'populated by intentions.' The bardicidal aspects of the modern competition in drama and literature can thus be seen as the long-term outcomes of particular struggles, intentions, and accidents (such as the fact that Jonson's own designs on Shakespeare have left him always in second place).

IV

The idea that the field of cultural production is a collective undertaking possessed of a deep historical dimension points to a more complex understanding of literary politics than is suggested by the triumphalism of bardicidal art and criticism, which tends to represent literary revisionism and revisionist interpretation as forms of political resistance. Triumphalist narratives (the archetype of which is the myth of progress) greatly oversimplify the relationship of present to past by treating the legacies of former cultures as burdens to be shaken off or as obstacles to be overcome by dint of heroic artistic self-fashioning. The past appears as a monolith of ills and oppressions rather than as a dimension of the context of present-day actions and thoughts. I have suggested that a more complete understanding must acknowledge not only the impediment that a past master like Shakespeare represents but also the various forms of strength that his work bequeaths to modern artists.[8] Plays like *Hamlet* and *Taming of the Shrew* embody forceful versions of political élitism and patriarchalism, but they also contain persuasive critiques of these standard Elizabethan ideologies. That means that when MacDonald attacks patriarchal authority from the point of view of authentic individuality and personal dignity, she is developing as well as contesting a line of thought out of Shakespeare. This is the case also for Smiley's *A Thousand Acres*, which builds upon – without acknowledging the indebtedness to – *King Lear*'s shrewd socio-political analysis of family dysfunction, and it is true also of *Last Action Hero*, which rejects what it sees as the ineffectuality of poetry (represented by Hamlet's inability to take revenge), but which takes up the issue of action and meaning so central to the play, not to mention ringing the changes on the themes of sonship and art and nature. This is not to suggest that modern artists are unoriginal in comparison with the Bard – after all, Shakespeare himself made his mark first as a bardicide, a poacher of other poets' property; as Robert Greene complained, he was an 'upstart crow beautified with our feathers . . . an absolute *Iohannes fac totum*, in his own conceit the only Shake-scene in a country' (quoted in Evans 1974: 1835). Rather, it is to point out that drama and literature are made, 'not out of bricks, but out of forms . . . already heavily laden with meaning.'

Instead of cleansing the modern body politic of the past evils embodied in Shakespeare, bardicides such as MacDonald or Smiley or Schwarzenegger participate in the somewhat vexed rituals of symbolic politics. By lining up to deal the fatal blow – in order to augment their own specific capital within the competitive field of cultural production – they cannot help but preserve Shakespeare's position as what Harold Bloom calls 'the centre of the canon.' In so far as the structure of the literary field seems to compel oppositional writers to celebrate Shakespeare's kingship, modern bardicide can be seen as an expression of the strain of nostalgic royalism or social élitism that survives within modern democratic political culture, especially in the United States.

'Talking back' to Shakespeare has, however, another side, one that can be well described in terms of Charles Taylor's thinking about the 'politics of recognition.' Taylor explains how recognition became a central feature of modern political culture when the hierarchical system of rank and honour gave way to the democratic emphasis on the authenticity and dignity of the person, attributes which are by definition universalist and egalitarian. I count on my significant others to recognize my individuality, especially because I have arrived at my sense of who I authentically am in dialogue with them. Without that kind of recognition, my dignity is at risk; worse still, misrecognition can undermine my sense of self. In this view, whole groups of people can be harmed by being misrecognized – 'a person or group of people can suffer real damage, real distortion, if the people or society around them mirror back to them a confining or demeaning or contemptible picture of themselves' (Taylor 1994: 25).

Since the bardicides I have discussed misrecognize Shakespeare when they attribute to him an exaggerated level of socio-political intentionality, it is ironic that their complaint is that he misrecognizes *them*, and ironic also that they demand he recognize them properly and that they undertake to rewrite his works so that he holds the mirror up to their authentic identity. Ultimately, of course, the misrecognition of Shakespeare is less important than the demand to be recognized by him, since that suggests the degree to which his plays have become authorial property, for whose political implications he must be answerable, and the degree to which he has become the significant other (or conversation partner) of writers, readers, and playgoers. He is able to take part in the lives of so many moderns in terms of one of the central features of modern political culture because of his iconic position, because of 'the semantic treasures . . . embedded in his works', and because the theatrical poetics of irony, which he developed to the top of its bent in the face of the challenge of writing for the new playhouses, has proven to be eminently translatable into a deep and complex authorial presence.

I suggest finally that it is more productive to think about the socio-political consequences of literature in relation to the long rather than the short term. Bardicides take the short view because it grounds their claim to be able to undo the harm canonical literature is supposed to have done to certain misrecognized groups and so bolsters the bardicides' own sense of political importance. But, with very few exceptions, cultural producers are incapable of making a political difference in the short run, largely because their work is bound within the artistic and literary field, and that field's political capacity is limited by the structure of its relations with the fields of power and class. To take a long historical view is to begin to see that playwrights like Shakespeare, Marowitz, and MacDonald have very little direct political agency, since the socio-political consequences of their work emerge only in 'great time', in a diffuse manner, and only by virtue of both their formal orchestration of the languages of heteroglossia and their poetic inventiveness. (Orchestration affords cultural consumers a degree of ownership of the languages which otherwise determine their identities; inventiveness suggests new models of personhood and collectivity.) As writers rather than legislators, however, cultural producers retain considerable powers of direct action, and they are able, according to the measure of their specific capital, to exert influence over the work of other producers. Specific capital is one last reason to take the long view. In order to grasp the social politics of literature, it is necessary first to develop an understanding of literary history itself (i.e., the history of the field), especially since modern writers seldom limit their literary raiding to the territory of their immediate contemporaries (Shakespeare himself used and was influenced by the ancients as well as the moderns) and since the history of the field – the history, not the field – cannot be contained within the fields of power or class relations.

Notes

1   I should note that neither Bourdieu's model nor my argument is meant to apply to revisionist treatments of Shakespeare by artists outside the cultural field of the developed world. An African poet like the Ugandan Taban Io Liyong uses Shakespeare because of his standing as a mainstay of European colonialist education and culture; the political situation of African literary revision is not well explained in terms of a competitive field in which African cultural producers do not take part.

2   For a full discussion, see my chapter 'The Populuxe Theatre' (forthcoming).

3   See Cissie Fairchilds (1993: 228–48). Her definition of the word, 'desire for cheap copies of luxury goods', differs from that of the term's inventor, Thomas Hine (1986), who uses it to refer to opulent features added to everyday, utilitarian goods.

4   Shakespeare's drama also tends to be populist because, like all vernacular literatures of the early modern period, it aligned itself with the culture of a particular linguistic community – a people defined by its language – and distanced itself from the élite, international culture founded on the knowledge of both Latin and classical literature. In the English case, this populist appeal included caricatures of élite, un-English Italian and French culture.

5   All Shakespeare quotations are from *The Riverside Shakespeare* (Evans 1974).

6   Ann-Marie MacDonald, *Goodnight Desdemona (Good Morning Juliet)* (1990). All quotes refer to this edition.

7   The manuscript is named for another ghostly father in the play – Carl *Gustav* Jung.
8   See the discussion of 'the pathos [of] the principle of serial reciprocity' in Bristol (1996: 121–46; quotation on page 145).

3

The problem of professionalism in twentieth-century stagings of *Hamlet*

CATHERINE GRAHAM

I fear I am an inveterate ham, and shall never be the conscientious interpreter of Shakespeare that I should like to be.

(Gielgud quoted in Gilder 1965: 59)

Even in my youth the actor was still on the fringe of society. He was to be patronized rather than accepted; he was an amusement, a plaything still looked upon as a rogue and a vagabond. Romantic, but not socially enticing, all right for placing a discreet hand beneath the mistress's skirts, but not conducive to walking up the aisle and sharing a golden band. Irving was the first individual actor to become socially acceptable, but even today there is an air about the profession which says 'wrong side of the sheets'.

(Olivier 1986: 30)

These words, penned twenty years apart by two of the most distinguished actors of the twentieth century, reflect one of the central dilemmas of the modernist actor: how to claim status as a professional and escape categorization as either an unfocused dilettante or a vulgar entertainer. In the cases of Gielgud and Olivier an important part of the answer to this dilemma was: 'play Hamlet'. For them, as for so many other twentieth-century actors, the performance of Hamlet and the claim to professionalism seem inextricably linked. In fact many critics, like Peter Stead in his 1991 biography of Richard Burton, go so far as to credit Gielgud's performance of Hamlet at the Old Vic in 1929 with inaugurating 'the new age of English acting' that marked modernist productions of Shakespeare and that was consolidated with Olivier's performance of the same role in 1938 (Stead 1991: 12–13). The choice of Hamlet as starring role was nothing new, of course; many actors before Gielgud and Olivier had chosen Hamlet as vehicle for demonstrating their talents. But, as Gielgud and Olivier's above quoted words attest, the ways in which actors sought to legitimate their work changed with modernism, and the way they chose to play Hamlet changed at the same time.

Whereas the nineteenth-century performer was most likely to aspire to recognition as a master of his craft or, even better, a romantic genius, the modernist actor, in keeping with the new mores of the industrial age, describes what he does as a 'profession' and aspires to be known as a 'conscientious interpreter' of texts and most especially of *Hamlet*. It would, in fact, be difficult to name a role that is considered the equal of Hamlet when it comes to measuring the mettle of a great actor in twentieth-century Europe or North America. Certainly there are other roles in the world repertoire that require as much skill and preparation as does Hamlet. But by the end of the twentieth century, as the quantity of scholarly texts and educational videos on the role attests, to discuss acting in the Western tradition is to discuss Hamlet and to play Hamlet successfully is to establish oneself beyond question as an accomplished actor.

But why Hamlet? Olivier argues that the role's interest stems from the fact that *Hamlet* is 'pound for pound, the greatest play ever written'. 'Once you have played it', he says, 'it will devour you and obsess you for the rest of your life. It has me. I think each day about it' (1986: 46). The role is certainly a rich one and there can be no doubt that, in live performance especially, it tests both an actor's stamina and his skill. The actor playing Hamlet must be on stage for virtually the full length of a very long play and only then engage in a vigorous and complex fencing match that leaves the stage covered in bodies. His moods must seem to change at a moment's notice and he must convincingly perform soliloquies and stage business that are the subject of more rigid audience expectations than anything else he is ever likely to be asked to play. Further, since Hamlet is now considered a young man's role, it is most likely to be played by an actor who is not yet viewed as being at the height of his powers. In the words of Joseph Papp, 'You haven't graduated until you've played Hamlet' (Maher 1992: xi).

But can the demands of the role and the age at which it is generally played account for the kind of obsession Olivier describes? Probably not. It seems more likely that the actor's fascination with Hamlet is not too different from the more general fascination that has kept the play on the world's stages for nearly 400 years. In Michael D. Bristol's account, 'the character of Hamlet and his extraordinary predicament continue to reflect a distinctively modern experience of subjectivity', that of an 'unencumbered sovereign subject with exceptional powers of intellect and imagination' who discovers that 'these resources are precisely the liabilities of a deracinated and fatally disoriented modern agency, unable to confront the massive encumbrances of its own historical past' (1996: 205–6). Viewed in this light, Hamlet's predicament cannot but resonate for the actor trying to establish himself as a professional. After all, the modern actor's struggle for professional recognition demands both an exceptional use of imagination and a particular approach to the encumbrances of those institutional and personal pasts manifested in theatre traditions and everyday habits of action. For the twentieth-century actor, playing Hamlet may be the crucial test of professionalism not only because the role requires superior acting skills, but because it allows the performer to confront the contradictory demands of professionalism and of acting.

To understand the actor's predicament in negotiating these demands it is perhaps useful to look at the historical situation that gave rise to the possibility of being a 'professional performer' in the modern period. Joseph Bensman, in his introduction to *Performers and Performances; The Social Organization of Artistic Work*, points out, for instance, that the very notion of the 'professional' is linked to attempts to free artists from the constraints imposed on pre-modern performers by the religious orders and aristocratic courts of which they were members or retainers. As early as the Renaissance, he notes, composers and musicians 'attempted to enlarge their areas of freedom by moving from court to court, seeking better conditions of pay, work, and artistic freedom, especially when their past successes produced rising reputations' (Bensman 1983: 20). It was in this same period that Shakespeare and the King's Company started producing theatre on a commercial basis in London, apparently providing their own training and support outside religious and aristocratic institutions. The increased artistic freedom that resulted from this dissolution of the patronage system in favour of the new commercial production of cultural goods in the early modern period has led to a persistent belief in modern culture, perhaps most thoroughly expressed in our century by Theodor Adorno, that the most important guarantee of artistic insight is the autonomy of the artist from collective structures.

But there is a cost to this autonomy for, while commercially organized artistic events free the artist from the constraints of patronage, they also militate against wide community participation in the creation of performances. As Bristol demonstrates in *Big-Time Shakespeare*, the sale of artistic skill in the early modern period not only affected the relationship of the artist to the high art of patronage systems, but to the more popular pleasures organized as games and pastimes. To make such art saleable in a commodity market, not only is the patronage of the nobility rejected, '[p]opular culture as the spontaneous activity of peasants and artisans is expropriated in the form of standardized, mass-produced entertainment' (1996: 113). Max W. Thomas' discussion of Will Kemp's nine day dance to Norwich in 'Kemp's Nine Daies Wonder: Dancing Carnival into Market' (1992) is an excellent demonstration of this process at work. Most importantly, Thomas pays close attention to Kemp's insistence on excluding participation by the amateur dancers who would have followed Kemp had the dance been performed as part of the carnivalesque activities of medieval festivals. His account demonstrates that the development of the historical category of professionalism in the arts depended not just on the techniques of the arts themselves, but on the broad development of commodity-based social structures.

Arguing from this point of view, Jean-Christophe Agnew contends that the historical importance of the Elizabethan theatres depends not simply on their new institutional status or the beauty of their performance texts, but on their development of conventions that reproduced the representational strategies of the growing commodity market. The theatres, he argues, flourished because they served as a laboratory for working through the difficulties of living in a commodity-based world (Agnew 1986:

12). Chief among these was a new strategy of social relations based on negotiation of short-term contractual relationships between individuals. Whereas the older feudal order depended on the belief that social roles should be carried out by people who were 'naturally' predisposed to play them, and that change should follow the repeating patterns of the seasons, the new commodity market demanded the possibility of rapid and non-iterated change, much like that exercised by the player in portraying different characters.

In *Hamlet*, this conflict can be seen in the struggle between the Prince and his mother, Gertrude. While Hamlet tries to think through his new situation and choose a rational course of action, even if this means feigning irrationality, Gertrude consistently argues for a simple acceptance of the iterated change of cyclic time. Her first address to Hamlet is a simple reminder that death is a normal part of the cycle of life. 'Thou know'st 'tis common. All that lives must die, / Passing through nature to eternity' she says, in an attempt to convince Hamlet to accept his father's death and uncle's succession (I.ii.71–3).[1] It is worth noting too that Gertrude's last line in this scene is a request that demonstrates her lack of faith in the apparent source of Hamlet's new habit of rational self-fashioning: 'I pray thee stay with us: go not to Wittenberg' (I.ii.119). As Brecht points out, it was at the University of Wittenberg that Hamlet had learned the 'modern' notion of rational reflection that would serve him so ill in a traditional world rife with violence (1964a: 202). This modern rationality stands in sharp contrast to Gertrude's way of being in the world. Throughout the play Gertrude speaks in favour of maintaining traditional relationships, whether this be in asking Hamlet's friends Rosencrantz and Guildenstern to visit her 'too much changèd son' (II.ii.36) or in mourning the fact that Ophelia has died at a point in the cycle of life where she would more normally have been married: 'I thought thy bride-bed to have decked, sweet maid, / And have strewed thy grave' (V.i.131–2). Hamlet's arguments in the closet scene seem to touch Gertrude most pointedly when he suggests that her marriage to Claudius is itself a break with the natural cycles of life and reflects her inability to see the true nature of the man who has killed her husband. Interestingly, while Hamlet's anger is apparently triggered by Gertrude's lack of reflection about the death of his father, the Ghost of that same father appears in the scene to criticize Hamlet for having asked Gertrude to reflect at all, and urges him to 'step between her and her fighting soul' since 'Conceit in weakest bodies strongest works' (III.iv.114–15). Hamlet obeys his father's order despite the fact that he himself is trying to use rational reflection as a means to step outside the 'natural' rhythms and relationships of his parents' world. Nowhere is this more clear than in the soliloquies, where Hamlet literally steps outside the action of the play to reflect on what his actions should be. Faced with the beginnings of a modern society in which appearances cannot be trusted and tradition is not a reliable guide, Hamlet works through his own dilemma in much the same way the commercial actor of the period worked through his. He steps outside the boundaries of traditional roles to invent a fiction that allows him to explore a new way of being in the world.

If such a reading of *Hamlet* tends to support Agnew's argument about the influence of broader social trends on the self-definition of the players' art, and vice versa, then by extension it also points to the need to recognize the difference between the social role of the early modern actor and that of his post-industrial-revolution counterpart. There can be little argument that our notions of both professionalism and of the social role of the actor have changed significantly since the industrial revolution. As Bensman underlines, professionalism in the arts is now not only a question of skill and flexibility but of specific institutional practices 'rooted in full-time training, systematic instruction, practice and rehearsal, and guided entry into performance' (1983: 20). As such, twentieth-century professionalism is as much an institutional as an aesthetic category and any claim an actor makes to professional status now depends not only on artistic skills but on guided entry into particular institutional applications of those skills. Further, Bensman argues, artistic disciplines are following the same path as most other institutions in twentieth-century society in demanding ever higher levels of technical proficiency and, as a result, stricter specialization. In Bensman's view this leads, in artistic as in other professional institutions, to the 'occupational psychoses' of specialists who 'develop loyalties and the trained incapacity and occupational blinders of their own field' (25).

But Albert Borgmann, in *Technology and the Character of Contemporary Life*, suggests that the strict professional specialization Bensman points to is not simply a result of the need for high levels of proficiency in dealing with increasingly complex knowledge systems. While it may now be impossible for any individual to be technically proficient in all the complex aspects of modern life (or modern theatre), this is not enough to explain the drive to narrowly defined professional responses to social problems, even in situations where broader knowledge is readily available. Borgmann blames this aspect of the drive to specialization on what he calls the 'device paradigm'. A device, in Borgmann's definition, is characterized by a 'sharp internal division into a machinery and a commodity procured by that machinery' (1984: 33) where the 'concomitance of radical variability of means and relative stability of ends is the first distinguishing feature' (43). The second distinguishing feature is perhaps more important: 'the concealment and unfamiliarity of the means and the simultaneous prominence and availability of the ends' (44). Specialization, then, is not always a response to the need for complex skills. It can also be a response to the ideologically induced desire to hide the burdensome machinery necessary to make a desired result easily available to large numbers of people. The device, in this view, is a technology designed to do one and only one thing, and, in response to the demands of the commodity-based society within which it functions, to freely circulate as an object that requires little or no maintenance of a type that would require ongoing human relationships.

As applied to acting this might mean that, while the professional may display a variety of new and exciting moves to create a performance text, the mechanism of these actions should remain relatively invisible and the spectator's reaction to the text should remain essentially stable. A wildly different reaction in the spectator may thus be taken as evidence of a simple lack of professional skill on the part of the performer, while the most apparently outrageous staging of Shakespeare may be completely acceptable to mainstream critics if it induces reactions similar to those spectators expect. In a similar vein, an acting technique that demands that the spectator consider the social relationships out of which it has arisen (as is so often the case in local amateur performances) may simply be taken as evidence of a lack of professional skill. As a result, twentieth-century actors are put in a double bind where they must master a particular set of skills and social relationships to be considered professional, but will have much more difficulty making a claim to professional status if acting technique and social relationships are at the forefront of our thinking about their work. This in itself may go a long way towards explaining why so many professional actors have been so reluctant to discuss in any detail how they actually go about acting a role.

The danger of such a vision of professional acting is much the same as that Borgmann identifies facing social thought that treats the device as 'an implicit guiding pattern for the transformation of human existence and the world': this 'liberation by way of disburdenment yields to disengagement' from the social world out of which the acting has arisen (1984: 76). This is clearly what started to happen when Will Kemp separated his professional practice of dance from the more participatory carnivalesque cultural activities of Elizabethan England. In industrialized societies, Canadian sociologist Dorothy E. Smith argues, this kind of disengagement, this deliberate separation of professional from everyday life, has become a crucial element in the definition of professional competence. 'As professionals', she says, 'we know how to practice and preserve the rupture between the actual, local, historically situated experience of subjects and a systematically developed consciousness of society. If we are to claim full and proper membership in our discipline, we must be competent performers of this severance' (Smith 1990: 52). According to Smith, the main job of the professional institution is to create 'facts' by controlling the 'organization of practices of inscribing an actuality into a text, of reading, hearing, or talking about what is there, what actually happened, and so forth' (71). In order to maintain control over these practices, the institution must not only carefully initiate newcomers into the intricacies of its particular machinery, but must vigilantly exclude those who can't be counted on to know in a way that is guaranteed to produce the appropriate facts. This, Smith argues, is most often accomplished by insisting on a strict division of mental and manual labour where those who have the ideas stand outside the actual physical relationships necessary to give them material form. The advent of this new professional division of mental and manual labour can easily be seen in the development of the role of the director in the theatres of the industrial revolution. Unlike the actor-managers of the earlier period, the directors of the new industrial era planned and organized the performance text without themselves actually taking part in the physical labour necessary to produce it. This left the actor in the position of carrying out the physical labour necessary to create a performance text on the basis of the director's visions and, as Tracey Davis has demonstrated in *Actresses As Working Women* (1991), in commercial theatres employing large numbers of female performers, this work was often carried out on an industrial model. How then, could a modernist actor hope to claim anything like professional status when his or her art depended on the use of the body?

A common solution, I would suggest, is the first one Smith points to. To prove his or her professionalism, the actor must 'practice and preserve a rupture between his or her actual local historically situated experience and the systematically developed consciousness' that underlies different schools of acting (Smith 1990: 52). This is, of course, easier said than done, especially when the school of acting in question also demands that the actor convince both him or herself and the audience that this consciousness is not the result of a technical system but of a highly personalized approach to the problem of interpreting a particular text. Nonetheless, belief in some kind of systematic approach to performing a role is crucial to actors who want to prove their professionalism because it is this system that allows them to preserve the rupture between mind and body that justifies their claim to control the theatrical device rather than being controlled by it.

And here is where playing Hamlet becomes a logical step on the road to professional recognition for the actor: it is a role that offers ample opportunities to demonstrate the deliberate control of the body by the mind that professionalism demands. If we look at the play in these terms, we cannot help but notice how often the body is mentioned as a problem for Hamlet. From his first soliloquy in which he wishes that this 'too too sullied flesh would melt, / Thaw and resolve itself into a dew' (I.ii.129–30) to his Mother's description of him in the final fencing match as 'fat and scant of breath' (V.ii.276), Hamlet is portrayed as a character whose ability to act on his conscious desires is thwarted by a body that is all too literally encumbered by the habits of its own historical past. Using sociologist Pierre Bourdieu's notion of *habitus*, which explains how dominant social relationships are unconsciously reproduced through everyday physical interactions between individuals, we might even describe the action of *Hamlet* as the playing-out of the main character's struggle to bring reflection to bear on the violent habits that maintain the social structures of a warrior society. While Hamlet may question the kind of agonistic contest of warriors that has lead to his father's death and that authorizes the father's demand that his son avenge him, his own first meeting with Horatio tells us that the habitus of the warrior drives many of Hamlet's own instinctive reactions. When Horatio tells Hamlet that the cause of his absence from Wittenberg is 'a truant disposition', Hamlet replies: 'I would not hear your enemy say so', implying that if he did hear someone speak ill of his friend, he would without question exact vengeance for the insult (I.ii.170). His abrupt killing of Polonius behind the arras also stands as witness to this tendency to react to a perceived attack without hesitation, especially since it comes immediately after his more conscious decision not to kill the King at his prayers. Yet by the end of the play Hamlet is able to engage in the duel that leads to his death, not as a habitual reaction, but as the result of the conscious choice reflected in the 'If it be now' speech. In instances like these Hamlet is a most useful role for the actor trying to prove his professionalism precisely because it not only allows but *demands* that an actor show an audience how reflection can be used to control a body encumbered by habitual responses to everyday social expectations. It thus allows the actor to demonstrate his most important professional skill: his ability to use mental processes to produce a rupture between the habits of the everyday world and the forms of action prescribed by the institution within which he claims professional status.

For the modernist actor, this rupture must be established in the context of an artistic institution that has long-established norms for performing Shakespeare's plays, norms so strong that they seem to many to be part of the playtext itself. Both Gielgud and Olivier, for instance, speak frequently about the expectation on the part of both critics and audience members that the performance text of *Hamlet* must not only include Shakespeare's words, but a particular style of acting. As Olivier puts it in *On Acting*: 'in those days there was a way of doing things. That's how they were *done*, and that's what the public came to see. They wanted their verse spoken beautifully, and if that was not how you delivered it, you were considered an upstart, an outsider' (1986: 44). Gielguid actually identifies some of these acting traditions as part of the habitus he himself has learned in the theatre. 'I have been and still am', he says, 'irritated by my actor's desire to make such a "curtain" of [the end of scenes]' (quoted in Gilder 1965: 54). Gielgud initially, and probably correctly, associates this instinctive move to create a striking picture at the end of each scene with the demands of the pictorial stage and the descending curtain of the nineteenth-century theatre. He goes on though, to announce his suspicion that these 'curtains' are the result of an unfortunate intrusion of personal desire on the actor's professional judgement: 'I fear we actors like them particularly because they bring applause more surely than a simple exit' (49).

For Gielgud in particular, this struggle between a personal desire for applause and a professional desire for correct interpretation is carried out in confrontation with traditional ways of playing Shakespeare and most especially with some of the traditional business associated with the plays. As Mary Maher points out, Gielgud 'was performing his Hamlet at a time when to be ignorant of what other actors had done with this role was tantamount to not doing one's homework; certainly the critics were aware of traditional business, and the actor was also' (1992: 12). Gielgud frequently cites the work of other actors in his discussions of his own directing and acting decisions, but he is never content with merely reproducing traditional moves. In his introduction to Gilder's description of his performance of Hamlet, Gielgud argues for a particular approach to the work of the master actors: 'just as a great teacher trains his pupils to adopt a correct method of study, and leads them towards the most sincere approach to an appreciation of style, so, it seems to me, an aspiring actor should be able to study these essentials from watching his masters in the craft.' What they should learn, he suggests, comes not 'from a great actor's mannerisms, or some brilliant but fundamentally personal expression of voice, gait, or carriage that he will learn, but from the master's approach to character, and from every moment in his performance in which he reveals or clarifies the text' (quoted in Gilder 1965: 42). It is on this point that Gielgud makes his real break from the traditional approach to acting with which he is so obviously familiar. As a modern professional, he is not content to carry on a tradition simply by imitating his predecessors' physical actions. Instead he insists that these actions should be approached as a guide to correctly interpreting the written playtext, which can only then be expressed through the actor's creation of his own version of the performance text. In moving from observation of performance back to the written playtext and only then to his own original performance, the professional actor participates in much the same kind of 'organization of practices of inscribing an actuality into a text' that Dorothy Smith describes as defining professionalism in the social sciences (1990: 71). While Gielgud sometimes uses another actor's stage business, as when he follows Irving in portraying Hamlet breaking the recorder he carries in the play-within-a-play scene, he only does so after assuring himself that a professional reading of the printed playtext justifies this action (Gilder 1965: 59).

For Olivier, the break with traditional ways of acting *Hamlet* is even more pronounced than with Gielgud. Where Gielgud struggles with his own desire to follow the traditional business and thus gain applause, Olivier is uninterested in tradition and legitimates his own work by comparing it with that of other professional institutions. In Olivier's own estimation, Gielgud 'was giving the familiar tradition fresh life, whereas I was completely disregarding the old in favour of something new' (1986: 44). That something new was a specialist's approach to acting and directing that simultaneously laid claim to a recognition of its distinctive machinery for interpreting texts and to a social position parallel to that of more established professions.

Olivier's foreword to *Hamlet, The Film and the Play* is particularly illuminating in this regard. This discussion of his own very famous film version of *Hamlet* starts with the line 'I am no writer', and goes on to tell of the Scottish critic who threatened to play *Macbeth* and make Olivier watch it if the great actor didn't stop trying to write essays. 'I must admit I saw the fellow's point – even though he was a drama critic!' Olivier replies, then concludes that: 'The cobbler should stick to his last, the player to his part, and the film-director to his film-script' (1948: 1). The foreword further demonstrates that an important part of Olivier's strategy for gaining recognition for the specialized machinery of his own professional institution is the organization of a quasi-industrial team of other equally specialized professionals to realize his interpretation of *Hamlet* in film form. Such an organization has clearly become a necessity in the kind of professionalized arts world Bensman describes, where higher levels of technical proficiency and stricter specialization are demanded of everyone. It is not surprising then that Olivier uses the same foreword in which he makes a claim for the separation of different professional spheres to thank a long list of collaborators, whose particular professional contributions he underlines in each case. These include Alan Dent, the script consultant and editor of the book; Roger Furse, the art director; William Walton, the composer whose music, Olivier believes, 'speaks most eloquently for itself'; Reginald Beck, 'that non-pareil of cutters'; and 'my inspired and highly inventive camera-man Desmond Dickinson'. As a group he describes them, in a language more reminiscent of industrial management than artistic inspiration, as 'the most loyal little committee that ever an actor-director has worked for and with'. Olivier's high regard for industrial forms of organisation is further underlined when he goes on to legitimate the decision to make a film version of *Hamlet* simply by pointing to the support of producer J. Arthur Rank who, in Olivier's words, 'was prepared to harness his vast and superb organisation to my film' (1986: 2–3).

Olivier is concerned, however, that within such an organization, every individual take a professional approach to his or her own specialized work. In *On Acting*, published almost 40 years after *Hamlet, The Film and the Play*, Olivier argues that this applies even to the most humble bit player:

> To achieve true theatre, you can't have one man up front and the acolytes with their backs to the audience feeding the great star with lines as dull as dishwater. What you must have is every character believing in himself and, therefore, contributing to the piece as a whole, placing and pushing the play in the right direction. The third spear carrier on the left should believe that the play is all about the third spear carrier on the left. I've always believed that.
>
> (1986: 22)

For Olivier, the machinery of professional acting can only work if everyone treats it seriously all of the time. If they do this, he believes, it will not be their personal 'star qualities' that will prove their value, but their deep grasp of the machinery of the profession itself, and it is this emphasis on the machinery of the institution that allows Olivier to associate acting with other kinds of professional activity. By demonstrating that acting, like other forms of professional work, cannot be successfully under-taken without particular institutional training, he lays claim to a professionalism based on procedure rather than on genius. To be a successful actor, Olivier seems to say, one must not count on personal charm or exceptional talent, but on consistently applying a particular institutional approach to interpreting a text. Olivier's evaluation of his own work at the National speaks to this. 'They were a sensational company,' he says, 'and they were a company in the true sense of the word. Any one of my team, at any time, could have taken the helm and steered a play into safe harbour' (1986: 240). Clearly, Olivier believes this skill was achieved by cultivating a respect for the interpretative machinery of the theatre itself, and not by mindless obedience to the whims of an actor-manager. 'My company *did* speak and *were* heard,' he insists, adding 'I was able to pass on to them what had been passed on to me. For, although I maintain we must forever be looking forward, it is still very important to hold on to our theatrical roots and listen' (240).

Olivier's willingness to listen extended not only to other actors, but to professionals from outside the theatre whose reflected authority might colour public perception of the social value of the actor's art. Here again, *Hamlet* was among his boldest experiments. In *On Acting* Olivier relates how, at the instigation of Tyrone Guthrie, who was directing Olivier's first Hamlet at the Old Vic, he and Peggy Ashcroft, the production's Ophelia, went to visit Professor Ernest Jones, 'the great psychiatrist, who had made an exhaustive study of Hamlet from his own professional point of view' (1986: 48). Olivier walked away convinced that the key to understanding Hamlet's dilemma was to recognize that the young man suffered from the Oedipus Complex. He was determined to demonstrate this to his audience, but warned the professor that he 'would not find the Oedipus theories overt' in the production. In Olivier's recollection, Jones heartily agreed with this approach, saying: 'You're not supposed to tell the audience with every wink and nod that part of the reason for your present predicament is that you still wish you were hanging on your mother's tits' (49).

Olivier's reporting of Jones' response points to two important elements in the actor-director's approach to professionalizing the theatre. First, it underlines the device-like nature of the enterprise. For Olivier, Jones explanation of Hamlet's purported struggles with the Oedipus Complex functions like the devices Borgmann describes: this method of analysis constitutes the concealed and unfamiliar mechanism of a specialist's knowledge system. Olivier, in turn, subjects this analysis to his own concealed and unfamiliar acting and directing techniques. The result is a performance text that makes this interpretation of *Hamlet* readily available to large audiences who need never be bothered by evidence of the mechanism that created it. Second, it shows how Olivier was able to interpret *Hamlet* in a way that emphasized both the mind's role in controlling the body and the necessity of turning one's back on tradition. By demonstrating that he could apply Freudian psychoanalysis to the performance of Hamlet, Olivier simultaneously associated acting with one of the most modern forms of professional meaning-creation and denounced the power of tradition through his censure of Gertrude, the only character in the play who consistently argues for a traditional approach to social relationships.

Of course, if Olivier is to be taken at his word, we should not rely on what he writes about *Hamlet* but should look instead at how he actually performed the leading role, for it was acting that he claimed as his specialized professional mode of social communication. Indeed, a comparison of Olivier's 1948 film performance of Hamlet and Gilder's description of Gielgud's 1938 Hamlet, yields interesting insights about the different approaches the two actors took to interpreting the role that was so closely identified with their struggles for professional recognition.

Olivier's performance is marked by a sharp distinction between mental and physical responses to the events that surround him. From the beginning of the film Olivier portrays Hamlet as a thinker in rebellion against the traditional uses of the courtier's body. This is emphasized from our first glimpse of Hamlet in the court scene, where his appearance is preceded by a visual description of the court in which the new King demonstrates his carnal nature by downing a drink and embracing his Queen before attending to matters of state. The scene is performed with great ceremony, all of which involves carefully choreographed movement: Polonius signals for trumpet fanfares, starts the applause that greets the King's first pronouncement and leads the courtiers to rise to their feet every time the King or Queen moves past them. In contrast, Hamlet sits perfectly still downstage of the main action of the scene. When the King first turns attention to him after granting Laertes permission to return to France, Olivier moves his hand from the side of his face to the arm of his chair in a manner clearly designed to draw audience attention to himself as the action shifts in his direction. But from this moment onwards he is perfectly still except when he moves his head slightly to respond to his mother's gaze, a move that is immediately contrasted by the courtiers who shift their whole bodies ninety degrees to follow the King as he moves past them to speak to Hamlet. When the King declares that Hamlet is closest to the throne, he turns his back on the Prince to face the courtiers, who in turn rise to their feet. The declaration made, Polonius again signals for a trumpet fanfare and all applaud, except Hamlet, whom the camera catches sitting perfectly still and staring at the ground just as he had before the King started to speak. His pose changes not at all except when he raises his head to respond to his mother's plea that he not return to Wittenberg and to accept her long and decidedly unmaternal kiss. After this he returns his head to its original position, his body having moved not at all, and is captured sitting perfectly still in the foreground of a long shot from above that shows the King, Queen and courtiers leaving the stage in a flurry of controlled motion. Where others simply act according to the dictates of tradition, Olivier seems to be saying, both Hamlet and the actor who embodies him must step out of this traditional world altogether to concentrate on the things of the mind. This impression is reinforced in the scene immediately following when the camera zooms in on Hamlet's face as the 'too too solid flesh' speech is heard in voice-over, clearly marking it as a private thought rather than a public declaration. It is only then, once the room is emptied of ceremony, that Hamlet rises from his chair and moves aimlessly about the space, only to be arrested by the sight of his father's empty throne, from which he turns away sharply as it reminds him of the short period of mourning his mother has observed.

This pattern of movement is repeated throughout the film as Olivier uses restrained movement to denote planned actions and portrays madness as a pattern of abrupt and directionless moves that often retrace the same ground and seem to follow no predetermined plan. Perhaps more importantly, he shows Hamlet physically evading courtly ceremony by climbing to the top of the castle walls where he again sits perfectly still to contemplate his next action. This move is often reinforced by the camera that zooms in on Olivier's head, as it does for the famous 'To be or not to be' soliloquy, where it seems to actually move into Hamlet's skull and show us the world through his eyes. But ultimately Hamlet, like Olivier, cannot win his battles by avoiding physical interactions, a point he first acknowledges indirectly when he instructs the players on how to use their bodies in a dumb show designed to challenge the king. The success of this endeavour is denoted in the film by a chaotic exit of King and courtiers that inverts the decorum of the first exit of the court from the council chambers, with Hamlet moving wildly about the room as the King and Queen rush up the stairs and the courtiers scatter. It is noteworthy though that Olivier's Hamlet can only control his own body once he is able to control Gertrude's: in the closet scene, Olivier shows us a forceful Hamlet who physically restrains a hysterical Gertrude in order to make her listen to his version of his father's death. Remarkably the Ghost, represented as a disembodied heartbeat, in turn pushes Hamlet to the ground when he interrupts this diatribe with a demand for the revenge the dutiful son has promised. The scene ends as Hamlet and his mother demonstrate their reconciliation around Hamlet's version of events by engaging in a more maternal embrace than that which ended the first scene. This frees Olivier's Hamlet to become the conscious warrior who can choose to participate in the fencing match with Laertes and so fulfil his oath to kill the King. Not surprisingly, Olivier/Hamlet does this in the most modern fashion, with a sensational leap from the balcony that shows the actor Olivier as the consummate professional, unfettered by tradition and taking complete control of his own body to make a spectacular finish in the familiar role.

Olivier's choice to make direct control of the body the centre of the role stands in contrast to Gielgud's more tradition-centred portrayal of the young Prince. Where Olivier used the opening court scene to establish a rupture between mind and body, Gielgud's performance turned more on Hamlet's need to control his responses to social tradition, just as the actor Gielgud struggled to control his responses to theatrical tradition. So, for instance, where Olivier stilled the body in the first court scene, Gielgud emphasized the difference between chosen actions and actions dictated by decorum. The audience's first view of Gielgud in the role, as chronicled in Gilder's exhaustive description, is against the background of an elaborately staged council meeting where 'courtiers and attendants stand about, their attention riveted on the King in his showy glory'. By contrast, Hamlet is 'a black arabesque of silent scorn' whose pose 'expresses by its stiff and slightly mannered line his unwilling submission to a formal necessity' (Gilder 1965: 89). In this production the King dismisses the court before addressing Hamlet directly, a choice that cannot but emphasize the difference between public and private behaviours. Yet in such a formal setting, the fact that Hamlet remains seated and forces the King to come to him, rather than respecting the usual formalities of authority, must read as a rejection of tradition. It is striking then that when the Queen approaches him, Hamlet rises to greet her, only to lose his formal composure as she speaks to him of his father's death. He closes the scene by kissing his mother on the cheek, and marking the King and Queen's exit with the formal bow that tradition dictates, despite his distaste for the position in which traditional decorum places him. The formal quality of this gesture is further underlined when 'the mask of manners that has protected Hamlet's face drops' as soon as the King and Queen have left the room (Gilder 1965: 90–5).

This is a pattern Gielgud used throughout the performance, showing Hamlet rejecting tradition only to fall into traditional patterns of action when he feels the need for a positive emotional response, and then slipping out of social intercourse altogether as his own emotions get the better of him. The problem of the play is thus posed as one of finding a correct relationship to traditional practices, one that will allow for rational evaluation of each situation with which the thinking actor is confronted, yet will not place him completely outside the social world in which he must act. Following this pattern, Gielgud's Hamlet confronts Gertrude in a much less physical way than does Olivier's. In the same closet scene where Olivier's Hamlet struggled physically to control Gertrude, Gielgud's Hamlet struggles against a decorum born of emotional entanglement as he attempts to convince his mother of the rationality behind his anger. He 'takes her roughly by the arm and pushes her down on the end of the bed' only to sit beside her, even more determined to 'make her see what he sees'. He rejects her offered embrace on 'to give the world assurance of a man', his hands flying up, 'pushing her off, repudiating her', as he goes on to paint a vivid word picture of his Father's death while gazing at the ground before him, then leaps to his feet in anger, leaving Gertrude to pull away and attempt to shield herself from his searing words with upraised hands (Gilder 1965: 181–3).

In keeping with this approach, Gielgud's Ghost does not physically overpower his recalcitrant son as does Olivier's, but reminds him how tradition demands that he direct his anger. The issue in this scene is not the repression of the body, but its correct and conscientious direction. So, when Hamlet attempts to follow the Ghost from the room, the sound of his mother's voice calls him back from the doorway where it has disappeared (Gilder 1965: 183–5). With this action, which echoes Gertrude's movement towards the door at the beginning of the same scene, Gielgud reminds us that no-one can solve the problem of tradition by refusing to face the material realities of his or her own world. If the tradition dictated by Gielgud/Hamlet's predecessors is to survive, Gielgud seems to say, it must be brought into confrontation with the realities of the modern world and not simply repeated as a habitual pattern of action.

Only after he accepts this does Gielgud's Hamlet become the rational being who has any hope of convincing his Mother, and more importantly the audience, of the reasonableness of both his emotions and his actions. As with Olivier's Hamlet, Gielgud's can only make the conscious choice to kill the King once he faces the lessons of the closet scene, but unlike Olivier, Gielgud creates a death scene in which Hamlet is reconciled with tradition. Having consciously chosen to kill the King with the very weapons the King has used against him, Gielgud's Hamlet embraces the mother who has argued for tradition throughout the play, then, with the help of Horatio, moves across the stage to Laertes' body as the effects of the poison visibly start to cripple his own. In Gilder's description, 'the poison is working on his body, but his spirit is indomitable' (1965: 227–33).

Gielgud, like Olivier, uses the last scene to demonstrate what for him is the crucial skill in the new professional actor: the ability to reconnect with a dying tradition by concentrating on a correct interpretation of the text before him. Following the tradition of his predecessors, Gielgud closes the play with a striking stage picture that must surely bring applause, but this is a new kind of picture. It is the picture of the new professional who establishes an emotional distance from the everyday needs of the body, firmly controlling it with the power of his indomitable mind. For Gielgud, as for Olivier, Hamlet has served as much more than a starring role, it has become a vehicle for the modern actor's struggle with the encumbrances of theatrical tradition and the proving ground for a claim to professional standing in a modernist world.

Note

1   All quotations of *Hamlet* are taken from Harbage (1969).

4

Translation at the intersections of history

JEAN-MICHEL DÉPRATS

As Antoine Vitez would have us remember, 'The stage director interprets the signs left on paper by people from bygone centuries (this is called the text), and also, or perhaps, above all, interprets the movements and intonations of the actors who are before him on the stage' (1988: 26). Thus, the theatre is an arc stretching between the past and present, between the age of a text and the reality of a body that exists in the present; the theatre, 'at the crossroads of the past and the present, unites a time-space continuum within itself' (Banu 1987: 13). To be sure, contemporary plays are performed, but Roger Planchon denies that true staging is involved here.[1] In any event, whether we are happy about the fact or deplore it, twentieth-century theatre is primarily devoted to going over the Classics, to rereading these 'broken structures', these 'sunken galleons' as Vitez describes them in a very fine essay. In his opinion, the purpose of contemporary staging is not so much to restore, or to reconstitute, as to transform, 'by using their parts to create something else.' Our work, says Vitez, is 'to show the fissures of time' (1976: 9).

Indeed, the question that arises for staging, which Vitez sees as the 'art of variation', is its relationship to these fissures of time, to a past that is lost. What the modern director must deal with is history, the distance between the period of the text and the period of the production. Should we bring the play up-to-date by making Shakespeare, Chekhov or Molière our contemporaries? Or, on the contrary, should we delve into the past to unearth the original context, and underline the differences and the distance that separates them from us? The choice is not limited to these alternatives, and this schematic presentation does not take into consideration the existence and overlapping of several temporal strata. The historical period depicted in a play is not necessarily that of its creation, and staging can refer to another period than that of the performance. Put simply, we can have *Julius Caesar* played in togas, in Elizabethan costumes, in suits . . . or in Wehrmacht uniforms. . . . This is when one is not choosing what Vitez calls 'costumes of eternity', or the types of costume Peter Brook chose for *Timon of Athens*, in which the costumes were not linked to a specific period, and clearly denoted *a prototype* of the social function or status of the characters.[2] The most successful choices are those in which there is an interplay of periods, a combination of references, and the most striking staging. These stagings superimpose several time-strata in the same sheaf of images and let us immerse ourselves the most deeply in our memory. This was the case for the staging of *Electra* in Chaillot in 1988: the costumes, the actors' gestures and the decor managed *simultaneously* to evoke Greece as it once was and as it was in the 1970s–1980s, the Greece of Antiquity and the Greece of the Colonels. In this show, which was extremely powerful in its polyphonic vibrations, Redjep Mitrovista's rather thug-like Orestes and Eric Frey's Egisthus (who wore a white suit and looked like a cross between a crook and a pimp) were quite out of place. In a polysemous production, actualization that was too obvious and univocal condemned these characters to function in an impoverished referential mode. Be this as it may, even if a staging gains from articulating several time-space references rather than working on one paradigmatic axis, it cannot be devoid of historical landmarks.

Nor can translation. Translations, like stagings, periodically reassimilate traces from the past as they are exemplified by the great classic works. And this task of translation, like staging, must perpetually be done over. 'I perceive this as the very image of Art itself,' says Antoine Vitez: 'the Art of the theatre, which is the art of infinite variation. Fresh interpretation must continually be produced, the whole play must be looked at again and re-translated' (1982: 6). The translator of older works, like the stage director, is astride the past and the present: he serves two masters,[3] and travels not only between two languages but between two periods – the time of the text and that of its reception. He can take a historical approach or can modernize it, thereby choosing to anchor it more firmly on one shore or the other, strengthening one allegiance to the detriment of the other.

In a majority of cases, the translator takes a clear stand in relation to two powerful and apparently antithetical options: distance or proximity, remoteness or closeness. Over and above lexicological choices – and the choice of words is never a purely linguistic decision – translation sets up a plan, which may or may not be deliberate, of how it will relate to the history of the language. There are basically two tendencies or ways of translating older texts. Either the text can be anchored in antiquated language, or the old text can be rendered in the most contemporary language possible. One can accentuate the author's time, or the reader's/ listener's time. This choice calls for an analysis of the text's relationship with the past. The historic approach emphasizes what is over, what is unique and discontinued. The actualizing approach, on the contrary, emphasizes underlying affinities; it underlines things that are permanent, and describes History as the return of the past, in a different guise. Vitez compares two diametrically opposed Russian translations of *Tartuffe* that were played in Moscow at the same time; one was by Lozinski, and the other by Donskoï.

> In Moscow, I staged *Tartuffe* using Lozinski's translation. . . . The objective of this translation is to make the reader and the spectator feel that the text and the characters belong to the past. The style evokes a rather domestic, provincial life. That is Lozinski's *staging*. However, at the same time *Tartuffe* was being played in Moscow, Lioubimov's *Tartuffe* was being performed using another translation. It was excellent also, but very different, being contemporary. This was not by happenstance: Lioubimov needs to say things that can be grasped immediately at a political level. Lozinski's *staging* is based on keeping distances and on historic insight, whereas Donskoï's shows closeness and depicts how situations are similar. In translation itself, therefore, there is a *staging* effect.
>
> (Vitez 1982: 7)

I would like to illustrate the different 'staging' effects of translations which approach texts from a historical or from a modern standpoint, and to analyze the textual processes by which this game of 'pretence' is established. For it appears to me that each approach, which is justifiable in and of itself, is the product of a deception or a strategy based on a specific falsehood. Translations of Shakespeare lend themselves well to this exercise.

The desire to translate Shakespeare into language that corresponds to sixteenth-century English is a legitimate one. What can be more honest than not pulling the work out of its original linguistic and cultural environment, and keeping intact the threads that bind it to its epoch and historical context? As Daniel Mesguich argues: 'History is embedded in textuality' (Mesguich and Vittoz 1977: 27). 'What is a modern French translation of Shakespeare's *Hamlet*? . . . It is surely not a translation of Shakespeare's *Hamlet* in modern French' (13). Moreover, the translator, who is the herald of the past, cares more about the history of the language than anyone else. 'Translating', Jourdheuil reminds us, 'can only be perceived as the inaugural gesture for the survival of a work' (1982: 35). The translator then becomes, in the words of Florence Delay, 'the teacher of what has been lost', and takes on the role of curator for the history of the language; in so doing, he responds to what is perhaps his strongest calling:

> Language is always what exists before oneself: it is the past. We need its memory. . . . Its protection is its past. And what do we know of its future? How many works from the Middle Ages, from the Renaissance, and from more recent centuries, have already disappeared! The translator of ancient texts can rekindle the existence of things that have been lost, bring to light words that have been forgotten . . . what has been lost can be rediscovered.
>
> (1982: 29)

Translation can then be described, in the words of Georges Banu, as 'the utopian attempt to bring the memory of the past back to life' (Delay 1982: 29).

It remains to be seen what means can be used for this resurrection; for making utopia viable, so to speak. The recently re-edited translation of *Hamlet* by Eugène Morand and Marcel Schwob provides a convincing example.[4] Schwob objects strongly to modernized translation: 'The critics here have not reflected on the fact that sixteenth-century style is no longer the one at hand.

Putting Shakespeare's period in today's mode would be about on the same order as wanting to translate a page from Rabelais into Voltaire's language. We have to keep in mind that Shakespeare was thinking and writing during the reigns of Henri IV and Louis XIII.'[5] And yet, their translation is only intermittently archaic and very slightly so. For instance, Hamlet refers to his mother who showers her husband with amorous attentions 'comme si son désir eût forci par sa pâture même.'[6] *Forci; pâture*: one of the words is rare, and the other belongs to the literary register. As we will see in numerous examples, the archaic effect is not the reflection of true historic and linguistic authenticity, but rather the result of rhetorical processes such as using an elevated literary level of language, resorting to rare words, and syntactic breaks. Further on, Polonius says to Ophelia 'combien l'âme est prodigue à prêter à la langue des serments' (Morand and Schwob 1986: 58; *Hamlet* I.iii.116–17). The turn of phrase *prodigue à* is not properly established in French. This is an example of syntactic licence, and is Schwob's invention. But it has a fragrance of yesteryear and it creates a slightly archaic impression. One of the questions that arises concerning texts that are deliberately archaic, is that of the authenticity of the language thus produced. It would appear that there is necessarily an aspect of artifice to be found in the recreation of archaic language.

Michel Vittoz, for one, is aware that he is working with artifice. In his translation, he makes an effort not to translate old into new and to recognize that *Hamlet* is a classic text. His archaic expressions are concocted; he is deliberately aiming at an effect in staging with an eye to literature rather than to authenticity. Furthermore, his adaptation is heterogeneous: he blends archaic language, in which Elizabethan English is translated into sixteenth-century French, with modern language that uses the latest 'in' word games, the purpose of which is to work with the language of the body and to make the signifier speak using some Lacan-inspired puns. 'Puis-je me Père mettre?' Polonius asks Claudius, whose place he is taking in order to question Hamlet.[7] 'Je ne suis que le pâle reflet de ton fleuret,' Hamlet says to Laertes (a translation of: 'I'll be your foil Laertes').[8] In this way, along-side Latin constructions, false syntactic archaisms (placing the noun complement before the noun), and true lexical archaisms (*oncques, remembrance, souvenance*), the translation also refers to current texts and uses organized/disorganized phraseology that is eminently modern. Set mid-way between Ronsard, Mallarmé, Maurice Scève and Lacan, Vittoz's translation belongs to no particular period: it is no closer to Shakespeare's time than it is to our own. The main effect is to distance *Hamlet* from us and to mark it as an old, archaic text, connected to dramatic rhetoric that we no longer remember except as a literary keepsake. The stylistic processes that are used here are designed to suggest what a great distance separates us from *Hamlet*.

Two short extracts illustrate the tone of this translation: the first is in Claudius' initial monologue, and the second is a sentence from the most famous monologue in *Hamlet*.

> *Claudius*: Combien qu'en la mémoire nous soit encore
> récente
> La mort de notre frère chéri Hamlet, et qu'il sied
> De maintenir nos cœurs en le chagrin, ainsi que
> le front
> De l'entier royaume tout à douleur contracté,
> C'est assez que notre souvenance aille vers lui avec
> sage tristesse
> Sans que gagne l'oubli de nous-mêmes.[9]

> *Hamlet*: Comme au soleil en nous s'achèvent les tourments,
> les mille atteintes par la nature à la chair portées,
> toute l'âme aspire à telle consomption. Mourir,
> dormir . . . Dormir, rêver peut-être, oui, mais au
> sommeil de la mort, les songes à venir, quand
> règne enfin la paix en notre fatal désordre, nous
> doivent retenir. Là se tiennent les égards qui
> prêtent à malfortune longue vie.[10]

This *artifact* is sufficiently elaborate to conjure up a recreated memory of sixteenth-century language. This is done by highly literary means (the French text is much more mannered than the original), and Shakespeare appears to be a mannered artist. It is striking to see how self-reflexive the translation is. It listens to itself; it watches itself translating, and acknowledges the artifice on which it is founded. In this instance, the translation is being staged by itself.

While they both employ techniques that create the impression of archaism, neither Schwob's nor Vittoz's translations of *Hamlet* is a naïvely natural and deliberately archaic translation that wants to pawn itself off as authentic. We are not presented with a translation 'the way that' one would have translated in a historical period different from the time when the translations were actually made. Examples of that kind of translation can be found in the attempts by Littré, Borchardt and Pézard to translate Dante into Provençal, in Old German and in Old French, respectively. For Antoine Berman (1985), these deliberately archaic translations are 'typical of the philological spirit when it wants to outdo itself.' If we compare André Pézard's translation of *The Divine Comedy* with Jacqueline Risset's translation for Flammarion, the contrast is striking (Pézard 1965; Risset 1985). Pézard has opted for studied language that purports to be the equivalent of Dante's Italian, and has created fourteenth-century 'pseudo-French.' The result may well be prodigious and prestigious; it is, however, totally unintelligible to a reader who is not a medieval specialist. The antiquating effect obliterates any other goal, in particular, the transmission of meaning. At this level of erudition, one may well ask oneself whether the hold philology has over us is not indeed *fatal* for our relationship to classic works, because it is the wellspring for translations that are basically *unreadable*, or more unintelligible, in any case, than Dante's original text would be for an Italian living today.

The main question is that of our relationship to the work. The deliberately archaic translation refuses to lie by translating what is old into something new. It does not attempt to erase the passage of time and, in this case, it even draws attention to the age of the text and displays it. In so doing, however, it tends to deny us access to the text. Its only horizon is erudition; its only literary affinity is the pastiche. We know that, on the one hand, there are antiquarians, and on the other, cabinetmakers of period pieces. Translating Dante or Shakespeare into fourteenth- or sixteenth-century French is ineluctably creating a period piece. 'The great problem in philological translation', says Antoine Berman, 'is that it has *no* horizon. By that I mean, not only in terms of the principles of translation, but by being *anchored* in the language and the literature of the culture into which it is being translated. The starting point for one's translation is always a certain *state* in one's language and culture' (1985: 134). When Yves Bonnefoy was asked about his translation of *Hamlet*, which was directed by Chéreau in 1988, he agreed: 'A text has to be translated into the language that is spoken today: there is nothing more dangerous than dreaming of translating Shakespeare . . . in an imitation of our own language at the turn of the sixteenth century' (1988: 5).

While the deliberately archaic translation refuses to lie about the passage of time intervening between author and translator, it remains based on a lie, or, at the very least, on fiction. The deliberately archaic translation substantiates the fiction of a translator moving about in a language – moreover, an artificial language – that is not his own. He is trying to translate in the way it would have been done in one period or another. The attempt is particularly risky when no contemporary translation has been made of the work. We have a translation of Montaigne's *Essais* by an erudite English grammarian, John Florio, who was of Italian extraction. But we do not have – unfortunately, or fortunately – any contemporary French translations of Shakespeare. After Shakespeare's death, we must wait a century and a half, until 1746, for the first French translations by La Place to appear, followed some thirty years later by those of Le Tourneur. A modern attempt to provide the French translation which a contemporary of Shakespeare's might have made is intellectually legitimate as a way of being faithful to the text. Translating Shakespeare in 'fictitious' French from the beginning of the seventeenth century is an attempt to reproduce the relationship of an English speaker in 2001 to a work that antedates him by four centuries. The contemporary aspect being aimed at in such a translation is that of the translation, the author, and the original recipients of the work. It risks, however, creating such a distance between its object and contemporary readers or spectators that it threatens to destroy the immediacy that exists between them and the text.

By contrast, the primary objective of the modern translation – more precisely, the deliberately modern translation – is to stay in touch, to fill the physical and mental gap that separates the public from the actors, and the text from its readership. The modern translation is not devoid of an initial falsehood either. Another kind of fiction must be created here. The text that is presented to be heard or read must give the impression that it was written today. The historicity of the original text has been occluded and short-circuited. This is the way that most translations are done, and it is for this reason that they must be redone every ten years.

The most obvious and deliberate modernized translations of Shakespeare are those of Jean-Claude Carrière. Those translations are themselves inextricably bound to Peter Brook's particular theatrical practice. In Brook's view, Shakespeare set up his text in such a way that the actors and the spectators were bound together by 'a constant flow of words. And these words are powerful ones . . . very strongly charged. [Thanks to them] . . . we are continually connected to one another.'[11] Brook is inspired by his ambition to 'connect' the scene and the spectators. In Brook's terms, this is done by establishing a clear French text that flows quickly, articulated around radiating words, with syntax that is less logical than prismatic (Vincent in Carrière 1974: 97). The most obvious characteristic of that text is that it is written in modern language, with 'sparse, modern terms that have a clear meaning for today's audience' (Brook, quoted in Carrière 1974: 108). There are no literary or unusual words; the sentences are incisive in their phrasing, and the vocabulary is commonplace. The *Timon* text by Jean-Claude Carrière was seen to be so direct and natural, that during one show in the suburbs, some young spectators thought they were seeing a modern play (Marienstras 1977: 35). Jean-Claude Carrière told us that a rock singer used one of the monologues from *Timon* without changing a word: the modern language with its perfect rhythm became a natural means of contemporary communication and expression.

Before analyzing the characteristics of this adaptation and the means that were used to make it contemporary, let us consider the analysis that is the cornerstone of this approach and this project. For Brook,

> the play is much less accessible in English than it is in French, but for the wrong reasons. Its archaic language no longer has a direct effect on the audience the way it did during the Elizabethan period. Certain passages are no longer understood by anyone other than scholars. . . . If archaic language moves to the fore, then it is a barrier that should be removed. This is what Carrière's simple and straightforward translation does.
>
> (Millon 1975: 88)

Seen in this light, the translation of a text into another language – far from being either a makeshift solution or a necessary evil, as it is often considered by people who take pleasure in insisting on the inevitable loss of meaning it entails – is an opportunity to create a more vital bond with a work that one can clearly not bring closer in its original language. Coming from another angle, Georges Lavaudant arrives at the same conclusion and expresses the same conviction when he declares:

> When I speak of the necessity of retranslating certain authors, it seems to me that we are touching a raw nerve. In France, fortunately (or unfortunately), we have the opportunity to translate Shakespeare. . . . If, quite suddenly, we heard the British dramatist's language in the same way we hear Rabelais and Montaigne, I am not convinced we would be as attracted by him. The curious alchemy that lets us 'modernize' Shakespeare through our translations is, after all, a golden opportunity. In the last analysis, perhaps we only like the poet from Stratford-on-Avon because of the permanent betrayal/recreation that his work is subjected to by successive translations. Could it be that playing Shakespeare is still a convoluted way of working on an unedited linguistic work, and perhaps, of playing a contemporary text?
>
> (Lavaudant 1984: 12–13)

In the case of Jean-Claude Carrière and Peter Brook, the decision to translate Shakespeare into modern language stems from a desire to establish a live contact that is free and natural with the audience. The choice of simple, non-literary words is not the only weapon in this strategy for a good text–audience relationship. In the translation of *Timon* (as in Carrière's translation of *Measure for Measure*), speed and concision are increased by a certain number of conscious breaks in the text. These breaks are adroitly spread out, and are sometimes linked to a play on words that is difficult to translate. 'In certain cases, Jean-Claude Carrière breaks up a monologue and distributes the text between several characters. . . . He abridges certain passages and ends up with a translation that is shorter and clearer than the original text. . . . He often breaks the Shakespearean sentence into pieces and multiplies propositions, ellipses, noun phrases and exclamations.'[12]

Take, for example,

                      Ay,
If money were as certain as your waiting,
Twere sure enough.[13]

In Carrière's translation, this becomes: 'Ah oui! Vous attendez! C'est sûr! Plus sûr que l'argent!' (1974: 48). As Richard Marienstras notes, 'The modernity of the French text is as much an offshoot of this syntax as it is of linguistic choices that are often successful: strong expressions, terms that actors can use for repartee or project powerfully without becoming breathless from the intricacies of an oratorical sentence, or bogged down by adjectives that are bunched together or split up' (1977: 36–7).

In addition to these changes in form that produce a clear, incisive and swiftly moving text, based on the frugal use of rhetoric, one can add other changes that affect the symbolic universe of the play. 'The text is prepared so that it can be stated energetically and received without ambiguity: whatever entrenches it too firmly in Elizabethan ideology has been expurgated' (Marienstras 1977: 38). An example is the response of a guest after a meal of stones and water: 'He's but a mad lord and naught but humours sway him' (*Timon* III.vi.106–7), becomes 'C'est un accès de folie, voilà tout' (1974: 59). The reference to the 'humours' that create Timon's agitation, which refers to the four basic humors that need to be balanced for equanimity, is not rendered. Some radiating words that relate to Elizabethan ideology are stripped of their historic content. Therefore, 'bond', a word designating reciprocal bonds, a complex system of obligations, is translated by *devoir*; 'bounty', the virtue of magnificence and liberality that characterized princes, is mistranslated by *bonté* (Marienstras 1977: 38). In her study of *Measure for Measure* in translation, Martine Millon also notes that key terms have lost their meaning: *mercy*, a word designating the Christian concept of mercifulness, which is part of the prerogatives and duties of the powerful, translated by *pitié*; *liberty* translated literally by *liberté*, whereas it means licence (1985: 117). A refusal to refer to the ideology of the period inevitably leads to inaccuracies and oversimplifications that reduce the symbolic significance and the moral universe of the play. Over and above the rhetorical processes which increase speed and concision (such as flexible syntax, concentrated and reduced meaning, frequent elimination of ambiguities, modification of the structure to the benefit of discontinuity, and reinforcement of immediate clarity), the changes that affect the historic referent help structure a timeless text. With this *interpretation*, the original text is always modern, unfettered by specific values or by a precise moment in History. This is clear in Peter Brook's summary of the *Timon* fable.

He does not say something like: 'In a society ruled by the love of money and egotistical calculation, an aristocrat is confronted by the consequences of his magnificence'; he says, rather, 'Once upon a time there was a man who tried to acquire love and friendship in such and such a way.' (Millon 1975: 89). In contrast to the historicism of the theatre, Brook describes a man and timeless human feelings to reinstate the human being in his trans-historical generality. The choices that are made in translation are at the service of this interpretation or ideology, for translation cannot escape from interpretation any more than can the actual staging.

When confronted with another kind of distance between text and audience, a distance not in time but in space, Jean-Claude Carrière's translation practice apparently indicates a middle path. He preserves certain specific cultural elements without multiplying the vistas, or referring us to what is incomprehensible and unfamiliar. His adaptation of *The Cherry Orchard* illustrates his desire to place himself at the crossroads. Christine Hamon reminds us that the Pitoeffs francised the text so much that its Russian reality was jeopardized. Elsa Triolet kept the Russian terms and explained them in footnotes. For his part, Jean-Claude Carrière adopted an in-between approach, which consisted in keeping the Russian word when it was very well known, like 'muzhik', and in translating more obscure words with periphrasis. 'Generally speaking, the predominant concern seems to be rejection of cultural markers that would show *The Cherry Orchard* as a historical and sociological creation, but also the rejection of excessive assimilation of the text. This ambiguous bias reduces and partially preserves cultural distances' (1985: 263–4).

Jean-Claude Carrière explains his approach as follows:

> *The Cherry Orchard* can be performed as a play with historical roots, in which we catch a glimpse of Russian life at the beginning of the [twentieth] century or, on the contrary, it can be played in blue jeans, in up-to-date costumes that will make it a completely modern play. In the play, we did not want to translate or stage just one image, but rather composite images and, at the same time, strengthen the relationship that the modern audience has with the play. If I keep 'versts' in the entire text, I will very gradually distance the text, whereas if I translate 'kilometers', no one will be bothered. On the other

hand, I kept 'kopek' and 'rouble' because everyone knows these words and there is nothing exotic about them. Ania says: 'I don't have a kopek.' . . . She might well have said, 'I don't have a cent' . . . but in that case the desire to draw the audience closer would have been too explicit.

(1982: 42)

The desire to bring the text closer to us which is too explicit, and too visible, can be seen in a great number of recent adaptations in which the language was too contemporary and too full of slang. For example, in Bernard-Marie Koltès' translation of *A Winter's Tale*, the worthy Camillo suddenly exclaims: 'Tout est foutu et bonsoir' (which comes from the bland 'yourself and me cry lost and so good night').[14] In Koltès' text, this is no more than one of a very few interruptions in the 'hoodlum' style, which he probably wants to use for effect as a break. A few 'fadaises' or a 'Fichez-la dehors' do not basically alter the continuity of a more formal register. In other cases, the systematic use of familiar language and slang that are part of everyday speech end up making all the characters appear vulgar. The desire to bring the text closer is dished out in facile humor, to wit Jean-Claude Grumberg's recent adaptation of *Three Sisters* in which Macha proposes to 's'en jeter un' and exclaims to Anfissa the nurse: 'J'en ai marre la vieille' (Grumberg 1988: 27; 41). There are also two instances in which the word *pékin* is used (this is Saint Cyr military slang): Macha says 'Aujourd'hui, il n'y a qu'un pékin et demi dans un calme de pierre tombale' (14), and, further on, Vershinin utters: 'Ici on écoute un membre de l'intelligentsia, qu'il soit en pékin ou en uniforme' (34). These create jarring notes, as would the use of Chtimi, a northern French dialect, or of a Marseilles accent spoken by a Cossack.[15] Such methods not only remove the text from its historical context, but they also run counter to the present Russian referent, at least as concerns the characters' names. This image of modernity that needs to use the most vulgar and violent slang is as equally impoverished and 'mythological' a convention as the hackneyed performances of desires and passions 'in the present' that can be found in certain films by Zulawski or Doillon. In one instance, to be modern, very colloquial speech is used. In the other instance, a conventional repertoire with demented bodies, strident hysteria, and extremes that run the gamut from muteness to shrieking and from slaps to embraces, is supposed to translate violent desire and sudden emotional impulses. Through language or on the screen, on paper or on the stage, *images* of modern times are created, through which we reappropriate the past. A textual or scenic representation of Shakespeare's or Chekhov's universe, refracted in the prism of modern sensitivity, comes on the heels of our predecessors' more noble Shakespeare giving us a harsher, more violent, and wilder Bard. The engagingly melancholic Chekhov of preceding decades is supplanted by a more direct Chekhov who is more scathing and more cruel. He is funnier too, sometimes. Contemporary Shakespearean staging accents everything sordid, rough, and primitive. We have Matthias Langhoff's *Roi Lear* in Babigny played in an innovative and stimulating theatrical mode (1987). We have Michel Dubois' *Titus Andronicus* played in a poor and epigonic mode in Chaillot (1987). 'Our' Shakespeare in French texts speaks more harshly, more abruptly, and more roughly than he did in preceding decades. He is stripped of literary affectations and of the 'wish to prettify things in a Giradoux-like mode', which led the Pléiade, for example, to translate the famous line from *The Tempest* 'Our little life is rounded by a sleep', by 'Notre petite vie, un somme la parachève.' In fact, a literal translation, 'Notre petite vie est entourée par un sommeil', would be simpler, more accurate and more fraught with meaning. In the 1980s and 1990s, Shakespeare speaks in stronger, more concrete terms.

Contemporary modernized Shakespearean translation moves towards more concrete and fuller language and, by the same token, towards rougher language. This raises the whole problem of how to translate obscenities. One of the main characteristics of translations from former decades was to water down, or sometimes to censure, the entire verbal stratum that referred to the body and to bodily functions, notably to sexuality. Since occluding these terms is systematic in François-Victor Hugo's translations, the current Pléiade edition, as we know, produces note after note at the end of its volume stating: 'obscene play on words'; 'untranslatable play on words.' At present, the tendency is rather to overemphasize obscene terms and put them in relief, setting aside more polite circumlocutions. It is striking, for example, to see how the phrase 'Aroynt thee, witch, the rump-fed ronyon cries'[16] (uttered by the first witch in *Macbeth*), evolves in a more and more graphic manner. The syntagma 'rump-fed ronyon' is successively rendered by:

La carogne au croupion bien nourri	F.-V. Hugo	(c. 1860)
La rogneuse au gros derrière	Maeterlinck	(1910)
La rogne à la croupe trop grasse	Jean Richepin	(1914)
La galeuse au gros fessier	Pierre Leyris	(1977)
Ce gros cul de matrone	Yves Bonnefoy	(1983)
La galeuse au gros cul	in my translation	(1985)

Finding the proper register for 'rump' poses a particular problem, because the term 'rump' occurs in the expressions 'Rump Parliament' and 'rump steak.' A translation with *cul* appears excessive, accentuating the verbal violence that is nevertheless clearly perceptible in its tones. The movement that leads successive translations to pass from *croupion* to *cul* in just over a century demonstrates quite clearly how sensitivity and taste have evolved, together with changes in perception and in how the original text is read.

The importance of the historical moment of translation in shaping how the Shakespearean text is being received and interpreted emerges clearly in Antoine Berman's remarks about German translations of Shakespeare:

> A. W. Schlegel and Tieck, for example, translate Shakespeare faithfully but, as Rudolf Pannwitz has said, without going far enough 'to render the majestic barbarism of Shakespearean verse' [Pannwitz 1947: 192]. This barbarism in Shakespeare that refers to things obscene, scatological, bloody, overblown . . . in short, to a series of verbal abuses . . . are aspects that the classical romantic German translation attempts to attenuate. It backs down, so to speak, before the Gorgon's face that is hidden in every great work.
>
> (Berman 1985: 93)

In his remark about Pannwitz' quotation, Antoine Berman only retains the word 'barbarism', omitting the word 'majestic', which balances his judgment and gives a nuance to 'the barbarism of Shakespearean verse.' It is interesting to note how this quotation describes the phenomenon of a certain modernity (obscenity, scatology, gore, extravagance), and draws the lineaments of a Shakespearean *interpretation* which, according to the commentator, defines the side of Shakespeare that speaks most clearly to our modernity. We invent Shakespeare for our own use, and every period is sensitive to one aspect or another, as is shown by how the works are staged, translated and read.

Translation, like staging, is not carried out by totally free agents, but by readers who exist in one moment in history and who, despite themselves, are governed by the sensitivity of a period, its literary tastes, and its relationship to the language. The different examples I have commented upon do not teach us, but confirm in a concrete way that 'a translation, like a performance, is a very ephemeral moment, which is contingent upon the approach one takes to a work' (Lasalle 1982: 11). This is why

> bringing a foreign text to the stage requires, as a first step, the creation of a new text as an affirmation that neither the translation nor its performance are definitive, and that they can only account for a particular dimension of the text at a given moment in its existence. This view is at odds with that of the editors who want a literary Utopia in which the translation is fixed forever.
>
> (1982: 11)

When a director decides, despite everything, that he wants to perform a theatrical work translated in an earlier period, one can see that he must deal with at least *three* temporal strata rather than *two*: that of the work, that of the translation, and that of the performance. In any case, he has to deal with two texts, the original *and* its translation. In answer to George Banu's question, 'Who is being put on the stage when we perform a great translation? Goethe, Nerval or Goethe-Nerval?' Vitez (1982) answers, 'If the translation is magnificent, then we stage the original and its translation. In this way, the translation also becomes a focus of the staging. In the case of Faust-Nerval, my work had to take into consideration the way in which the French Romantics looked at Goethe' (7).

Translations can also work with multiple temporal strata. The translator has the option, as does the director, of designing a complex structure with multifaceted syntax, in which language reflects the past, the present and the imminent future. This is the case, for example, in Klossowski's translation of the *Aeneid*. As he translates Virgil, Klossowski encounters the historic 'sites' of our language: the sixteenth-century poets, Maurice Scève, Racine, Corneille. However, his translation encompasses a vast and modern poetic horizon that covers the range from Mallarmé to Bonnefoy, including Claudel, Saint John Perse, the Surrealists and Jouve.[17] 'For its part, translation anchored in this type of poetic soil can change the future of poetry by revealing latent linguistic possibilities in the language' (Berman 1985: 134). At this juncture, translation unfolds in a double linguistic time frame: 'it must reinvest the language with a feeling of its history, going back to its roots, and it must open it up to a future full of unsuspected possibilities' (146).

Translation, like staging, is indeed a mark of the past, transformed by the subjectivity of another period and the sensitivity of the present that gives it shape. If we can consider translation as a *relationship* rather than a means of *transport*, archaism and modernism are no longer antinomic terms: they merely express two ways in which the present can establish its links with the past. Archaism is an imaginary construction which builds up an image of the past. Modernization is another form of memory, out of which a different relationship is forged with the past, but it cannot escape from history. In both cases, the truth of the translation must be envisaged, not in terms of adequacy, but in terms of manifestation.

Notes

1 'One can only be a stage director for "Classics". . . . There is no such thing as a critical production of a work by Brecht or by Genet. These works have appeared at the same time we have, so it is impossible to put them in perspective. The hidden "why" in staging the "Classics", works from the past, is perspective or historic hindsight' (Planchon 1977: 53–4).

2 Banu (1977: 98) Banu also comments on 'the coexistence and alternation of elements belonging to well-defined moments in history' and describes the theatrical space in *Timon* as a 'summing-up space' that appropriates elements from the Italian theatre, from Elizabethan space, Greek space and Medieval space (67–71).

3 The intrinsic condition of the translator is to perpetually find himself 'between two shores': between the poet and the academic; between the creator and the literacy critic; between the artist and the craftsman; between the original tongue and the mother tongue; between the literary and the literal.

4 Morand and Schwob (1986). This translation was staged for the first time in May 1899 at the Sarah Bernhardt Theater, with Sarah Bernhardt in the title role.

5 *Quatrième de couverture* [Jacket copy], Morand and Schwob (1986).
6 Morand and Schwob 1986: 47 See *Hamlet*: I.ii.144. All references are to the Arden edition (Jenkins 1982).
7 Compare *Hamlet* II.ii.170. These Lacan-like plays on words that appeared in the first version of the text, presented in Grenoble and Nanterre in 1977, were eliminated in the 1986 version by Papiers that was used for the new staging of *Hamlet* in the Saint Denis Gérard Philippe Theatre. The play on words is no longer there.
8 *Hamlet* V.ii.252. In my translation I have used a kind of portmanteau word: 'Je serai ton fleuret valoir', since *foil* is used to mean both the sword and a foil for something.
9 Compare *Hamlet* I.ii.1–7. I am quoting the 1977 version, parts of which had appeared in the journal *Silex* (Vittoz 1977: 9). The version published in 1986 brings the text closer to us by eliminating certain archaisms and syntactic breaks: 'et qu'il sied' becomes 'et qu'il convienne'; 'en le chagrin' becomes 'dans le chagrin', etc. (Vittoz 1986: 64).
10 *Hamlet* III.i.66–9. The revised version is quite different (Vittoz 1986: 104–5).
11 Interview for *Shakespeare et Peter Brook*, Broadcast prepared by Isidro Romero, Richard Marienstras and Peter Brook for the Institut National de l'Audiovisuel, 1974–5.
12 Marienstras 1977: 36–7. The previous remarks and those that follow, as well as the examples mentioned, are taken from his detailed study of Jean-Claude Carrière's translation.
13 Compare *Timon of Athens* (Oliver 1963: III.iv.46–8).
14 Koltès (1988) Compare *The Winter's Tale* (Pafford 1966: I.ii. 410–11).
15 Vitez uses this example (1982: 9) Vitez often comes back to the difficult problem of translating a dialect, and recommends under- rather than over-translating.
16 *Macbeth* (Muir 1960: I.iii.6).
17 See Berman (1985: 146).

5
Women's work and the performance of Shakespeare at the Royal Shakespeare Company
SARAH WERNER

Directors and theatre professionals today often speak of the right timing in producing a play – directors will explain that they chose to produce *King Lear* because it speaks to our current society, or someone will explain the resurgence of *Titus Andronicus*, for instance, as being rooted in its relevance to today's world and its problems. Richard Halpern refers to this practice of locating Shakespeare in our time in his account of the modernist notion of 'historical allegory'; part of the modernist legacy is seeing Shakespeare both as belonging to the remote past and as being an immediate presence, in which 'immediacy is always generated from and against historical difference' (1997: 5). Halpern argues convincingly that our view of Shakespeare at the end of the twentieth century remains strongly influenced by the modernist beliefs of those who studied him at the beginning of the century. But to understand Shakespeare's place on the modern stage, we must put alongside the modernist literary tradition the history of modern theatre. The two work together to give us a sense both of how Shakespeare is shaped in our theatres and how that shape is limited by the modernist parameters that make them possible.

One of the hallmarks of modern theatre is its interest in the spectator. As W. B. Worthen has put it, modern drama and modern theatre 'cast the spectators, so to speak, as part of the spectacle' (1992: 1). Worthen approvingly quotes Arthur E. Quigley, who describes a modern theatre

that gives priority to offering audience members the opportunity to participate in a particular mode of social inquiry. Such
participation requires audiences members to respond to the
challenge of reconsidering their role as audiences as a first step
in reconsidering the nature of the theatre and the nature of the
larger worlds in which they and it participate.

(Quigley 1985: 52-3; Worthen 1992: 3)

While literary studies began to consider Shakespeare in terms
of an 'historical allegory', modern dramatists began to use the
spectator's relationship to the drama as a way of investigating
the constraints of the outside world. The meeting of these two
developments paved the way for the state of today's Shakespeare
on stage, in which audiences are encouraged to see themselves
and their lives on stage in his plays and to take the lessons they
learn from the theatre home with them.

But while these two notions of the modern revitalized
Shakespeare and made his plays an indelible part of our modern
culture, they both failed to investigate the same thing. Both
rely on notions of audience and audience reaction – whether that
audience was reading or sitting in a theatre, their lives outside
the play determined the meanings that the play generated. But
neither questioned who that audience was. If they didn't assume
a timeless historical truth that was embodied in our present lives,
they did assume that there was something that could be thought
of as 'the' audience and 'our' lives. When feminist theory and
activism entered the world of Shakespeare on stage, however,
notions of a stable 'the' and 'our' soon disappeared. What male
directors had assumed was the meaning that could be gathered
from Shakespeare was contested by women whose experiences
of life and the plays were vastly different. In 1985, these differing
views met at the Royal Shakespeare Company (RSC), and led to
the brief existence of the RSC's Women's Group. In the history of
the Women's Group, we can locate the pressures that feminism
puts on modern Shakespeare.

The RSC Women's Group was a short-lived enterprise that
began approximately in the fall of 1985, and ended with their
production, directed by Susan Todd, of Deborah Levy's *Heresies* at
the Barbican Pit in the 1986/87 season. Although there had been
earlier informal gatherings of women's theatre work by RSC actors
in fringe venues and a Women's Theatre Workshop as part of the

1983 Barbican One Year On Festival, the Women's Group was the first company-sanctioned attempt to bring feminism under the umbrella of the RSC. Tracing the history of the RSC Women's Group is not a straightforward task. Since very little has been written about the group (aside from some examination of *Heresies* in the context of contemporary female playwrights), information about its history must be entirely reconstructed from participants' memories of it. Many of the participants, however, are reluctant to talk about their experience in the group. And because the group was at times acrimonious, some of those willing to discuss it are particularly eager to justify their side of the story. Moreover, the passage of ten years has altered how the participants see that history. Everyone who spoke to me emphasized that she or he did not remember many details about the group. What they did remember, which was cumulatively a great deal, is not necessarily factual evidence. Even the most concrete part of the group's history, their final production of *Heresies*, is not easy to access. Because I did not see *Heresies* in 1986, I have had to reconstruct the play from the archival video footage, the published script, the promptbook, reviews, and Susan Todd's recollections. What follows, then, is an interweaving of the various stories that make up the history of the RSC Women's Group – personal voices, company culture, and societal values that describe one moment of intersection between feminism and modern Shakespearean theatre.[1]

The RSC Women's Group had its origins in a weekend devoted to women's theatre work during the Fourth RSC/W. H. Smith Festival in the autumn of 1985. The Fortnight, as the festival was called, was a two-week event sponsored by W. H. Smith and created and run by RSC actors. According to the actor Fiona Shaw, that year 'it was agreed that rather than have the thing over-burdened with the majority of men which were in the company, that there would be a special weekend held for the women, of which Juliet [Stevenson] and I were put in charge.'[2]

During the course of planning for the Fortnight's Women's Weekend, Shaw and Stevenson began to hold meetings with other women in the company to discuss the relationship between femi-nism and theatre. The weekend itself was envisioned as a chance to focus on women directors in Britain. Shaw and Stevenson invited them all 'to come to Stratford and knock on the door' – in other words, not just to come to the conference, but to aim specifically for getting work at the RSC. Although not a great number of women directors came, the weekend on 19-20 October 1985 maintained this goal of improving the chances for women within mainstream theatre. The first day of the Women's Weekend was devoted to plays performed and devised by women and the second to talks and debates about women's roles in theatre. The weekend gave the women in the company a chance to perform but also opened discussion about the scope of their future work, especially on the final day as reported by Julia Pascal:

> But the afternoon was an open forum which took the debate away from academic analysis into a more pragmatic arena. What can actresses do in a power structure where the artistic control is dominated by white Oxbridge men? The debate explored the problems actresses encounter when they are not allowed to be directed by an equal quota of female directors. As Fiona Shaw said, 'What is being said at the RSC is that a good director is a male and a bad director is a female. The hiring system tells you that. We want to do something to redress that balance.'
>
> (Pascal 1985)

While supportive of the Women's Weekend, Pascal's report also anticipated the vast problems that would face the RSC Women's Group. Getting women directors in the front door of the RSC did not address the complexities of the challenge. While, according to Shaw, hiring female directors seemed radical to the company's male hierarchy, simply substituting female directors for male directors would do little to redress the inequality of power within the company.

If simply increasing the numbers of women at the RSC would not change the nature of the company, the absence of women was an indication of the company's antipathy towards women's appropriation of Shakespeare and male power, and so a likely focus for attention. The Women's Weekend came at a time when there was growing concern in the theatre community about the opportunities for women in the theatre. In January 1984, the Conference of Women Theatre Directors and Administrators (CWTDA) released a report by Sue Parrish on 'The Status of Women in British Theatre, 1982-83' which found that 'the more money and more prestige a theatre has, the less women will be employed as directors and administrators; the less likelihood that a play written by a woman will be commissioned or produced, excepting Agatha Christie; and the less women [*sic*] there will be on the Board' (Parrish 1984: b). The implications of this are profound for women, concludes Parrish:

> These facts taken together confirm that women are the least subsidised artists and workers in the theatre. This raises serious questions about equality of opportunity; of expression. This has in turn fundamental implications for the legitimate aspirations of women in theatre: for women directors to direct Shakespeare, and other classics, which are also their heritage: for women writers to write plays for main stages: for women actors to be offered parts which extend beyond playing a man's mother, wife, mistress, sister or daughter: and for women administrators to run their departments as equals, not as super secretaries, in whichever structures they choose.
>
> (1984: c)

Sue Dunderdale's summary of the report emphasizes that because women are part of the public which funds these theatres, they deserve to have equal access to those funds, a point that Fiona Shaw echoes when she later summarizes the goals of the Women's Group: 'it was a feeling that the RSC, which was a subsidized company by a country that was 53% women, would somehow reflect the preoccupations of the country totally.' Dunderdale ends her summary with a direct call to action:

> We must seek out and support the women who are managing to find work; and we must start to pressure those who award subsidy to make demands about access to and control over that subsidy by women. It is up to us to ensure that the situation revealed by the survey is not allowed to continue.
>
> (1984: 11)

Although there is no specific mention of the CWDTA report in accounts of the Women's Weekend or in Shaw's description of the formation of the Women's Group, the weekend and the subsequent group were clearly participating in the same culture that led to the CWDTA report.

Although the RSC management might have been taken aback by what they perceived as the actors' assault on the company, the group's concerns were neither out of the blue nor unfounded. At the time the Women's Group began in 1985, only one woman had made any sort of impact on the RSC: Buzz Goodbody was an important part of the RSC until her death in 1975. Subsequent female directors Penny Cherns, Jane Howell, Sheila Hancock and Di Trevis, however, did only one production each. The CWDTA report found that in the 1982/83 season, the artistic, associate and resident directors were all men, three of the four assistant directors were men, the administration was entirely male, and 70 of the 80 board members were men (Parrish 1984: 12). There was quite clearly little opportunity for women in the RSC, and the emergent Women's Group was understandably determined to change that. Although a narrow focus on hiring female directors would not radically change company identity or operations, it was the most obvious place for the Women's Group to concentrate their discontent.

After the Fortnight's Women's Weekend was over, the RSC women continued their meetings, culminating in a meeting with Terry Hands, then co-artistic director of the RSC. Shaw, Todd and Genista McIntosh (who had been the RSC Planning Controller from 1978 to 1984 and who briefly rejoined the RSC in 1986 as Senior Administrator) all describe a scenario in which the women began by putting their complaints to Hands. Hands, however, describes the meeting as something which he initiated and of which he was in control. Saying he had been aware of grumblings about the lack of opportunities for women within the RSC, Hands addressed them, 'trying to give a historical perspective and equally admitting that there was something that should be done.' Hands describes himself as a facilitator of the women's demands: they had complaints, so he wanted to give them a way of solving the problem. Having laid out a sketch of why theatre history had led them to this frustrating position, he then claims to have taken himself out of the picture: 'And then I left it and waited. I'm not sure there was anything else really I could have done.'[3] McIntosh explains the dynamics between the women and Hands rather differently: 'Because he's quite devious and quite clever . . . he kind of nodded in their direction without ever really putting anything tangible behind it.' 'In the end', she says, 'it was probably misguided to imagine that they were ever really being given per-mission to do anything much.' Hands essentially saw the women's demands as coming from a desire for better roles, a desire that all actors share; in his eyes, their frustrations were not so much gender-specific, as actor-specific. If there was going to be a group project, Hands saw the necessity of hiring women to direct and manage it, but he did not see the group as anything other than a chance to create a one-off piece of theatre with strong roles for women.

A few months after this, Lindsay Duncan, Fiona Shaw and Juliet Stevenson are purported to have given an interview in which they criticized the RSC for its lack of opportunities for women within the company. This interview, reportedly published in April 1986, is not in the Shakespeare Centre's RSC press clippings.[4] The Centre does, however, have a follow-up article by the theatre industry paper, *Stage and Television Today*, about the interview and the actors' subsequent reprimand. Reporter Angela Thomas claims that 'their remarks are being widely seen as a symptom of the growing discontent of women about the lack of opportunities for them in the theatre' and summarizes the actors' complaints as follows:

> In an interview with *Theatregoer Magazine*, the three actresses have highlighted the need for more women directors within subsidised theatre as well as the lack of any female influence on major policy decisions. They also claim that the RSC's so called 'women's project' was purely a reaction to another article which criticized the lack of women in the company. And they noted that the men at the top were more willing to give an inexperienced man, whether writer or director, rather than a woman the chance to learn his craft within the company.
>
> (Thomas 1986)

The industry paper supported the women's position by pointing out that the newly released report of the Directors Guild of Great Britain on the earnings of women directors upheld their complaints and by noting that 'women who do break through [into top companies] often find they are left to work on what are regarded as the less prestigious productions and their salaries remain well below those of their male counterparts.'

Hands was evidently furious with the actors and, says Shaw, sent them each 'an incredibly cross memo – for a moment we thought we were all going to lose our jobs.' Hands' sensitivity to their public criticisms (according to Shaw, he felt that 'we had washed our dirty linen in public') stemmed from his feeling that the company, under siege from the press, was facing enough difficulties without the actors adding to them. Although Hands now has no specific recollection of the *Theatregoer* interview or his reaction, he does agree that in light of press hostility and their financial crisis, he was likely to have been angry with the three actors: 'When anybody, male or female, chooses that moment to rock the boat, the timing is not appropriate. And it's not appropriate when you've actually said to them, "Look, have your own group, do your own thing" and they don't do it. That's when confused thinking becomes dangerously naïve. And as you would with a child, you smack its bottom.'

Hands' use of a parental metaphor here is, I think, unintentional. But his anger at the actors' interview was related as much to his sense of the RSC as a family organization as to his feelings of being under siege. As Hands said in an interview published a few years later than this incident, 'Our organization is built on personal relationships, making the whole structure analogous to a family. As a family we have our problems and our tensions, but we work together with the common aim of providing a service to the public' (McCullough 1988: 124). He repeated these feelings in our interview in 1996. Director Susan Todd suggested that the uproar over the interview was closely related to the company's dynamics as a 'family': 'They hate it at the RSC when any members of the company speak out. It works on loyalty very much; very familial.'[5] Loyalty to the company certainly was important to Hands, who insists that problems should have always been brought to him first and only as a last resort to the press.

The patriarchal structure of the RSC played an important role in determining the opportunities for women within the company and the ways in which the women reacted to it. Colin Chambers explicitly draws out how the idea of family worked in the company culture:

> The metaphor that still occurs is that of the family, and the traditional implications hold true. The Company remains a male-dominated hierarchy, with those who are definitely parents and those who are definitely children (and if they happen to be secretaries and women, which is most often the case, they will be servicing their wise, humanist 'fathers' with cups of tea or coffee). The family asks for and expects loyalty,

but looks after those it considers its own, especially in dealing with 'outsiders' like the Arts Council. It is riven by rows, and a lot depends on personality, though in public the family keeps face.

(1980: 17)

Chambers' perception of the paternalism of the RSC renders the idea of the women in the company wanting a revolution highly plausible. But Hands' own description of family values gives a sense of how cosy the RSC could also feel:

It was in those days very, very much a collaborative organ-ization, and people really were sounding boards for each other, and critics for each other, and helpers in terms of crisis and need. So it was a good place to work on many levels. It was very, very much a family. And you would have disputes, catastrophes, and wonderful moments of joint celebration.

It was also a family in a more literal sense, 'a place where a lot of people had babies' and a place where there was 'a family in the creche and the kind of bubbly life.' Hands' vision of a place where actors could go to have babies (because the company offered a contract of two years' steady income) is a pleasant one: the RSC becomes a place that supports its actors, supporting them precisely because it is the parent and they are the children.

Chambers' and Hands' contrasting descriptions of the RSC family reflect the ambivalent feelings women in the organization may have had about the Company. In many ways, the relationship between Hands and the Women's Group played itself out as the script of a paterfamilias and his rebellious adolescent children. Genista McIntosh describes the RSC of the 1970s and 1980s as being a patriarchal organization, 'in the sense that the company was, and to some extent remains, obsessed by its history and its sense of being a family organization', and Shaw's description of the group's relationship with Hands certainly echoes that: 'You see we were always maneuvering, wondering whether we were affecting him here, and actually he may have been oblivious most of the time. There was a sense of punching Daddy.' Their status as actors defining them as children, and their status as women within the patriarchal structure doubly reinforcing their distance from the source of power, the members of the Women's Group had their demands for change continually absorbed back into the RSC. Everyone I spoke to about the group brought up the idea of the RSC as a family of his or her own accord; the family ethos of the company was clearly fundamental to the working methods and vision of the RSC, as well as to the women's desires to rebel (or not to rebel, in some cases) against that structure. Shaw's description of 'punching Daddy' suggests that much of the group's energy was spent simply trying to get attention instead of imagining any clear alternative to the family.

As the furore over the interview died down, the women began following up Hands' invitation to put something together for the winter 1986 season at the Pit. At this point, the group invited Susan Todd to work with them, largely at Stevenson's behest. Todd had a long history with feminist theatre. She was a founding member of the Women's Street Theatre Group, the Women's Company, and Monstrous Regiment, one of the most influential feminist theatre groups in Britain; she worked as well with the Women's Theatre Group, an equally important long-standing feminist theatre collective. Todd, in fact, has been described by performance critic Lizbeth Goodman as one of the 'few key individuals' who influenced the development of feminist theatre in Britain.[6] Todd also had a history of connections to the RSC, starting as an assistant director to John Barton in 1968/69. Although she did not return to the company until 1983, she was one of the first women directors inside the Barbican, having been brought in by McIntosh and the actor Harriet Walter to direct a production of Shirley Gee's *Typhoid Mary* for the Barbican One Year On Festival in March 1983.

This production of *Typhoid Mary* led to Todd's return to the RSC as a director for the Women's Group. Juliet Stevenson had played Mary. When the women's group started looking for a piece to do, Stevenson went to Todd. Todd is now not entirely clear whether Stevenson had specifically invited her to work with them, or just used her as a sounding board. Her initial reaction was 'a very mixed one of irritation, annoyance, rage that this big institution, of which I had been part in my early days as a director, was wanting to reach out to embrace what it saw as the latest fashionable something.' Nevertheless, Todd was determined to take part: 'I thought, "Well if there's bloody well going to be resources available to do a feminist piece at the RSC, I'm bloody well going to do it."' Regardless of whether Stevenson intended to ask her to join the project, Todd made it quite clear that she thought she deserved to be in on it: 'I'm sure that I gave Juliet to understand that if any such thing was going to happen that I should certainly be involved in it, because I considered myself to be, and indeed I was, a leading figure in feminist theatre at that point.'

When Todd met the group in March or April 1986, she found a group of women who had little in common other than 'a kind of vague feminism' and 'considerable discontent at the poverty of roles assigned to them within the company in every respect.' Although Todd could sympathize with the actors' feelings of marginalization, she also saw it as the inevitable result of being in a classical company: 'You're talking four or five women's roles for every twenty-five men's roles.' Her impatience with their political sense is tied to her own sense of the proper way to be a female artist:

> I regarded the women within the RSC with a certain amount of healthy suspicion, in the sense that they could not but be women who were striving to fulfil their ambitions within a very male-dominated domain. And they had not, up to that point, struck out for themselves into the feminist domain, and discovered what it was to work autonomously as a female artist.

If Todd was resentful at not having had the chance to become part of the RSC as a young director, as some group members have suggested, she might have felt that her own experience as a struggling fringe director justified her impatience with what she saw as the RSC women's comfortable, nationally subsidized artistic lives. If she had had to struggle in order to realize her feminist politics, then it might have been tempting to see these actors, who were outside the feminist theatre movement, as only having a vague kind of political awareness. Shaw, in contrast to Todd, remembers those early meetings as 'intellectually very vibrant' and 'terribly exciting,' full of the sense that 'we were changing the world.'

Todd saw the group's lack of feminist theatre experience as a hindrance to their effectiveness in creating a feminist project. While the RSC was far from an institution that encouraged feminist explorations, Todd's reference to the 'proper' way to be a female artist points to the ways in which the women at the RSC found themselves politically and artistically without foundation. Her skepticism about female artists working within a male tradition is shared by many feminists within the worlds of theatre and scholarship in their search for appropriate targets for feminist investigation. Thus in *Contemporary Feminist Theatres* (1993), Lizbeth Goodman's definition of feminist theatre excludes work done by female actors in male-authored scripts. She implies that the only valid arena for feminist theatre practitioners is within female-anchored projects where women are the actors, directors and playwrights. But such an exclusion denies feminist actors who want to work within classical theatre the space to create feminist theatre. Actors at the RSC, whose attempts at feminist work were not perceived as appropriate by either the RSC or by feminist theatre, found themselves caught in an impossible position, asked to disavow either their company or their feminist politics.

Of course, not all the women actors at the RSC were interested in feminist theatre or feminist politics. Although the label as the RSC Women's Group implied that all RSC women were involved and united, in fact they had little besides the RSC in common. Memories differ: Hands remembers hearing a lot of discord after he left his initial meeting with the women; Shaw remembers that 'there was a group that was very "anti-" the group, but who were in it anyway,' and Stevenson remembers the group's diffuseness as frustrating and almost disabling: 'We sat around as a group of actresses who had not chosen to be together, who had not selected each other because we were like-minded, because we shared an ideal or a dream or a vision. . . . Most of the time we were functioning there was fear, mistrust, frustration, ambitiousness' (quoted in Woddis 1987: 14). The creation of the RSC Women's Group was convenient for separating their particular theatrical project from the rest of the RSC's work. The label also reinforced women's secondary status within the company as contained by but separate from the neutral (rather than clearly marked as male) RSC.

The false unity thrust on the group *was* accurate in reflecting their separation from and challenge to the RSC. Although the group's women did not agree on what they wanted their project to be, their belief in the possibility of a theatre project led by women marked them out as different. This difference from the main company became explicit in the group's emerging sense that, rather than do a naturalistic drama, they wanted something that was more on 'an epic or mythic canvas.' Todd in particular was keen to 'go down a different path, where the theatre aesthetic would be as foregrounded as the material and content of the piece.' Her intention reflects that of many feminist theatre practitioners and theoreticians, among whom there was a growing sense that the theatrical traditions of naturalism and realism were inherently linked to patriarchal ideology.[7] Certainly in the performance of Shakespeare at the RSC, determination of what is natural has tended to work from patriarchal assumptions.[8] The Women's Group's search for an 'epic or mythic' theatre project meant that they were not going to rely on the traditional aesthetics of the RSC, which strove for a naturalism that was also appropriate for Shakespeare. Theirs was a search for a theatrical form that would equal the power of Shakespeare without relying on the masculinist ideology surrounding his plays.

Out of this interest in doing something that 'broke out of the constraints of naturalism', Todd went to see Angela Carter, who had reworked a series of fairy tales in her 1979 story collection *The Bloody Chamber*. After describing the Women's Group to Carter, Todd asked her advice about an appropriate piece. Carter's response, as Todd remembers, was, 'It's a bloody place for doing bloody Shakespeare. You want to do Shakespeare. Do *Macbeth*.' Although Carter was not willing to write a script, she did agree to work as a consultant with the group. When Todd went to Terry Hands, however, he rejected an all-female *Macbeth* out of hand: 'Terry just went, "Well, no. We, I mean, no. I, well, we, no. No, definitely not."' But he did not offer a good reason for his refusal, aside from insisting that the group should do a new piece. Todd is not sure what his objection to the piece was, offering that it is possible that Hands rejected the idea because it was not substantial enough, or that she did not make a strong proposal, or that he 'just didn't want a bunch of women doing Shakespeare.' According to McIntosh, Hands' objections to the piece were grounded in RSC notions about what is appropriate for Shakespeare:

> The objections that were raised by Terry were firstly, that it wasn't a very good idea anyway. But also that it was one of the popular plays, and we didn't give those plays to people who were sort of first-time directors. So there was a whole RSC ideology/ mythology about how you do the plays of Shakespeare that came into play the minute they said, 'The thing we want to do, is what

you do, boys.' And the boys went, 'Oh no, we didn't mean that; we didn't mean *that*, we meant do something girly.'[9]

Hands himself does not remember any suggestion about *Macbeth*, although he says now using Shakespeare as source material for a new project could have been a good idea, even though *Macbeth* itself might have been a difficult play for the group since it is Macbeth himself who drives much of the action of the play. Hands rejects the idea of an all-female version as 'silly.'

Although it might be true that Hands felt strongly that the group should present a new work, that does not contradict McIntosh's assessment of his response. The RSC ideology of how to do Shakespeare evidently stemmed from artistic concerns about creating a house style for the company and from financial worries about keeping the company solvent. The RSC continually faced financial problems; in the 1985/86 season only 41 per cent of its costs were covered by grants from the Arts Council and other sources.[10] Without strong ticket sales, the company could not continue to operate. This need for public appeal led the company to see big popular Shakespeare productions as their best source of income; the RSC began to spend more money on sets and costumes in order to lure audiences away from lavish West End productions. *Macbeth*, as a popular Shakespeare tragedy and one of the set texts for school exams, was a ready source of income for the company, not a production that the RSC was likely to risk having fall short. The administration's sense of what was sellable, appropriate Shakespeare meant that the play had to be reserved for a more classical and serious treatment than could be entrusted to women with little experience in producing Shakespeare. The play was, in fact, directed by Adrian Noble for the 1986/87 Stratford season.

After Hands' negative reaction, the group realized that, in McIntosh's words, 'the only way they were going to get it past first base was by coming up with something that wasn't going to be threatening in any area to anybody else's territory.' Although the group formed in the first place to challenge the RSC administration's belittling assessment of female directors, the women surrendered their claim to equal status when they did not insist on doing a Shakespeare play. Although a non-threatening 'girly' production does create opportunities for women to work, such a production fails to challenge RSC preconceptions about the value of such work. The separation of women from the company's main work suggests not just that women do theatre different than Shakespeare, but that they cannot do Shakespeare either. When the Women's Group came back to Hands not with another Shakespeare project, but with something completely removed from the realm of classical theatre, they missed their chance to claim Shakespeare as legitimate for women to produce and stage.

The project next proposed was one that did not tread on any RSC toes: a staged version of the Cinderella myth written by Timberlake Wertenbaker in collaboration with Marina Warner, who at that time was researching her book on fairy tales, *From the Beast to the Blonde*. The Cinderella project gathered steam until Wertenbaker learned that neither Shaw nor Stevenson had actually committed themselves to it. Says Todd of this difficulty, 'Timberlake, being Timberlake, said quite rightly, "Well if they're not prepared to commit themselves, nor am I." And she was very adamant about that.'[11] Todd was unable to convince either Shaw or Stevenson to stick with the project: 'Juliet wept and stormed and wept and said, "I have to leave the RSC, I can't stand it any longer, it's just killing me, I can't bear it." She felt the place was just consuming her and that even for a women's project she was not prepared to stick it out.' Shaw, when asked about it now, explains that she left the group when she was offered the RSC national tour (playing Beatrice in *Much Ado About Nothing* and Portia in *Merchant of Venice*), because she wanted to get out of London and to concentrate on classical roles. While Shaw is clear that her decision did not stem from dissatisfaction with the group, but rather from professional career choices, McIntosh suggests that she and Stevenson left the group once it became apparent that its revolutionary potential was an illusion:

> I suspect that in both their cases, and in the others who dropped away, it was that it was fun while there was a real possibility that you could have got into the inner sanctum. And when they began to see that actually they were still outside the walls and were being thrown a crumb, it didn't seem worth doing to them.

Todd was clearly angry and disappointed when Shaw and Stevenson 'abdicated,' not least because it meant the end of the

Cinderella project, which Todd was (and still is) convinced was 'the right idea.'

By this point (June 1986), it was becoming crucial that the group start work on a project in order for it to be ready by December. There was pressure to come up with a title to put in the new brochures, and planning meetings were already underway to allocate resources for the new season. But according to Todd, 'nobody [from the group] came with a lively idea.' Todd herself was becoming increasingly frustrated and unhappy with the group, finding their meetings 'grim' and 'pointless' and feeling as if 'it was going to be a miserable undertaking.' Terry Hands urged her to stick with it. Todd's final hope was playwright Deborah Levy, with whom Todd had worked closely in developing a piece called *Pax* for the Women's Theatre Group in 1985. Levy had been discussing her ideas about a new project with Todd, a piece about the relationship between an architect and a composer. Todd was keen to work with Levy again, so she proposed to Levy that she expand the piece for a group of actors as the RSC Women's Project. Levy agreed, and so *Heresies* came to be the piece finally premiered as the group's culmination.

After choosing a cast to work with, Todd and Levy started a series of intensive workshops, working with the actors to 'discover more about the potential of the material.' This collaborative working process was common with feminist and socialist theatre groups: Monstrous Regiment, Women's Theatre Group and others routinely developed material in collaboration with playwrights and group members. In order to explore the character and plot of *Heresies*, Levy and Todd devised material for four weeks of workshops with the actors, including improvisational sketches in 'the spirit of a building' and imagining scenes from the prehistory of the play's narrative, exercises that Todd described extensively in her program notes for *Heresies*. At the end of the workshops, Levy took what the actors had 'encountered' as well as her original ideas and 'used them as a well to draw from in writing the play.' In her program notes, Todd argues that ultimately, the point of such a working method is

> not only to produce a play at the end of it all, but to dynamically alter the actors', writer's and director's relationship to the material. Our feelings as a group toward the characters, and toward the play's content, are of greater depth and much

greater responsibility than is generally possible. I think that altered relation produces a more satisfying exchange between the stage and the audience.

Despite Todd's enthusiasm for the revolutionary potential of the group's working process, most of the actors found it an alienating experience. Many of them simply did not have experience of working in this way, and their discomfort contributed to tensions already present in the project. Looking back, Todd describes it as 'not a good rehearsal process': 'People were not able to commit themselves to the process of working in a new vein, and where everything has to be invented.' A few actors who were more familiar with working collaboratively in workshops with a writer managed to feel at ease, but Todd blames the others for not being willing to work with an open mind: 'they couldn't, they wouldn't come towards that effort.' The workshops' production of material also created problems for Levy. After taking into account the variety of issues that had come up in the workshops (our relationship to the past, what we hand on to the future, the place of money in our culture, the relationship between Eastern and Western Europe), the script ended up more of a conglomeration of ideas than a clear-cut development of themes. The piece badly needed to be rethought and edited, and although Todd and Levy both recognized this (for the published version of the play, Levy cut three characters), the actors were very resistant to losing any of their lines. It is easy, however, to sympathize with the actors' desire to hold on to their lines; after an uncomfortable four weeks of workshopping a project that was designed to create better roles for women, the last thing an actor would want is to end up with a bit part.

The final play was a piece built around twelve characters, each representing – and clearly labeled in the program as – a type: Cholla, the Displaced Person (Caroline Goodall); Mayonnaise, the Courtesan (Susan Tracy); Pimm, the Architect (Roger Allam); Mary, the Housekeeper (Ann Mitchell); Leah, the Composer (Susan Colverd); Violet, the Educator (Paola Dionisotti); Edward, the Lonely Businessman (Clive Russell); Betty, the Mother (Miriam Karlin); Bridie, the Student (Stella Gonet); Lindiwe, the Fortune Teller (Nimmy March); Marissa, the Body Conditioner (Tina Marian); and Roman, the Hairdresser (Penelope Freeman). Roughly, the plot of the play centered around Pimm and Leah, who had once been Pimm's piano teacher. Pimm had had a daughter with Cholla, an emigré from Hungary; Cholla, a friend of Leah and her lover Violet, had taken their daughter and left him, and was now cleaning offices. Pimm was currently having an affair with Mayonnaise, Edward's wife, but wanting to find his daughter. Mayonnaise, whose only friends in the play are her fortune teller, hairdresser and aerobics teacher, tracks down Cholla and kidnaps her daughter; her own mother, Betty, unexpectedly shows up and meets Edward. Meanwhile, Bridie, an Irish political activist, comes to visit her sister Mary, Pimm's housekeeper. By the end of the play, all of the women end up at a concert at Leah and Violet's house for the première of the piece which Leah has been composing throughout the course of the play. The plot is clearly a complex one, even convoluted. But the play is less concerned with a straightforward narrative than it is with the relationships between the characters, and the contrasts between their worlds. It is not in any sense a naturalistic drama: the characters are representative types as well as individuals, and the language they speak is poetic and highly expressionistic.

This form coincided neatly with Todd's stated desires to avoid a naturalistic, domestic drama. Like Todd, Levy wanted to explore the aesthetic language of theatre. In her program notes, Levy describes *Heresies*' aim as: 'to explore a theatre language that uses poetics, physical and visual metaphors and the abstraction of domestic situations, but which is nevertheless rooted in the political and personal conflicts of our culture now.' Levy felt that naturalism was dead as a language for theatre, and deliberately chose to use archetypes in her work, instead of more traditionally realistic characters, in order to 'get out of lamentable obsolete naturalism onto a much bigger canvas, psychological and cultural' (Charitou 1993: 227). Although not completely happy with the end result of *Heresies*, Levy did ultimately feel proud that her work was presented at the RSC: 'work in that form at that time had never been put on there, and I'm glad it was' (quoted in Charitou 1993: 228).

Although the play's creators saw its experimentation with form as an opportunity to discover a new type of theatre, reviewers for the national press saw *Heresies* in terms of failures rather than possibilities. With their repeated complaints that the play was more concerned with ideas than with realistic characters and dialogue, the reviewers' insistence on traditional relationships between author, actor and character and their resistance to feminist politics kept them from recognizing *Heresies* as creating a new theatrical aesthetic. A couple of reviewers found the play's experimental ambitions worthy of praise. John Peter saw the play as 'striving for a blend of literary writing and performance art that will make sense in the theatre', while Marina Warner recognized *Heresies*' links to earlier forms of narrative, describing it as 'an intricate masque, in the manner of Commedia dell' Arte' that pulls various character types into a single plot much as 'an improbably medieval romance does' (Peter 1986; Warner 1986). But more characteristic of the press reaction was Milton Shulman's assessment that the dialogue is 'pretentious', the characters 'unlikely' and 'incredible', and 'the end result is not so much a pseud's corner as a pseud's kitchen, in which naïve feminist notions are brewed and half-baked' (Shulman 1986).

According to the consensus of the national press, real theatre is naturalistic, has speech that sounds like what we hear in the real world, does not have melodramatic coincidences, is centered on a few characters who have clear relationships to each other, does not espouse political views, has a single author who is the progenitor of the work, and above all, is done by men. All of these conditions are clearly suspect: Shakespeare, after all, abounds in absurd coincidences and is certainly not written in naturalistic speech. As for whether or not a play espouses political views, this is an impossible criterion for separating good theatre from bad. All plays voice an ideology, though it is only when that ideology does not readily align with that of the viewer that it becomes visible as espoused politics. Lizbeth Goodman argues that particularly with women's collective theatre groups, mainstream reviewers 'criticized devised or collectively written plays as "weak" due to what they perceived as overt politics superseding artistic form', and Susan Carlson makes a similar argument about reviews of women's plays (Goodman 1993: 54; Carlson 1991: 177ff.). Elaine Aston notes that feminist playwright Sarah Daniels' work is often criticized for not following traditional dramatic structures, and that 'she is repeatedly accused of statement-making rather than (good) play-making' (Aston 1995: 397). Shulman, for whom the collision of non-traditional theatre with feminist ideology resulted in something that was clearly not recognizable as good theatre, reacted to *Heresies* in a way typical of the (male) reviewing establishment.

With the end of the *Heresies* run, the Women's Group disbanded; indeed, the group had ceased to exist from the moment that *Heresies* was cast, since the majority of women had not been part of its visionary origins. Whatever the ambitions of the group were in its heady early days, those ambitions were never to be realized once the project was confronted with management dictations and the defection of founding members. By the time *Heresies* came to be performed, the Women's Group had become simply a name for the women doing a one-off project. Although their statement in the program notes points to hopes for future productions, there seem to have been few actual desires for such a thing. Certainly since that time there has been nothing comparable at the RSC. If the main goal of the RSC Women's Group was to increase women's participation in the RSC and to increase the visibility of women's concerns in their productions, the group must be said to have failed. Susan Todd, ten years later, says that the Women's Group had absolutely no lasting effect: 'The waters closed over, and the institution went on exactly as before, with no change.' Genista McIntosh also feels that the group did not change anything, and though with time the RSC has changed, the difference is not great. 'There are still no women at the top of the organization,' she points out. Until the June 1996 appointment of Katie Mitchell as Artistic Director of The Other Place, senior artistic management was entirely male, and with the exception of the two female producers, the top executive staff is male as well.

The one thing that both McIntosh and Fiona Shaw point to as having changed is the number of female directors working for the company. Since 1986, there has been a definite increase in the number of women who have directed at the RSC: Di Trevis, Deborah Warner, Phyllida Lloyd, Katie Mitchell and Gale Edwards have all directed productions for the RSC in the last ten years, with two of them doing main stage productions of Shakespeare (Trevis' 1988 *Much Ado About Nothing* and Edwards' 1995 *The Taming of the Shrew*), and with Warner often being credited for revitalizing the RSC. But the presence of a few female directors does not change the RSC ethos. The power to alter company identity rests with the Artistic Director and, perhaps, the core group of returning directors. With the exception of Mitchell, the women who have directed at the RSC have not become part of the company structure.

It is unlikely that it was ever possible for the group to change anything at the RSC. Even aside from the tensions within the group and the lack of agreement about politics, the structure of the group and its relationship to the RSC precluded any serious revolutionary potential. The RSC Women's Group was, as its name suggests, completely contained within the RSC. And if the women wanted to punch Daddy, as Shaw suggests, Daddy was never going to give them the tools to actually unseat him. According to Todd, there was never any serious intention to alter the RSC's relationship to female artists: 'I don't think Terry or any of the dominant RSC voices, including Genista McIntosh at that time, had any notion of including women in the organization in a way that mattered creatively.' McIntosh herself agrees that it was never really possible that the Women's Group would get what they wanted:

> It was an unequal struggle. They wanted Terry to say, 'I give in.'
> And he was never going to. And so a tremendous amount of
> energy went into trying to achieve something that actually
> wasn't achievable. Whatever kind of capitulation in some way
> they felt it was possible to achieve, really it just wasn't going to
> happen. And the mark that has been left by that is so faint, that
> even I can barely discern it.

In a May 1986 interview with Susan Carlson, RSC literary manager Colin Chambers spoke about the divided response in the company administrators about how to include more women in their work:

> We have discussed and do discuss quite often how should the
> company overcome its clear bias. And then you get caught up
> in this argument to do with positive discrimination as against
> something supposedly called quality. . . . There are roughly two
> positions inside the company. . . . One is that we must in some
> way encourage women to be represented, but that they must go
> through exactly the same process of selection or competition
> or whatever as everybody else, i.e., the men. The other is that
> this very process is precisely the process that excludes them.
> And that you have got to do something much more radical and
> actually interventionist, and that is a much bigger risk.
>
> (Carlson 1991: 332)

These questions are the same ones that faced the Women's Group: work within the company, or aim for something more radical and interventionist? But by starting off within the company and looking to company management for encouragement and endorsement, the group was never going to be able to do something radically outside company policy. The opening of Michael Coveney's *Financial Times* review of *Heresies* might be snide, but is nonetheless accurate: 'Women in last year's RSC Stratford company banded together first in a spirit of opposition to the male hierarchy and second in an attempt to create a work together, supported by that hierarchy' (Coveney 1986). Supported and endorsed by the very system that they were criticizing, how much of a revolution could the Women's Group have created? It is of course understandable why the women of the group wanted to be supported by the hierarchy of the RSC, since it was that hierarchy that guaranteed their livelihood. And as Hands' angry reprimand of Shaw, Stevenson and Duncan indicated, there were indeed potential repercussions for attacking the company.

By failing to challenge what were the criteria for a good director, the RSC Women's Group left in place a system that defined women's work as ill-suited to Shakespeare. Those women who were hired as directors, whether or not as a direct result of the group, had no more power to challenge the company structure than those directors still outside the RSC. In order to challenge successfully the RSC's male ethos, the Women's Group would have had to take on a series of larger issues: not only the company's belief that real Shakespeare is gender-neutral, but the pressure to conform to the company's homogeneous family values and the reaction of critics hostile to feminist theatre's challenges to traditional aesthetics and politics. The RSC's vision of itself and of Shakespeare, in the layers of artistic, cultural and economic considerations that define its terms, does not readily allow feminist challenges to the patriarchal bard. And although nobody involved with the project speaks explicitly of the traditions of modern theatre, the universalist notions embedded in modern notions of Shakespeare and audience clearly participate in this exclusion of feminist politics.

Notes

1 My research would not have been possible without the willingness of Terry Hands, Genista McIntosh, Fiona Shaw and Susan Lily Todd to be interviewed about their experience of the Women's Group, and I am grateful to them for making room for me in their busy schedules. The librarians at the Shakespeare Centre were indispensable for their help in pursuing the group's history through the Centre's archives. But the person I am most indebted to is Lizbeth Goodman, who generously gave me her press file on *Heresies* and spoke with me about her experiences researching the group. Without her earlier work and her encouragement, I would not have discovered the group's existence, let alone been able to pursue its history.

All articles about, and reviews of, the RSC Women's Group and the projects leading up to it have come from the collections of Genista McIntosh and Lizbeth Goodman, and from the press clippings archived in the Shakespeare Centre; none of the press clippings have page numbers for the articles. Many of the reviews, however, can be found in the *London Theatre Record* (see vol. 6, no. 25/26 and vol. 7, no. 1).

2 Fiona Shaw, interviewed by the author, London, 5 September 1995. Unless otherwise noted, all quotes from Shaw are from this interview.

3 Terry Hands, interviewed by the author, London, 18 April 1996. Unless otherwise noted, all quotes from Hands are from this interview.

4 I have been unable to track down the existence of this magazine, let alone a copy of their interview Although the *Stage and Television Today* article reports the title of the journal as *Theatregoer Magazine*, there is no history of a publication under that name in Britain. There is an American newsletter with that title, but although I searched through the archives at the New York Public Library, I did not find mention of the interview. It seems unlikely that the American magazine is the one in question, as Shaw clearly remembers the interview being published in a glossy, widely-read industry magazine. I have looked through back issues of a number of such journals, but have not as yet found the interview.

5 Susan Lily Todd, interviewed by the author, Totnes, Devon, 24 November 1995. Unless otherwise noted, all quotes from Todd are from this interview.

6 Goodman (1993: 57). For a history of British feminist theatre, see Goodman and Wandor (1986).

7 Recently Sheila Stowell (1992) has argued for the recuperation of realism as a vehicle for feminist drama, pointing specifically to early suffrage plays.

8 I have explored this issue as it relates to actor training elsewhere; see Werner (1996: 249-58).

9 Genista McIntosh, interview with the author, 17 May 1995, London. Unless otherwise noted, all equations from McIntosh are from this interview.

10 *The 110th Report of the Council, 1985/86*, Royal Shakespeare Company Executive Council, Geoffrey Cass, chair, 4 November 1986.
11 Susan Carlson, who interviewed Wertenbaker on 3 May 1986, writes that Wertenbaker 'turned down an offer to write for [the RSC Women's Group], having envisioned that the tensions of collaborative work in the subsidized theatre would be exaggerated there' (Carlson 1991: 288). I have not spoken with Wertenbaker, but this reasoning as stated by Carlson would not be incompatible with Todd's assessment. The date of Carlson's interview suggests that the time frame Todd recollects for the group is slightly inaccurate.

6

Shakespearean performativity

W. B. WORTHEN

This theater reminds many people of Shakespeare's Globe; my
only question is, can we use it for playing Shakespeare?

Freddie Rokem (1998)

I

When Stephen Greenblatt confessed 'a desire to speak with the
dead' (1988: 1) some ten years ago, he expressed a common
longing, a hunger that has also shaped the most notorious theater
built in recent memory: Shakespeare's Globe Theatre on the
Bankside. The texture of the structure promises to satisfy our
appetite for such discourse with the dead (or at least with the
creations of the dead, Hamlet, Ophelia, Shylock, and so on): an
early-modern structure frames the return of early-modern subjects. In its meticulous reconstruction of building practices
and ongoing research into the use of period costumes and staging, the Globe reflects a desire to see performance releasing
original 'Shakespearean' meanings; the Globe is a monument to
an understanding of dramatic performance as the embodiment
of a textualized 'past', expectantly (or inertly) awaiting the chance
to speak. At the same time, the Globe also enacts the ineluctable
presentness of performance, the ways performance speaks with a
difference. Despite the oak and plaster, the Globe is everywhere
traced by the passage of history: it's down the street from the

original foundations; it holds fewer, bigger, and quite different people; the hair-and-lime plaster uses goat hair (cow hair today is too short); the thatch is chemically treated; the lath and plaster conceals a modern firewall; sprinkler heads dot the ridgepole; the exterior timbering is whitewashed (a concession to modern 'Tudor' sensibilities); there are actresses, intermissions, numbered seats, toilets, ushers, ice cream, the restaurant, the cafe, the gift shop. The Globe epitomizes a host of attitudes toward history, not least the commodification of 'pastness' within the economy of international tourism; it 'works' as a theater because it epitomizes a contemporary sense of dramatic 'performativity.'[1]

The common understanding of dramatic performance is thoroughly informed by a sense of the 'performative': words on the page appear to cite a range of appropriate behaviors, behaviors which evoke an agent, a fictive subject, a 'character.' The citational aspect of dramatic performance – what Austin took to be its peculiarly etiolated, hollow quality – is precisely what it shares with all verbal performance; the text is naturalized to behavioral regimes that lend the words appropriate significance, force, as performance.[2] The Globe expresses one dimension of the historically volatile ensemble of values and behaviors that might be called 'Shakespearean performativity' today: the sense that the performance of a Shakespeare play can, or should, evoke the pastness of the text and what the text represents – early-modern values, behaviors, subjects. Reconstructing both the material frame and the spatial and proxemic relations of 'Shakespeare's factory', Globe performance claims a kind of historical privilege: there, we can begin 'to see how his [Shakespeare's] plays were originally intended to work' (Gurr 1997: 34), as though the framing structure will release the behaviors that made the plays 'work' from their captivity in the text. Yet much as contemporary performance also claims a continuity between the matter of Shakespeare's plays and contemporary forms of identity and behavior, performance at the Globe also occupies a rich intersection between theatrical means of encountering the past (Shakespeare, summer Shakespeare, nonShakespeare theater) and a sweeping range of nontheatrical performance: living history reconstructions (Plimoth Plantation, Colonial Williamsburg, the Ironbridge Gorge Museum, and many others), participatory re-enacting (of Civil War battles in the US [Horwitz 1998] and the UK, for instance), and the 'theming' intrinsic to staging the past (and the future) at Disneyland, Walt

Disney World, and their many spinoffs. The surprising popularity of the Globe surely stems in large part from its well-advertised commitment to historical accuracy. At the same time, Globe performance depends on a complex of theatrical and non-theatrical, aesthetic and pragmatic behaviors, practices in which the historicizing impulses of Shakespearean performativity are enacted in the democratic and destabilizing conduct of a living public.

Richard Schechner has argued that 'Performance means: never for the first time' (1982: 40), but while Schechner suggests that what performance 'restores' is behavior, the Globe expresses a pervasive desire to see performance restoring something else, using behavior to restore the pastness apparently located in the text. What distinguishes Shakespearean performativity from some other modes of theater today is the premium placed – by performers and audiences, in conventional and experimental productions – on the identity of the verbal text, and the belief that its meanings inform, guide, or are animated by stage performance. In part, perhaps, because of Shakespeare's dual canonicity as theater and as literature, it is now conventional to understand the performance of a Shakespeare play in relation to a prior understanding of the text – a performance 'of *Hamlet.*' Yet how the text appears to motivate the practices of performance is hardly uniform, either in the history of theatrical performance or on the contemporary stage. The force attributed to the text in a performance is not a stable or essential aspect of dramatic performativity; the genre of a performance determines how (or whether) a sense of 'the text' emerges as a distinct element, has a relevant 'force.' Even in the relatively restricted stylistic repertoire of contemporary Anglo-North American theater, different texts appear to exert different kinds of force: whether 'experimental' or otherwise, Shakespeare productions function the text in distinctive ways, different from the approaches typically taken to Greek drama, or to Chekhov, or to Beckett, and different as well from the more flexible policy usually adopted for other early-modern playwrights – Jonson, Middleton, Kyd. The force of texts is constituted differently again in nontheatrical arenas of dramatic performance, such as film and television. Television scripts are dispensable material *for* the performance (as, arguably, the scripts of early-modern plays were in their day). Devised by writers, not 'authors', these scripts have little value outside performance; the performance can't be *of* them in the way we see a performance *of Hamlet* (Patrick Stewart can't really give a faithful or an unfaithful performance of 'Jean-Luc Picard'), in part because television doesn't operate as a repertory medium (the cast of *Friends* won't be doing *Seinfeld* next year), and also because the scripts are not reconceptualized in another sanctioned institution – literature – that would incorporate them as 'works' and lend them an independent identity.

While dramatic performativity in the West may, as Jennifer Wise argues, arise at the interface between writing and enactment, the function of the text in the force of performance is extremely variable, even within a relatively discrete historical and cultural moment. If the force attributed to the dramatic text in performance is variable, so too is the belief that the text's 'history' can be recovered or restored by performance. This 'historicizing' capacity is the mark of *modern* Shakespearean performativity, emerging fitfully in the eighteenth century when the identity of the Shakespearean text outside the theater came to bear on Shakespearean practices in the theater, and extending through the dominant theatrical innovations of nineteenth-century performance: the use of the mise-en-scène to frame a historically 'accurate' picture of Shakespeare's dramatic setting, and the cognate use of the 'Elizabethan' staging to frame an 'accurate' realization of Shakespeare's theatrical practices.[3] 'Modernized' Shakespeare – a tradition extending from Barry Jackson's modern-dress productions of the 1920s through the 'eclectic' staging common today – merely reciprocates the sense that the Shakespearean text is freighted with its past, and that this history must be confronted, restored, or updated.

The notion that dramatic texts – at least 'literary' dramatic texts, like Shakespeare's – might bear their historical origins into performance not only sustains projects like the Globe, but characterizes Shakespearean performativity in the modern era. Irving's Anglo-Saxon *King Lear*, William Poel's picture-framed Fortune stage, and the authentic underwear of the Globe's 1997 *Henry V* all evoke a modern confidence in the restorative power of performance, and a modern anxiety as well: the fear that much as performance operates in the here-and-now, it risks losing a validating connection to the past, a past located in the 'text' that the performance is said to enact, to be of. The Globe frames the question of the historicity of performance in a particularly urgent way. However we understand the subjects of Shakespearean dramatic writing, can performance really make them speak to us? The extraordinary popularity of the Globe testifies to the desire to evoke a 'Shakespearean' past in the present behaviors of performance. In his recent book, *Big-Time Shakespeare* (1996), Michael Bristol provides an unusually cogent account of the historicizing capacity of performance and a vigorous argument for the importance of regarding performance in this way; at the same time, he also demonstrates some of the difficulties that arise from trying to see the text's past inhabiting the present of performance. *Big-Time Shakespeare* makes a shrewd case for the ongoing work of Shakespearean writing, a case that depends not merely on the continuing renegotiation of Shakespeare's texts by successive readers, critics, and performers, but on properties of the texts themselves, their openness as 'discursive formations' which are not 'limited to expressing the concerns and interests of a narrowly circumscribed historical period. They have potential for generating new meanings in successive epochs' (1996: 11). Bristol captures this ability of texts to stage a dialogue across history – at once to say something determinate, while at the same time remaining open to later interrogation – in his vivid translation of Mikhail Bakhtin's *bolshoe vremja* as 'big time' (10). Taking the uncritical celebration of textual indeterminacy and the 'abolition of the author' (54) as representative of a willful evacuation of the materiality of writing, its character as labor, Bristol frames literary artifacts as 'the deliberate and purposeful work' of human agents (18), in order to expose the ethical dimension of writing-in-history. Literature provides equipment for living by enabling a continuous, dialectical understanding of the history of the subject, one that enables 'the inheritors of Western modernity to understand their complex situatedness as fully as possible' (140) by enabling them – *us* – to engage in an ongoing dialogue with the past through the reading and performance of Shakespearean drama.

Within the wider aims of this complex and densely-argued book, Bristol suggests how negotiating the historical 'big time' can also be understood as the purpose of playing.[4] Motivated by the conviction that 'To suggest that a verbal artifact as complex as for example, *Hamlet*, contributes nothing of its own to the practices of exegesis, interpretation, and stage performance is to trivialize those very practices' (1996: 27), Bristol locates the historicizing

potential of dramatic performance at the origin of the professional
theater: playwriting and stage production were reciprocal elements
in the wholesale invention of a new mode of cultural production:
the entertainment industry, the big time. Theatrical entrepreneurs of the 1570s and 1580s were able to transform the 'familiar
performance practices' of traditional communities (both popular
fairground performance and perhaps also the similarly occasional
performances commanded as an aristocratic privilege) into 'cultural merchandise' (36). More to the point, theatrical enterprise
transformed both 'the commodities of spectacle, narrative, and
conviviality' and the audience who purchased them, an audience
now cast as 'self-reliant consumers', able 'to enjoy cultural goods
at their pleasure . . . without the time-consuming burden of direct
participation'(37) implied by more traditional forms of performance. Selling performance as alienated commodity, the theater
both depended on and helped to create a new kind of subject:
the 'socially undifferentiated consumer of cultural services' (37).
As 'founding documents in the history of modern show business',
Shakespeare's plays contribute to this 'pattern of long-term
continuity' (30) in the institutional formation of theater, a business
dependent both on a monetary economy and on the increasing diversification and alienation of early-modern urban life.
Shakespeare's colleagues invented an industry whose product
(performance) and audience (consumers) are recognizably those
of the theater industry today.[5]

In this view, contemporary performance can use Shakespearean drama to open a historicizing dialogue with the past because
stage production today participates in the institutional continuity
of the theater industry, an industry in which Shakespeare's plays
were 'founding documents.' For performance today to take up a
dialogue with Shakespearean drama in this way, however requires
a continuity between the performative function of the texts in
the early-modern theater and in contemporary Shakespearean
performativity. Shakespeare's plays were also 'founding documents' of another emerging industry – dramatic publishing.
Although Bristol works to 'analyze the complex relationship
between these emerging media [theater, print] without assigning
a privilege either to a theatrical or to a bookish Shakespeare' (30),
in order for later theaters to perform the meaningful, non-trivial
recovery of a 'past' lodged in the text, the 'residual' (43) printing
of plays must be taken to register the integrity and identity of

Shakespearean writing, writing everywhere compromised by other, disintegrating factors. It's hard to claim this integrity, of course: Shakespeare's plays 'were created not as autonomous works of literary or even dramatic art as we now understand such notions, but rather as a set of practical solutions to the exigencies of a heterogeneous cultural market' (49); indeed, the 'participation of collaborators, revisers and other secondary creative agents' so inflects any understanding of Shakespearean writing that it is impossible to disentangle Shakespeare's 'singular creative agency' from such 'derivative forms of participation in artistic production' (52).

Nonetheless, by defining this participation as 'secondary' or 'derivative', Bristol can regularize the relationship between dramatic writing and theatrical performance along modern lines, and so preserve the idea that Shakespearean writing – *any* writing – can have been a 'founding document' of this theater, a theater whose principal commodity – *performance* – was not yet exchangeable with a competing 'literary' valuation of *drama*.[6] To situate the text at the origin of early-modern theater, that is, we must take 'literature' to assume 'its present institutional shape of a bookish community of writers and readers' in the early modern period (45), and take the relatively marginal printing of plays to reflect the integrity of the dramatic text and its emerging 'literary' status.[7] Yet plays had monetary value, value as property, only when they could be sold to a company who knew how to use them; as David Scott Kastan points out, 'Inductions and epilogues speak regularly of the play not as the author's but as "ours", property and product of the players' (34), a proprietary notion reflected as well in the often-garbled attribution of authorship on early-modern title pages (35). Publication appears to represent the 'derivative' by-product of a much more valuable commodity: performance.

Understanding performance as capable of recovering a history located in the dramatic text requires a recognizable correlation between early-modern and contemporary 'Shakespearean performativity', as though the early-modern theater enunciated the force of its texts, its 'founding documents', rather than merely consuming them; the provisional identity of these texts would be guaranteed by their incorporation as 'literature', and their value be convertible into a derivative product, theatrical performance. In Bristol's view, performance engages the ethical dimension of dramatic writing if only we understand it to preserve this relationship; 'the *longue durée* of Shakespeare's cultural authority is the

product of interactions between a body of incompletely determined works and a resourceful theatrical ingenuity. Shakespeare's
works are themselves an important instance of derivative creativity
highly responsive to its own moment of contemporaneity' (Bristol
1996: 61). Much as Shakespeare's 'company routinely engaged in
the various forms of derivative creativity' (65), so too 'Garrick's
productions, like those of his predecessors [and successors], were
a sophisticated pastiche of Shakespeare's poetry fused with
contemporary performance techniques' (69). Performance is, for
Bristol, the application of an institutionally derivative ingenuity to
the theater's founding documents; this relationship sustains the
historical development of the stage in the West (and incidentally
explains the theater's increasingly subordinate relation to literary
production), and opens the opportunity for truly Bakhtinian
historical dialectic. If the performative relationship between texts
and performance in the early-modern theater is continuous with
our own, then every 'staging of a Shakespeare play results from a
dialogue between the historical moment of its creation and the
contemporaneity of the *mise-en-scène*' (13).

I take *Big-Time Shakespeare* to make a strong case for the ongoing
historicity of Shakespeare's work, and to account for the historical
feel we usually anticipate from Shakespearean performance,
a tension between a 'then' attributed to the language and the
'now' of performance. Despite this vivid account of the commodification of traditional *performance* as the instigating moment
of theatrical capitalism, Bristol's effort to redeem theatrical
performance from triviality depends on taking performance as
institutionally 'derivative', relying for its force on something else
– the text. Although texts *do* have this kind of force in some kinds
of dramatic performance today, often in the realm I'm calling
'Shakespearean performativity', this use of the text is not intrinsic
to the performance of drama, nor is it uniform through the
institutional history of Western theater. Nor is it entirely clear that
the text had this kind of force in Shakespeare's theater, given the
commodity-status of dramatic scripts – sold as a manufactured
goods (like cloth or lumber) used in making a finished product
(clothing, houses, theatrical performances) – and the extremely
tenuous purchase of printed drama on 'literary' identity in the
period. My reservations, though, are not really with Bristol's canny
interpretation of the evidence (still less with the desire to locate
the ethical and historicizing work of performance), but with the

sense of dramatic performativity that this view of the historicizing capability of the theater seems to demand. The unsettled 'literary' status of dramatic texts in Shakespeare's theater points, at the very least, to a different understanding of the relation between texts and performance, a different conception of dramatic 'performativity' than is common even in Shakespearean theater today. But to account for the historicity of performance as an effect of the dialectical tension between the determining force of the text and the derivative ingenuity of the theater requires us to understand the history of 'Shakespearean performativity' not as a record of dynamic change, but as fundamentally continuous with its dominant practice today, a sense of 'performativity' given force by its text.

Bristol raises the stakes for our understanding of the Globe, of Shakespearean performativity, and of the theatrical vitality of classical drama in general: how to imagine performance in the present evoking something more than merely present behavior, without at the same time conceiving the stage merely as a museum of performance. Let me phrase this a little more schematically. To see performance evoking a force intrinsic to its text defines performance as 'derivative'; yet 'derivative' theater bears with it the possibility of enacting a historical dialogue between the present of performance and the historical alterity of the text, its representation of early-modern 'character', for instance. To see performance as an independent (though related) mode of production, fashioning texts into something else (behavior), releases the stage from the obligation (indeed, from the ability) to reproduce the text, or the ways we may understand it offstage; yet this understanding of performance appears to sacrifice the belief that performance can reproduce a 'history' inscribed in the text – however much its productions smack of history, they evoke only a suspiciously modern, commodified 'pastness.'

While it may seem that this second alternative merely replicates the Disneyfication of history and identity characteristic of contemporary commodity culture (it's not just the Globe that's the problem; it's *all* Bard World out there), an understanding of performance as 'derivative creativity' should give us pause as well. For the notion of 'derivative creativity' implies that the dramatic text supplies the 'lawful or pre-ordained structure' which is then evoked by the 'spontaneous expressive individuality' of the stage (Bristol 1996: 23). 'Derivative creativity' implies that text can in fact supply this structure – of meaning, of history, of character – to performance. But does performance, even Shakespearean performance, really work in this way?

II

Though most often invoked in literary and dramatic studies for her reading of the performative dimension of gender and sexual identifications, Judith Butler unpacks the relationship between language and enactment in ways that bear directly on the historicizing potential of dramatic performance. Taking hate speech, pornography, and don't-ask-don't-tell to locate a contemporary politics of the performative, Butler traverses the zone where speaking crosses in ambiguous and contradictory ways into the sphere of doing, the zone, in other words, where behavior appears to derive its force as *action* from the text it performs. Butler's reading of the scene of speech develops from Derrida's rereading of Austin, the sense that illocutionary speech – the 'I do' of Austin's familiar example of the marriage ceremony – can never be thought of as occupying completely original ground. The conditions that make 'marriage' happen are not under the sovereign control of the speakers or their text, 'I do'; for 'marriage' to happen, 'I do' must be spoken within ceremonial and ritualized behaviors that cite and reiterate an entire range of heteronormative social institutions (see also Parker and Sedgwick 1995; Worthen 1998).[8] Yet in a variety of public and legal contexts, perhaps most dramatically in the case of hate speech – speech that in itself is held to cause injury – we understand words alone to have the force of action, behavior (indeed, this is how many people think of Shakespeare's texts, as containing the force of stage behavior). The doctrine of 'fighting words' implies that hate speech is a consequential – perlocutionary – form of speech: it causes something to happen (a fist fight, a smoldering house). But hate speech is also understood to commit an injury in the act of being spoken; to the extent that it puts its recipient 'subject in a position of subordination' (Butler 1997: 26), hate speech accomplishes an illocutionary act, becoming 'an unequivocal form of conduct' (23).

Although both senses (perlocutionary, illocutionary) of hate-speech-as-action evoke familiar models of dramatic signification (the text implies certain stage behaviors as its perlocutionary consequence; the text illocutionarily encodes stage behaviors in itself), Butler argues that the reduction of speech to conduct mystifies the ideologically citational character of behavior. For instance, *speech* is regarded as unequivocal *conduct* in order to proscribe homosexuality in the military (don't-ask-don't-tell implies that telling is doing, illocution). At the same time racist *conduct* has been regarded as the exercise of free *speech*: burning a cross on a black family's lawn is not taken as illocution (hate speech as conduct), nor as perlocution (fighting words), indeed not as conduct at all, but as protected, free speech.[9] The 'text' of the speech-act – a racist epithet, 'I do', or 'I'm gay' – is incapable of determining action in itself, or of constituting a performing subject. To perform the speech is not to cite a text but to invoke a context which determines the nature of the act and implicates a subject as well. 'If agency is not derived from the sovereignty of the speaker, then the force of the speech act is not sovereign force' (Butler 1997: 39); its meaning cannot be traced either to the independent authority of the text or of the speaker, but to the ways in which the act of utterance – and the acting of the utterance – calls into practice an available regime of social relationships.

Kenneth Burke might say that Butler privileges the explanatory force of the *scene*, rather than the *agent* in determining the meaning of speech *acts*; 'performative' regimes mark the subject's absorption into the scene and mark the site of potentially resistant agency as well (Burke 1969). Although Butler's construction of performativity is sometimes criticized as too far removed from actual performing bodies, this concise mapping of speech acts enables a searching rereading of the sovereignty – even the incomplete sovereignty – of the text in dramatic performance, and of how the text can bear the past into the theatrical present. Speaking produces language as behavior, as action; the language ('I do') gains the force of performance through the citational character of the social and behavioral regimes, the performances, that register it as action. Much as 'the performativity of the text is not under sovereign control' (Butler 1997: 69), dramatic texts cannot exert 'sovereign' force on their performance; dramatic performance becomes meaningful by deploying the text in recognizable genres of behavior, behavior which finally determines what the text can mean as performance.

Butler's reading of hate speech implies that the text of the play can only be conceived as engaging with action – let alone performing one – through its engagement of a living ritual context, a context of behavior. To this extent, Butler's reading of performative speech sharply qualifies the 'derivative' status of the stage, the performance *of* the text as a restoration of inherently textual meanings or of the 'past' encoded there. Acting, for instance, is perhaps the epitome of citational behavior: the familiar conventions of stage performance determine to a large extent the kinds of 'meaning' the text can be said to have onstage. Contemporary 'Shakespearean' characterization – a careful attention to how the minutiae of the verbal text can be physicalized in a single character 'journey' – attributes considerable force (usually 'psychological' force) to the text, both in rehearsal and in performance. This way of performing is not implied in the text, but forms one of the ritual contexts of modern Western theater, conventions of behavior shared by modern actors and audiences as a just representation of the Shakespearean real. Peter Thomson has argued that the demands of early-modern London playhouses for new material, and the pace with which new material had to be brought to the stage, imply a different relation between acting and writing in Shakespeare's era. Thomson suggests that in such a milieu, 'it was by no means the priority of working playwrights to create a gathering of subjectivities – what later criticism would call "characters"' (1997: 324–5). The actors expected to read a text (if they read it), not for its detailed representation of an individualized subjectivity (as modern actors eager to particularize their acting do) but for the ease and effect with which a given side could be phrased within a conventional regime of performance behavior, a line of business – comic old man or woman, clown, fool, a lover or a tyrant or a part to tear a cat in – that would take best advantage of the actor's marketable skills as a performer. The side provided the actor with material that enabled him to perform, to sell his line more or less effectively. Thomson's remarks suggest that while many texts – sides – were essential to composing the performance, the performative function of the authorial script, in the force of performance was somewhat different than it is today, at least as far as Shakespeare is concerned. Playwrights created 'text' to be used in the production of the salable commodity: performance.

Again, Thomson's evidence might well be construed more

elegantly than I have done here; my point is merely that the circumstances of early-modern performance imply a different (not entirely different, but different) positioning of 'the text' in the behaviors I'm calling 'Shakespearean performativity.' For this reason, although early-modern texts may encode a range of alien or familiar values, and represent alien or familiar modes of subjection, it is far from clear how Shakespearean performance today can evoke these textual implications. Performance in the theater is not the citation of texts, but the incarnation of texts as behavior: the 'text' never appears *as* a text in performance, but only as it is transformed into something else, someone lying, pleading, commanding, wooing, seducing, and so on. If acting were merely 'speaking', the release of performatives fully inscribed in the text, we'd all be great actors – as would anyone able to read aloud. Performing a scripted drama involves the insertion of its language – often of resistant, materially remote language and equally recondite habits of action – into the elaborate citational behaviors of the stage. Dramatic performance becomes meaningful through the conventionality of stage enactment, much as 'I do' gains its force to legitimate and legalize 'marriage' only within certain legal and ritual constraints. The text provides no 'instructions' for its performance; these instructions are embodied by the traditions, rhetoric, and *genre* of performance invoked to transform the text into performance. For Dryden, the genre that was capable of rendering *The Tempest* performable was opera, and we need only remember that for a century or more *Macbeth*'s witches appeared amid a corps de ballet to understand the principle that in performance a play's apparent meanings are constituted by something outside or alongside the text: the behavioral regimes that seem to make it meaningfully performable. While the organization of a text like *Hamlet* can surely tell us many things about the constitution of subjects in Shakespeare's era, what *Hamlet*-in-performance tells us will depend on how the text is embodied in behavior we recognize as germane to the theater and that implicates social behavior (and the force of the text) in recognizable and conventional ways.[10]

Appearing to arise both from the determinacies of the text and from the unforseeable contingencies of performance behavior, 'character' is at once a site where the historical dimension of the drama is most strongly felt, and where the citationality of performance most directly challenges the theater's ability to recover or

restore that historicity. By inventing powerful means for representing 'character' Shakespeare 'invented the human as we know
it' (Bloom 1998: 714); the mere notion of an individualized 'self'
registers an exploitative construction of Enlightenment philosophy channeled through market capitalism; the intermittencies
of dramatic character model diffuse sensibilities of self-fashioning
subjects struggling for position in the elusive power grids of a
now-distant culture: as even a cursory reading of recent scholarship attests, reading for the 'character' of early-modern subjects
entails a profoundly political encounter with history.[11] Indeed, the
controversy regarding early-modern subjectivity marks one place
where we can see how an understanding of Shakespearean
performativity deflects, even trivializes the historicizing work
of performance. For Alan Sinfield's shrewd suggestion that 'These
people were very different from us, but not totally different'
(1992: 62) poses two related lines of inquiry: how early-modern
'people' are registered in the formal qualities – 'character' – of
Renaissance drama, and how – or whether – these 'people' can
speak on the modern stage.

Harold Bloom, to take a clearly polemical example, repeatedly
treats 'character' and 'role' as synonymous terms, implying a
continuity between the textual and theatrical forms with which
Shakespeare registers 'the human' (see Bloom 1998: 404). Yet
despite his loving recollection of Ralph Richardson's Falstaff,
Bloom's stage is not the space where Shakespearean identities
are fashioned, for two reasons: 'In the theater, much of the interpreting is done for you, and you are victimized by the politic
fashions of the moment' (720). The actors, director, and
designers read the play, and in framing the text in stage action,
they put a lot into play; it might seem that performance exceeds
the text, gives us *more* to interpret, a different range of things to
interpret than reading does. Yet Bloom understands the text as a
kind of illocutionary encyclopedia, a compendium of legitimate
stage conduct: the theater's work should be to realize these performatives, and even under the best conditions a given performance
can realize only a narrow range of the text's illocutionary capacity.
Bloom understands the stage as an etiolated version of reading:
its force depends almost exclusively on the text that it 'interprets'
as performance. At the same time, though, that Bloom locates the
force of performance in the text, the text's illocutionary force isn't
forceful enough to *determine* stage behavior. For although Bloom's

Shakespearean text contains all legitimate stagings, it is none-theless susceptible to appropriation, to being traduced by merely politic and fashionable performances. Reading, for Bloom, implies full-time access to the multiplicity of Shakespearean meanings (All Shakespeare All The Time), while performance can articulate only one Shakespeare at best; at worst the thing that treads the boards is some belated monster of our own lapsed imagining.[12]

Bloom expresses a conventional, and contradictory, sense of Shakespearean performance; what he resists is performativity itself. Bloom understands performance as derivative, as capable of evoking the force of the text; at the same time, though, the theater's capacity to betray the text points to something else, the relative independence of performative behavior from the 'intrinsic' meanings of the script. Indeed, it's precisely this 'performativity' that appears to prevent theater today from gaining access to the Shakespearean past. Bloom's claim that Shakespeare invented 'the human as *we* know it' (italics mine) should imply that Shakespearean drama is continuous with our behavior, that our ways of enacting ourselves as human subjects in the theater should be at least partially transparent to the Shakespearean discourse of character, of the subject. But while 'we' are Shakespeare's inheritors, Bloom finds the contemporary theater's strategies for representing meaningful behavior to be only intermittently capable (if that) of registering an authentically Shakespearean humanity. There can be only two explanations for this failing: 1) We no longer understand, and no longer represent, our humanity in precisely Shakespearean terms – while performance was *once* (in Richardson's heyday; but in Irving's? Cibber's? Betterton's? Burbage's?) capable of deriving appropriately from the force of Shakespeare's texts, it no longer does so, so that performance is merely irrelevant to authentic Shakespearean meanings; and/or, 2) the theater is (and has always been) incapable of resolving our continuity with past modes of subjection *as they are registered by texts*, because performance necessarily constructs the force of the text as theatrical behavior, behavior which must appear politic, fashionable, *our* behavior in order to be significant. There is, of course, a third possibility: 'we' are simply no longer human at all, at least in the 'Shakespearean' sense, presumably like the great majority of the world's population.

Understanding Shakespearean performativity principally as a mode of textual transmission surprisingly limits the theater's capacity to evoke history – the true Shakespearean subject, like or unlike 'us' – because stage acting isn't determined by textual meanings, but uses them to fashion meanings in the fashions of contemporary behavior. If performance cannot recapture a more-or-less 'modern' Shakespearean subject from the text, it seems unlikely that the theater can restore a radically different early-modern subject either, a subject (in the equally polemical account of Francis Barker, for example) constituted through social and economic relations and represented through literary and theatrical means that are essentially removed from our own.[13] Contemporary Shakespearean performativity places considerable weight on the Shakespearean text, attributing to the text a significant force in determining the meaning and value of a performance. As a result, performance which does not appear to restate 'textual' meanings – either because contemporary theater is stylistically (Bloom) or historically (Barker) incapable of doing so – can engage neither with Shakespeare nor with history. Yet as we have seen, this 'force' is a consequence of how contemporary Shakespearean performativity constitutes appropriate performance; it is neither innate to theater nor to dramatic performance, nor is it even uniform across the spectrum of contemporary performance, dramatic or otherwise. Theatrical performance can never be 'historical' in this sense, as a means of recovering meanings inscribed in the text, because theater does not cite texts; it cites behavior. To the extent that the historicizing potential of Shakespearean performativity is identified with the independent force of the text, 'history' in the theater can only appear suspiciously theatrical.

To say that Shakespearean performance is not somehow involved with history seems odd, even trivial, even to me; for all that it's a modern kiss, surely a kiss is still a kiss (or is it?). This impasse arises, I think, from the historicizing force attributed to the text in our contemporary understanding of Shakespearean performativity. This force replicates a longstanding tendency to regard the merely incommensurable relationship between writing and acting, literacy and orality, as a fully 'schematized opposition' (Roach 1996: 11). Theater relies on conventionalized performance practices that evolve over time (even in relatively conservative performance traditions) and that derive their power – the scandalous sense of what 'works' – from behavioral genres which embody and transmit their own dynamic of historical change. A more powerful understanding of the historicity of performance would begin by recognizing the historical contingency of onstage and offstage behavior – how acting responds more directly to changing social behavior than to changing ways of reading classical texts – and also recognize the contingent relationship between Shakespearean drama and other kinds of performance with which it shares the stage: with jigs, clowning, fencing, sermons, bearbaiting, and pageants in Shakespeare's day; with contemporary plays, performance art, film, and other forms of live and mediatized performance today. Refusing to regard the Shakespearean text and its performance as 'transcendent categories' means acknowledging instead 'that these modes of communication have produced one another interactively over time' (Roach 1996: 11), and continue to do so. Whether it's possible to recapture early-modern subjects in contemporary performance seems to me at best an open question; however, to imagine dramatic performance as having any historicizing, restorative capacity requires a fundamental rethinking of Shakespearean performativity and the relations between 'text' and 'performance' it frames.

Shakespearean performativity today occupies a typically modern disjunction between texts and performances; expressing pervasive Western attitudes toward language, print, and the body as modes of communication, as well as toward the institutions of literature and theater, this tension cannot merely be thought away. At the same time, this sense of dramatic performance appears to frustrate the desire to locate the historicity of performance, in part because it treats the text as a stable (though interpretable) thing, and performance as a set of changing, indeterminable interpretive practices. Literary criticism is usually correlated with stage practice in this way, as the work of J. L. Styan (1977), Gary Taylor (1991), and many others suggests: changing ways of reading the text open it to previously invisible performance possibilities (feminism leads to feminist Isabellas onstage); changing performance practices (epic theater) produce the text in unanticipated ways, and so open unanticipated ways of understanding what the text means (feminist Isabellas onstage encourage feminist 'readings' of *Measure for Measure*). Such narratives, however, tend to preserve a derivative relationship between text and performance; at the very least, they preserve these categories in 'schematized opposition.' Yet Shakespeare's texts today are the site of a kind of revolution, both in how we understand texts as objects in literary and social history, but also in how we understand the practices by which texts – Shakespeare's or anyone else's, then and now – come to have a public identity as artworks. Does the relationship between text and performance become somewhat less 'schematized' if we imagine a more 'interactive' relationship between textual and performance *practices*?

The second quarto text of *Romeo and Juliet* contains a well-known stage-direction, one that's typically eliminated from modern editions of the play: '*Enter Will Kemp.*'[14] It's understandable why editors modify this stage direction: although Kemp was the best-known comic actor of his day, later becoming more famous for his Morris-dance to Norwich in 1600, 'Will Kemp' is not actually a 'character' in the play *Romeo and Juliet*, at least as we understand those terms today. Directed not to the character but to the actor, the stage direction marks a hole in the text, and reminds us of what's never there in the text – its performance. At the same time, it also sets the text alongside a performance history (clowning), preserving an intersection with this tradition in the rich opacity of the unspoken line, '*Enter Will Kemp.*' A recent production of *Romeo and Juliet* (directed by Peter Lichtenfels, who is co-editing the play with L. A. C. Hunter for Arden), cast a gifted comic actor with experience in stand-up comedy, Christopher Peak, in the role of Peter, Kemp's role. It's impossible, and probably irrelevant to imagine reconstructing Kemp's behavior: given the specific density of Kemp's dances, jests, and jigs in Elizabethan culture, even if the Bankside Globe could find an actor to reconstruct his performance, could it really signify to us *as* live behavior today?[15] Peak improvised some routines during rehearsal, which were more or less 'set' in performance, while routines were improvised anew every evening. Reminiscent at once of Grock, of Beckett's Didi and Gogo, of circus, Peak's clowning was (again to call on Roach's terms), not an imitation of Kemp, but a *surrogation* of Kemp's function, using an embodied performance to mark a history outside the text, a history also traced – just barely – within it (Roach 1996: 3).[16] Peter bulked unusually large in this production, in part because Lichtenfels used him to introduce the play, and left him onstage at other times not specified by the text. Hamlet – particularly in the 1603 quarto – was skeptical about charismatic commodities that Peak brought into the play:

Let not your clown speak more than is set down. There be of them I can tell you that will laugh themselves to set on some quantity of barren spectators to laugh with them, albeit there is some necessary point in the play then to be observed. O 'tis vile and shows a pitiful ambition in the fool that useth it
(Shakespeare 1998: 9.17–21)[17]

Peak's acting disrupted the narrative, split the 'focus' usually sought in modern stage productions, altered the tone of the surrounding drama, and thoroughly pleased us, his barren audience.[18]

Peak's acting was certainly a historicizing activity, though I don't imagine many people took it that way. What Kemp did onstage as Peter is unknown, but what the stage direction marks is hardly a moment of undetermined free play. It marks a moment where, perhaps, we can gain access to the 'performativity' of Shakespeare's theater, its quite different way of constituting texts and performances. To 'perform' that moment – '*Enter Will Kemp*' – will inevitably be an act of surrogation, a performance in the idiom of contemporary behavior, whether that behavior is the modernized Elizabethanism of the Globe or, as in Peak's case, a concentrated effort to engage in clowning, performance with a distinctive lineage and history, a genealogy that includes Shakespeare's clowns, both actual (Kemp) and fictive (Peter).[19] While no performance of Shakespeare today is likely to stand fully outside 'Shakespearean performativity' (how could it?), Peak's performance seemed less to derive from the text than to strike an 'interactive' relationship between text and performance. Peak's clowning opened a dialogue with textuality, with a contemporary 'editorial' understanding of Shakespearean writing as a social practice: that the texts – all of them, good and bad – respond to and record the densely pragmatic circumstances of their creation, including their use-value to performers like Kemp. This understanding of texts and performances would no doubt be unrecognizable to Shakespeare and company. Yet by using the text to instigate (not control) this aspect of the performance, *Romeo and Juliet* was, perhaps, doing the dialogic work of history, entering the 'big time' through the means of Shakespearean performativity.

No lath, no plaster, an industrial set, hip costumes (especially for The Artist Formerly Known as Tybalt), and a clown: is this really history?[20] It's neither reconstruction, nor derivation; the text inspires moments of surrogation – Peak doing Kemp – that are neither governed by the text, nor seem to recover or restore 'original' behavior. Nonetheless, the performance responds to a contemporary understanding of the material difference of early-modern textuality, within a relatively familiar structure of Shakespearean performativity. In this limited sense, this production perhaps points to an alternative understanding of Shakespearean performativity, one not constituted as expressing the force of the text, but arising at the interface where texts and performances, language and bodies, engage, represent, resist one another. Although Shakespeare performance generally encodes a restrictive, determining understanding of the text's role in performance, a fascination with the interactions and interruptions between bodies and texts might be taken to be one of the hallmarks of performance today. 'Texts' are visible everywhere in contemporary performance, though usually visible in ways that imply a very different 'interaction' than is common in stage Shakespeare. In Suzan-Lori Parks's play *Venus* (1997), for instance, Saartjie Baartman, the Venus Hottentot is doubly spectacular: she is embodied onstage as an object of voyeuristic inspection (and abjection), but also narrativized, in the extensive reading of historical 'extracts' by the Negro Resurrectionist. The sense that the Venus has been absorbed into a textual history is emphasized, too, by the play's repetitive dialogue, in which snatches of 'speech' are rendered again and again, creating a chorus of commentary that, somehow, both describes the Venus and never touches her. Anna Deavere Smith's performances depend on the written, audio-, and video-texts of her 'informants'; using supertitles to identify each 'speaker', Smith scrupulously reproduces the precise conduct of her subjects, their vocal and physical mannerisms – acting becomes a way to register, textualize, and even alienate the gestural regimes of everyday behavior. Anne Bogart's *Going, Going, Gone* (a staging *of* Albee's *Who's Afraid of Virginia Woolf* that retains the gestural regimes of the Burton-Taylor film, but uses a new verbal script); DV8's *Enter Achilles*, a dance work that develops the habitual attitudes and gestures of British pub culture as its choreographic 'text'; Robert Lepage's *Elsinore*, all of Beckett's short works for stage and video; the striking presence of 'text' in the visual economy of the Baz Luhrmann *William Shakespeare's Romeo + Juliet*: although these examples all express different ways of constituting the 'text' relative to 'performance', they also express a shared fascination for the slippage between bodies and texts in performance, a fascination evoked in different ways by the Oxford *Shakespeare*, by the controversial nature of Shakespearean performativity today, and perhaps even by the surprising return of J. L. Austin, Superstar, to the discourse of literary and social theory. Regardless of whether we can use performance to recover the 'alien history' of early-modern subjects (Barker 1984: 15), contemporary performance is preoccupied with concerns that bear directly on Shakespearean performativity. Indeed, the friction between texts and enactment in contemporary performance might help us to find the pulse of Shakespearean performativity, the changing force of the text in Shakespeare performance. This force must change, of course; it's always changing: in the theater, if we want to speak with the dead, we can only do so through the recalcitrant behavior of the living.

Notes

1 My thanks to Barbara Hodgdon and Robert Weimann for their careful and helpful comments on an earlier draft of this essay, and to Michael Bristol for inviting me to write about Shakespeare and modern performativity and for his forbearance with the results. I have discussed the Globe, theme parks, and reenactments at greater length in 'Reconstructing the Globe, Constructing Ourselves' (forthcoming); on building practices, see Greenfield (1997), and Orrell (1997); on plaster composition, see Mulryne and Shewring (1997: 27); on tourism, see Kennedy (1998); on 'pastness', see Kirshenblatt-Gimblett (1977: 5, and *passim*).

2 Austin excluded theater from the category of felicitous performance, but his notorious sense that 'a performative utterance will, for example, be *in a peculiar way* hollow or void if said by an actor on the stage' (1975: 22) points, as Jacques Derrida (1982) and Judith Butler (1997) have both argued, to the conventional status of all utterance.

3 Dramatic pictorialism (reproducing the dramatic setting in stage sets and costumes – Macbeth in kilts, Caesar in togas) and theatrical antiquarianism (reproducing the physical environment of Shakespeare's theater, as Poel and successors down to the new Globe have done) express a modern understanding of the historicizing capability of Shakespearean 'performativity'. For an excellent reading of the antiquarian stage as historicist inquiry, see Schoch (1998); on Victorian pictorialism and on Edwardian efforts like William Poel's, see Mazer (1981); on modern-dress and eclectic staging, see Berry (1989: 14–23); on the impact of modern design, see Kennedy (1993).

4 My focus here on Bristol's understanding of the institutional development of theatrical performance responds to his effort to incorporate performance into a dialogical Shakespearean history; his more urgent critique of the 'death of the author' (1996: 49–54) and of textual 'indeterminacy' (21–9) as ways in which literary scholarship both evacuates the historicity of literature and reproduces contemporary modes of commodification (of literature, subjectivity, experience) are, it must be said, much more central to the thrust of this excellent and provocative book. See also Kastan (1999: 32–3).

5 As Kastan remarks, one sign of this transformation is suggested by the fact that even antitheatrical writers like Prynne and Northbrooke make a distinction between plays performed in private, recreational, not-for-profit settings, and the professional theater (1999: 158); in a subsequent discussion of the closing of the theaters in 1642, he notes that Parliament not only waited two years to close the theaters, but defeated an earlier bill for theater closing 'on the grounds that playing was a "trade" that should not be inhibited' (204).

6 Margreta de Grazia notes that the emergence of an early capitalist economy did not immediately transform laborers into modern industrial workers, whose 'labor' was entirely convertible into 'wages'. Insofar as many early-modern workers both received important forms of non-monetary compensation, and seem to have regarded wages as a means to subsistence rather than surplus wealth, the 'capitalist system of equivalences' (1995: 83) that would produce a convertible 'exchange' between different commodities (such as linen and paper in Marx's example, or perhaps between printed and performed plays) was still in the future. My thanks to Celeste di Nucci for drawing my attention to this provocative article.

7 On the precarious economics of play publication, see Blayney (1997). Noting the relative absence of published drama between 1576 and 1587, William Ingram argues that the formation of the theater industry preceded an interest in publishing plays; the University Wits 'seemed to understand, better than the commercial playwrights who were their contemporaries, the importance of publication' (1992: 241).

8 Indeed, it might be noted that 'I do' is actually very rarely spoken as part of a wedding service today; this 'text' nonetheless persists as part of the general regime which the performative dimension of weddings appears to cite. I'm grateful to Carol Rutter for this timely observation.

9 Still other kinds of speech *are* prosecuted as racist *conduct* 'in those cases in which racial minorities come to stand for the source or origin of sexually injurious representation (as in rap)' (Butler 1997: 40)

10 There are many examples of plays which took some time to find appropriately expressive behavior in the theater: *Troilus and Cressida* and *Waiting for Godot* provide two very different instances, but Ibsen's plays, too, were thought to be unactable by a generation or so of actors, in large part because their language seemed to frustrate the available technology of acting (see Cima [1983]). Moreover, much as

it is said to embody textual implications, the gestural and movement vocabulary of stage performance is also a means of representing the semiotics of social behavior, and changes in acting style clearly respond more to changing social dynamics than they do to changing ideas about Shakespeare's texts. In Betterton's time, the teapot stance of the stage embodied contemporary habits of social interaction without literally reproducing them; today, actors onstage rarely speak face-to-face, without opening out to the audience, signaling 'intimacy' through a behavior – turning away – most of us would regard as impolite offstage.

11 Maus provides an exemplary summary of this debate (1995: 2–3).

12 Whether this plenitude of interpretive possibilities is ever really visible to a reader is itself questionable; see Fish (1995: 47–52).

13 For Barker, the privacy of the bourgeois subject is an invention of the revolution of capital, following hard on the English civil war; Shakespeare's plays embody a thoroughly 'alien history' (1984: 15), more cognate with the 'artisanal' (18) apparatus of the early-modern theater than the slick business of the contemporary stage In particular, the spatial relations of this theater – 'There is no well-founded division between those who perform and those who are spectators, between the subjects and objects of communicative sight' (26) – stand apart from the privatizing spatiality of the modern house, in which the occluded audience looks into a manufactured space of visibility, confession, and disclosure from a privileged zone of psychological and social privacy. The alien subject of the Shakespearean stage may be recoverable as an object of scholarship (as in Barker's striking reading of Pepys on *Hamlet*), but must remain remote from any modern performance practice.

14 In the Riverside text (Evans and Tobin 1997), the stage direction occurs between IV.v.101 and IV.v.102.

15 On Kemp's career and performance style, see Wiles; his discussion of the complex meanings of the jig in Elizabethan culture is especially illuminating (1987: 44–6).

16 Peak describes his work in this way:

> I worked with Peter [Lichtenfels, the director] very early on in the process, ironing out his ideas about 'Peter' and the clowning. If Shakespeare wrote the clown roles more open-ended, allowing them to work into the structure of the play while still utilizing improv and familiar bits, then we thought we would try that. So for my part I set most of the routines in rehearsal – the piss-pot, etc. But the one place I left open to manipulation was during the Romeo–Nurse scene, when I exited the stage [into the audience]. Each night I would start working on the next evening's production, trying to top whatever I had done the night before [Peak went into the audience and engaged several members of the audience, sometimes bringing them onstage]. I know that by putting that kind of pressure on myself I will be more creative, plus I had to work in secret because I didn't want the other actors to

know what was coming. I figured the more shocked they were, the
more the audience would buy into it. A lot of these ideas did come
from working in clubs [i.e., as a stand-up comedian], but they also
come from my experience in theater. I know that the danger of
performance isn't as prevalent in the theater, but in clubs it's what
everyone is anticipating. It's all the same people, I think, so I
figured given the opportunity the house would respond, which
would add a dimension to the show that I believe Will [Kemp?
Shakespeare?] probably intended.

(Peak 1999)

17 Hamlet's complaints in Q1 resonate somewhat more strongly against
Kemp's line of performance than the more familiar versions do:

And then you have some again that keeps one suit of jests, as a man
is known by one suit of apparel, and gentlemen quote his jests
down in their tables before they come to the play, as thus: 'Cannot
you stay till I eat my porridge?' and 'You owe me a quarter's wages',
and 'My coat wants a cullison', and 'Your beer is sour', and
blabbering with his lips and thus keeping in his cinquepace of
jests, when God knows, the warm clown cannot make a jest unless
by chance, as the blind man catcheth a hare.

(Shakespeare 1998: 9. 21–8)

18 Lichtenfels remarks that although he had not originally intended to
use Peak in this role,

during the summer, Lynette and I worked very hard at 'constructing' our first eclectic copy of the forthcoming edition and
that is where the idea of Will Kemp being cited in quarto 2 began
to take real root in my mind I was especially interested in
exploring what the role of Peter might be, and how that ties into
breaking up the rhythm of the play, whether it kept comedy alive
(all commentators say that the comedy dies after Tybalt and
Mercutio are slain).

(Lichtenfels 1999)

Working with Peak, Lichtenfels reports beginning with 'the
Peter/Will Kemp reference in quarto 2', and thinking 'that the
clown's function might be to be a direct link to the audience', he
noticed that Peter's

dialogue seemed underwritten to my ears. That may have been
unfamiliarity on my part – because so many of the scenes he is in
are usually cut in production. But I also began thinking whether
many of the clown's roles in [Shakespeare's] plays are underwritten, and whether that might mean that part of the latitude a
clown had/took was to be given a basic scenario (whether
improvised and then scripted, or scripted) and then work with
that, [like] lazzi [in *commedia dell' arte*].

(Lichtenfels 1999)

My thanks to Chris Peak, Peter Lichtenfels, and L. A. C. Hunter for sharing their thoughts about *Romeo and Juliet*, and this production with me.

19 On genealogies of performance, see Roach (1992).

20 Although I've highlighted Peak's work as epitomizing a critical relationship between the text and performance in this *Romeo and Juliet*, a full reading of the historicizing 'work' of this clowning would have to relate it to other dimensions of this complex production: the production had a contemporary, industrial setting; it had two complete casts (one all-male, one all-female), who performed the play in alternation for two weeks, and were then recast (with only a few hours' warning) in two 'mixed' – though still, in some roles, cross-dressed – performances.

7

Heresies of style
Some paradoxes of Soviet Ukrainian modernism

IRENA R. MAKARYK

In an interview in *Gambit* in 1970, Edward Bond remarked that, as a society, 'we use the play [*King Lear*] in a wrong way. And it's for that reason I would like to rewrite it so that we now have to use the play for ourselves, for our society, for our time, for our problems' (Hobson *et al.* 1970: 24). For Bond, 'wrong' Shakespeare is academic Shakespeare, while 'right' Shakespeare is a transformed and contemporary Shakespeare. Bond's clear-cut division of approaches to Shakespeare is quintessentially modernist in its rejection of 'museum' Shakespeare in favour of a reworked classic for our time. In both his rejection of an 'academic' or literary Shakespeare and in his division of approaches into right and wrong may, surprisingly, be heard the echoes of Soviet Ukrainian modernism – the labelling of performance styles using moral, or even theological, terms.

Writing nearly fifty years before Bond, the great Soviet Ukrainian director Les' (Oleksandr Stepanovych) Kurbas (1887–1937) conceived of a production of *Macbeth* in terms almost identical to those of Edward Bond's *Lear*. In 1924, Kurbas observed that

> Our approach to Shakespeare naturally must be the approach of our day. The restoration of Shakespeare in the manners and customs of his time is formally impossible and in essence unnecessary. The whole value of the scenic embodiment of a

classical work in our day lies namely in the ability to present a work in the refraction of the prism of the contemporary world view.[1]

Re-worked or 'deformed' classics (as some of his detractors styled it) were the especial purview of Les' Kurbas who, more than anyone else in Ukrainian theatrical history, is associated with the performance of Shakespeare. A polymath, Kurbas was an actor, director, playwright, translator, pedagogue, theorist, cinematographer, musician, and costume designer. Himself an 'epoch' in the Ukrainian theatre, as one of his contemporaries referred to him (Tokar 1933: 61), he influenced hundreds of artists involved with the theatrical and cinematographic arts. Introducing Shakespeare into Ukraine after a century of tsarist prohibitions, Kurbas prepared four plays (*Romeo and Juliet*, *Macbeth*, *Othello*, *King Lear*) and did preliminary work on five others (*Hamlet*, *A Midsummer Night's Dream*, *Twelfth Night*, *Timon of Athens*, *Antony and Cleopatra*), intending, eventually, to produce the whole Shakespearean canon; however, the only play which was actually staged in its entirety was *Macbeth*. Kurbas produced four variants of the play, the fourth of which, staged in 1924, was the most radical, and is the subject of this paper.

Of the same generation as T. S. Eliot, Eugene O'Neill, Erwin Piscator, and Charlie Chaplin, Kurbas also shared some of their ideas. Anti-bourgeois and anti-materialist, he sought spirituality in art, a recovery of wholeness in a fragmentary world. Trained in philosophy, Germanic and Slavic philology in Vienna and L'viv (Western Ukraine), he had travelled many times to Western Europe. A life-long voracious reader and a lover of art, he was influenced by the ideas and the works of a plethora of theorists, philosophers, writers, musicians, and artists, among them Henri Bergson, Edmund Gordon Craig, Georg Fuchs, Oscar Wilde, Max Reinhardt, Arnold Schönberg, Paul Cézanne, and Pablo Picasso.

Having seen Europe, Kurbas was not interested in a world limited to the adulation of Moscow and St. Petersburg. He spearheaded a theatrical movement 'away from Russia', the 'dead centre', as he called it, toward the West. Shakespeare and non-Ukrainian works as a whole were, for Kurbas, particularly useful in focussing attention on style, which was, in his view, the central issue of modernism. Rather than re-creating a Western European repertoire, Kurbas, in turning to Sophocles, Molière, Goldoni,

Schiller, Hauptman, Kaiser, or Shakespeare, intended to explore and mine aspects of style in his search for a new theatrical grammar for the new Soviet Ukrainian reality.

To appreciate its distinctiveness and comprehend its radical-ness, Ukrainian modernism must be set within its particular historical context. Unlike some Western European variants of modernism, Ukrainian theatrical modernism was not simply concerned with the restoration of a medium, a genre, or a mode. Nor was it a mirror of its Russian counterpart: with its rich theatrical legacy, Russian modernism could, with confidence, look forward toward the creation of a new Soviet Russian culture. By contrast, Ukrainian modernism was an attempt simultaneously to revivify, recreate and rethink a whole theatrical tradition suppressed since the eighteenth century.

The details of Ukrainian cultural repression under imperial tsarist rule are still not widely known and consequently some of its most salient features need to be rehearsed here. In brief, Ukrainian theatrical history may be encapsulated by the exchange between Duke Orsino and Viola.

> *Duke*: What's her history?
> *Viola*: A blank, my lord.
>
> (*Twelfth Night* II.iv.109–10)

The colonization of Ukrainian culture reached its apex in the nineteenth century with two particularly harsh tsarist edicts (ukazes) in 1863 and 1876, which, among many other inter-dictions, imposed a complete embargo on the publication and importation of all books (including the Bible) in Ukrainian; the removal of all Ukrainian books from libraries; and – significantly for our purposes – a total ban on the performance of plays in Ukrainian, whether native or translated.

Thus, both foreign works, such as Shakespeare, and native Ukrainian works endured a simultaneous prohibition. It is there-fore not at all surprising that in Ukraine (as in most European countries, although for very different reasons), Western drama and Shakespeare in particular would become associated with national and cultural revival,[2] and, further, that they would constitute literary and theatrical models preferable to those of their long-time masters.

Complicating the blank of Ukrainian theatre history was the ubiquitousness of the imperial presence. Thus, at the same time as Ukrainian productions and translations of Shakespeare were strictly forbidden, Russian performances continued on the stages of Kyiv. By the early twentieth century, some relaxation of the most strict edicts had taken place, including the possibility of performing plays, but only as long as the subject matter was confined to peasant life (so-called 'ethnographic' plays), and only when a Ukrainian play was performed on the same bill as a Russian. Full liberty came, perhaps paradoxically, only with the chaos of world war, civil war and revolution.

In the midst of such turbulence, Les' Kurbas staged the first Shakespearean play, Macbeth, in Ukrainian, in 1919–20, along with numerous Western classics and contemporary modernist European plays. All the '-isms' of the West – modernism, realism, expressionism, naturalism – as well as all of Western drama were now suddenly available for exploration and recreation on the blank slate of the Ukrainian stage. Thus, Volodymyr Vynnychenko, prose writer and political activist, as well as Secretary General and Vice-President of the first, short-lived autonomous Ukrainian state could write, 'Truly, we were like the gods . . . attempting to create a whole new world out of nothing' (1920: 258).

By 1924, when relative political stability followed the cessation of violence, with the creation of the Soviet Republic of Ukraine, and the government's active policy of Ukrainianization, aesthetic questions came to the forefront. Newspapers and journals carried extensive polemical debates concerning the relationship between politics, art, and nation, debates about realism and modernism, the place and significance of dramatic and literary classics in a new post-revolutionary Soviet world. With more freedom than was possible in over 200 years, and more freedom than was to come until the 1990s, a variety of aesthetic and political positions were hotly debated in public fora by Symbolists, Futurists, Neo-classicists, VAPLITE (Free Academy of Proletarian Literature), and many others.[3]

An active contributor to these debates, Kurbas declared his rupture with aestheticism on the one hand, and, on the other, his full endorsement of the proletarian revolution. These views were reflected in his establishment of a new theatrical company, The Berezil' Artistic Association. Its very name suggested it political roots: 'Berezil'' was the archaic Ukrainian word for March, the month associated with revolution.

In an interview, Kurbas explained that the main task of Berezil' was to engage in the 'ideological *perestroika* of the spectator' by destroying the remnants of the old naturalistic theatre and by focussing, instead, on the technique and texture of spectacle. Most inimical to art, he frequently argued, were realism and 'psychologism.' In his battle against these two tyrants, Kurbas intended to deploy a Shakespeare not found in the academic theatres, but one 'refracted in the prism of the contemporary worldview.' 'Theatre, before the revolution, before the turning point in art, was easel painting with theatrical devices. In the theatrical frame, as in a painting, we saw that same absolute correspondence to the real world; in the frame of the theatrical picture we saw an illusion. Now, there is no painting.'[4]

Opposed to the 'ukrainianophilic historical-ethnographic theatre' as well as to the prudently cautious Europeanized pre-revolutionary theatre, Kurbas argued that the theatre needed 'to create a new, not a passive, man' (quoted in I. 1924). Hitherto, he explained, the spectator had been 'educated by authoritarian tsardom in a spirit of piety toward the dominant culture' (Kurbas 1925a: 118). That piety and passivity needed to be set aside for a more critical, reflective stance on the audience's, as well as the actor's and director's parts. He urged Ukrainians to draw back from 'double provincialism' and colonialism (1927: 260). Left-leaning but not communist, Kurbas declared that Berezil' stood for 'action, organization, tempo, Americanization, *le dernier cri* in scholarship, and for the present' (1923: 230).

Anti-aesthetic, anti-academic, anti-naturalist, the theatrical art of the avant-garde embraced experiment rather than 'museum' culture. Non-Ukrainian texts were to be mined pre-eminently for their style. Experimentation was essential to 'sharpen the axe, to improve the instrument; experimentation is unavoidable for a theatre which intends to go forward and to be the model for many theatrical collectives which have recently been created in Ukraine.'[5] Like other modernists, Kurbas's interest in style meant a fascination with what Gordon Craig termed 'noble artificiality': inherently theatrical, not literary forms, such as the circus, vaudeville, Grand Guignol, cabaret, and mime. Style became an interpretive, an ideological, but also a moral tool: an avant-garde style was the only right style for the times, argued Kurbas. 'Avant-garde' thus meant both the expression of a left-wing political stance aimed at the total repudiation of bourgeois culture, and a radical, ground-breaking offshoot of modernism focussed on experimentation and process.

The fulfilment of this double task may be seen in its most extreme form in Kurbas's 1924 production of *Macbeth*. Shortly after the première, one of the actors, Vasyl' Vasyl'ko, recorded in his diary that a 'bomb went off, throwing such sparks into the audience that even on the second and the third day [all of] Kyiv shouted "*gvalt*."'[6] From the point of view of Vasyl'ko and many of the actors, as well as a good portion of the audience, *Macbeth* was a tremendous success, as the thundering ovations indicated.

But not everyone loved the production. Those critics who detested the production accused Kurbas of 'sacrilege', 'vivi-section', and serious 'error.'[7] Why did this production elicit such sharply-polarized responses? In interviewing theatrical historians in 1995 in Kyiv, I was surprised to learn that even today this production has many detractors. What was it about the style which led critics then and now to categorize it in moral and theological terms as 'wrong' and 'blasphemous'?

First, let's consider the production. The *Macbeth* which opened on 2 April 1924 presented a full-frontal attack on the illusionist theatre.[8] Disruptions, contrasts, juxtapositions, minimalist costumes, montages of stage action, atonal music – these were to help ironize the moral tale of an ambitious man. Kurbas employed various techniques to create a cubist expressionist production (Bennett 1990: 33), which would reflect his beliefs about audience, actor, and art work. A self-conscious creation of fragments to be re-assembled by the spectator, this production (as one of the sympathetic critics observed), intended to kill the remnants of the bourgeois theatre (Desniak 1925: 116).

While only twenty-three pages of the director's copy have survived, they reveal a consistency in their cuts; these appear to be excisions aimed at simplifying the emotional range of the play by omitting small choral scenes and, most importantly, by eliminating Macbeth's heroic concluding speech. The whole production was austere and harsh. In Vadym Meller, the artistic director, Kurbas discovered a like-minded friend and colleague who shared his artistic interests and could translate them into reality. Like Kurbas, Meller studied in the West. After a very successful first exhibition, he had been invited to show his works in the *Salon d'Automne* together with Picasso, Gris and Bracque.[9] For the 1924 *Macbeth*, Meller created enormous placards (four by four metres high), bright green shields of stretched canvas, on which giant modernist red block letters announced 'Castle', 'Precipice' (the translator's word for 'heath'), and so forth, recalling both medieval-renaissance locality boards,[10] and contemporary political posters. Their starkness urged the audience to creative completion: to imagining what each of these locations might be like. Their size dwarfed the actors, and diminished their usual centrality on stage, suggesting that the characters were subject to forces other than their own individual wills, to other discourses, interpretations, and frames. Raised or lowered when needed at the sound of a gong, the screens served as more than background. Lowered at the same time, they indicated the simultaneity of the action in different parts of Scotland. At other times, they moved in slow, stately rhythm to underscore the emotions of the lead actors, to emphasize tension, the dynamics of the action, or even to interfere in the action – as, for example, when they physically blocked off Macbeth's attempt to follow Banquo's ghost – represented by a searchlight beam.[11] Fragments of furniture, chairs, and a throne were, like the screens, lowered and raised when needed. The actors were often lit by the harsh light of projectors, and moved in a 'restrained' way, and the whole rhythm of the production followed this general style (Hirniak 1982: 196–7).

Like the stylized and bare stage which both suggested place and yet also mocked any such certainty, so the costumes were spare and theatrical, emphasizing the duality of the actors (as characters and as people) and of their time frame (both time present and past). Wearing either militarized garb or contemporary work clothes very like those worn by many people in the audience, the actors were distinguished from them only by a few ancillary articles: stylized bits of medieval or renaissance clothing, such as tunics and cloaks, decorated with appliques in a modernist interpretation of heraldic designs.

At the centre of this production was the 'naked' actor – the major experiment in this version of *Macbeth*. Kurbas's challenge to the actors was to display the perfection of their technique by turning their roles 'on' and 'off' at will. The pure craft of acting was laid bare without the attendant 'mysteries' of sustained, realistic character, illusory sets, grand costumes, extensive music, and numerous props.[12] In Renaissance fashion and with similar effect, actors' roles were doubled or tripled. Thus Yosyp Hirniak, for example, played Donalbain, the Murderer of Banquo, and the Doctor; each role carried over associations from the previous one, contributing to the spreading of guilt in the realm, and limiting the audience's habit of dividing the characters into goodies and baddies. The mechanism of acting itself was openly displayed: each actor came on stage at his or her own pace, sometimes greeting the audience, and assuming his role only when he was properly positioned. Similarly, after performing his part, the actor exited as 'himself.' Thus, in the first scene, the witches came on stage wearing wide blue-grey trousers and red wigs. Mysterious little electrical lights flickered in their costumes and around their eyes when they uttered their prophecies. A surreal violet blue light was used to emphasize their horrible grimaces. Like priests, they held censors in their hands, thus immediately announcing the bitingly satirical thread of the interpretation. But, after this eerie scene, the screen with the word 'Precipice' disappeared from sight, the violet light vanished, and the witches calmly left the stage as actresses who have done their 'number' (Rudnitsky 1988: 112).

The sleepwalking scene was performed with the same emphasis on actor in and out of role. Liubov Hakkebush proceeded to centre stage, where she placed her candle, took off her mantle, shook her head until her long dark hair tumbled around her shoulders, and only then proceeded emotionally to 'Out, damned spot!' Similarly, after Macbeth delivered his powerful soliloquy in Act I, scene vii, he seized his dagger and turned to go to kill Duncan. Taking a few steps, he resumed his identity as Ivan Mar'ianenko the actor.

The 'on-off' technique proved to be extremely hard on the actors. Actress Iryna Steshenko, who played one of the witches, wrote in her memoirs of the difficulty of maintaining a balance between restraint and involvement in the role (Steshenko 1969: 170), while Liubov Hakkebush, who played Lady Macbeth, was admonished at rehearsals for descending into pathology and bad taste in creating the sleepwalking scene (Avdieva 1969: 153). Indeed, the inclination to overdo their acting segments was one of the dangers of this technique, as Kurbas reminded them; all acting, he emphasized, proceeds from thought, not emotion (Samiilenko: 1970: 64).

The 'on-off' principle was repeated again and again in the production, thus isolating and drawing attention to key moments in the play, as well as to the points of transition – forcing the audience and the actor to a cerebral response to the play, to a focus on the constituent parts of theatre. Every aspect of the production was placed in quotation marks, every theatrical convention was questioned, including the idea of the tragic hero. The traditionally heroic Macbeth was portrayed by Ivan Mar'ianenko (hitherto noted for his tragic roles) as a common, unimaginative soldier, dressed in contemporary clothes, including sloppy puttees. This Macbeth combined simplicity of character with single-minded cruelty; his doubts were not indicative of a conscience, but were rather a revelation of his fearfulness, a fearfulness revealed right after the regicide, when he threw himself at his wife with the very same knife he used to murder the king. Duncan was presented as a drunken fool, whose death at first seemed if not deserved then at least not completely reprehensible. Both Macbeth and his wife counted on the fact that most of Scotland would not discover their crimes, and the knowing rest would keep silent out of fear. (The resemblance to Stalin's future institutionalization of terror, and the population's fearful, silent compliance seems uncanny in the whole interpretation.)

Lady Macbeth was more austere than her husband. Not a romantic young beauty, but a mature woman without passion for her husband – who seemed, rather, to annoy her with his fearfulness – Lady Macbeth was ugly and sharp-featured, in love only with power and herself. When Macbeth left to kill Duncan, she followed him, comfortably holding the dagger like a practised killer (Kuziakina 1969: 193). The Macbeths were understood as products of their time – a Scottish Middle Ages which Kurbas interpreted as inherently and instinctually spiritually hollow and cruel. The only moment which contained a remnant of traditional tragedy was the sleepwalking scene. Dressed in white, Hakkebush seems Ophelia-like in photos taken of this scene. While in the rest of the production she was costumed in restrictive, unattractive clothing (a dark, shapeless three-quarter length robe over a white shift, pleated at the bottom, vaguely recalling a Ukrainian peasant's costume), and a severe headpiece (a white kerchief held in place by a metal band), in this scene, she wore only the long white shift over which cascaded her long, unfettered hair. Robbed of the dignity of her usual severity, she was subject to the hallucination of an imminent assassination on herself.[13] The consequences of her past cruelty were apparent in the stark contrast to previous scenes. Here, she was palpably terror-striken by her inability to achieve real power or to control events.[14] That this was not a scene of pathos is suggested by the response of the drama critic I.Turkel'taub, who faulted Hakkebush for being too mannered and her acting too 'cold' (1924: 4).

Grappling towards a new relationship with the audience, Kurbas wished to break down drama into its constituent sub-systems, forcing the audience both to re-examine the individual materials of the theatre and then to re-constitute them into a new whole. He employed some devices to destroy traditional audience expectations and engagement (as, for example, the 'on-off' device), while others were to draw the audience in at moments when they least expected it. Thus, for example, he had the witches wired so that small electric lights lit up as they moved in their deliberately exaggerated 'witchey' way. But, when it came for Banquo and Macbeth to speak to the weird sisters, the witches were lit up from behind, casting huge shadows onto the audience. The thanes spoke to these shadows and thus to the audience which, after being alienated and amused by the odd beings, now just as suddenly found itself implicated in the dark world of *Macbeth*.

The closest link between actor and contemporary audience was provided by major additions to the text: three intermedia and dumb shows. The Porter (played by Ambrosii Buchma), called the Fool in Kurbas's production, appeared in the intervals between the acts. During the first interval, Buchma was dressed in fool's cap and traditional fool's clothing, with exaggerated make-up, including a bulbous nose which occasionally lit up. The Porter's costume clearly linked him to the Old Vice of medieval drama, the attendant of the Devil – a connection confirmed and developed in an additional mimed sequence following Act I scene 3 (that is, just after Macbeth and Banquo first encounter the witches) in which cardinals cavorted on the stage and then turned into devils by the simple process of revealing their cowls on which were painted devilish faces.

Buchma as Porter performed clownish tricks, acrobatic jumps and dance-steps, after which he always spoke with individual members of the audience. In her memoirs, fellow actor Natalia Pylypenko compared Buchma to a rubber ball, which flew across the stage, seemingly weightless and unpredictable, at one time flying up to the ceiling, at another descending by the trap door and shooting up again (1968: 15). Buchma made seemingly impromptu speeches on contemporary political and social issues (such as the deposition of the Tsar, the League of Nations, various religious superstitions, even backstage theatrical disputes); these were Kurbas's analogy to Shakespeare's references to the Jesuits' equivocations. Every day, the director insisted, the jokes and references had to be changed. The actor Stepan Bodnarchuk was responsible for transforming items in the morning newspaper into couplets by nightfall. In this, as in other elements of the theatricality of the production, Kurbas was consciously reaching back to the rich, old medieval and renaissance traditions of the audience–actor relationships. In permitting the Fool some creative freedom, Kurbas was also consciously drawing upon English fools like Will Kempe renowned for his impromptu conversations with the audience and his extempore comic remarks. Buchma shared with Kempe the lively combination of acrobatics, wit and physical clowning.

In the fourth act, during the intermedia referred to as 'Haymaking', Buchma entered as a Peasant, reaping energetically as he went and singing a harvest song. Here, from the scenes of bloody-mindedness, Kurbas moved the audience in a Shakespearean manner to consider the apparently undisturbed (or compliant) common man. Rather than any sentimental or folkloric association, the simplicity of the peasant's task both contrasted with the violent, over-the-top actions of the main characters, but also connected them. For, of course, the Reaper was also the Grim Reaper, mowing down 'the rays of light, [and] extinguishing them with his broad sweeps.'[15] Fatigued by the work, he would then approach members of the audience sitting on bleachers in front of him and take cigarettes from them; thus he connected the main plot and the intermedia to reality itself.

The Fool's third and last appearance occurred in the final moments of the play, when Macduff comes out carrying the head of Macbeth. Still wearing his Fool's makeup – the mocking, grinning face – Buchma came in costumed as a bishop, in gold tiara and white soutane. He then crowned Malcolm to the solemn music of an organ ironized by the delicate sounds of the piccolo and the rougher harmonium. Just as he did so, a new pretender approached, killed the kneeling Malcolm, and took the crown. Without pause, the bishop once again intoned the same words, 'There is no power, but from God.' As the new king began to rise, a new pretender murdered him, and the ritual was repeated once again.[16]

The mixture of burlesque, acrobatics, buffoonery, and Grand Guignol – linked to Futurism and Dadaism of the West – was intended to focus attention on and interrogate the material and form of the theatre most radically by employing a world classic – hence a text regarded with some piety. While in some quarters the production was acclaimed as a 'great triumph' and a work of genius (e.g. Mohylians'kyi 1924: 282; G-tov 1924: 6), in others, it was simply 'a scandal.'[17] The Kyivan audience, which had recently endured a Macbeth-like period of rapid and bloody exchanges of power (nine between 1917 and 1920), was forced to exercise a very renaissance type of activity. This 'history' play induced the spectators simultaneously to apprehend Ukraine, Shakespeare's England, and Macbeth's Scotland. Shakespeare was their con-temporary. Was he also their prophet? Whom was the production satirizing? Whom was it destroying? How were the issues of cons-cience, power, loyalty, treason, silent complicity, and destruction of innocence supposed to be interpreted in 1924 with the recently (21 January 1924) dead Lenin, and with the backroom power struggles which ensued? How could it be that the bloodiness and ineffectualness of the Tsar (Duncan) was, in the end, indis-tinguishable from the Soviet power that took his place (the Macbeths and the Malcolms of the world)? Where was the morality of the new regime? Was it possible that regicide was neither romantic nor heroic, and that evil was simply banal, repeatable, and unconnected to ideology?

Kurbas's intention – to problematize all the elements of theatre (the classic, plot, role, character, hero, time, space, acting, prop, costume) – was, as I have already noted, an attempt to re-conceive the whole notion of theatre. In his view, this was the only right way of going about the task of creating a new Soviet Ukrainian culture. Whether one considers him a naïve convert to the new order or an aesthetic idealist, Kurbas believed that the struggle had to be, could only be, the struggle to reinvent all systems; and this aim could only be achieved by constant experimentation. The avant-garde style was intended to make audiences think critically and to unite them in analytical thought through their complicity in the action. Devices which broke down the conventional barrier between stage and audience, actor and character, were, in Kurbas's logic, rupture on behalf of a new communion. But this harmony could only be achieved by the special cooperation of the audience which had to fill in the hermeneutical gaps. It required then, not a suspension of disbelief, but a very special and shared belief – a belief in the possibility of forms emptied of traditional associations and codes in order that they be recreated and filled with something entirely new.

Contemporary critics and spectators unsympathetic to modernism focussed on the discontinuity and unpredictability of the production. They found it cold, exclusionary, élitist. Even with his pre-production articles, puffs, and his brief statement of purpose before the curtain, Kurbas was not entirely successful at creating the kind of new audience–actor relationship he intended. The vociferous polemic launched in the press (which lasted over two months) was in part a debate about the modernist style and its relationship to the notion of the classic. Kurbas was accused of 'blasphemy' in his treatment of Shakespeare, of completely annulling a theatrical classic, of presenting a 'cold; and unfeeling production' (Hirniak 1982: 193; 197), of showing life as it shouldn't be, instead of how it should.[18] Shakespeare in his hands, according to the critics, was simply Mr. Wrong.

But what was 'right' Shakespeare? In an article castigating the production, Iakiv Savchenko defined the 'correct' tradition of staging Shakespeare as, first of all, a realistic recreation of Elizabethan theatre; secondly, as a tradition of strong actors playing in a heroic-romantic style; and, lastly, as a production which centres all the attention on the main characters (quoted in Avanti[19] 1924). 'Right' Shakespeare, then, appeared to be very close to old traditions and conventions of the commercial theatre. Savchenko's prescriptions suggest the unity between audience and stage of a simple garden variety based on the idea of the stage as representing reality or, more accurately, a heightened reality. The idea of style as potentially wrong or right seemed to rest on the bedrock of a particular understanding of community and, further, on the strength of the social fabric. Considering itself under ideological siege from within and from without (not having yet recovered from world war, civil war and revolution), the 'right-thinking' Bolshevik polemicists of the Soviet Union in 1924 had little tolerance for a notion of theatre (or art) that was not unifying or celebratory of great deeds. Ironically, in a country in which God was proclaimed dead, only moral and religious terms could be found to convey the depth of their condemnation of modernist Shakespeare.

Curiously (from Kurbas's point of view), his peers also attacked his *Macbeth* for being too bourgeois, for taking the 'bourgeois aesthetic' to its 'absurd' conclusion by not reflecting objective reality but only hinting at it, by presenting a system of signs, marks and ideas instead of concrete reality; and, finally, for creating overly abstract forms.[20] Art for art's sake – the principle which really was under attack here – was a movement that did not strike deep roots in the East, where art had always generally been approached from an ethical (religious or social) perspective.[21] The critics' offensives were, in part, a reflex regression to ethical models of criticism developed over the past two centuries (and perhaps most notoriously found in Tolstoy's critique of Shakespeare). The traditional, ethical approach to the arts also fed naturally into the new political terminology of error, heresy and deviation.

The Futurist Mykhail Semenko correctly pinpointed the cultural crisis of his time as a crisis of theory (1924: 222–9, cited in Ilnytzkyj 1983: 337). With little thought given to the part culture would play in the Revolution, its leaders had no consistent cultural policy, let alone a theory. Lenin's only interest in culture, for example, was exhibited by his insistence that cities be plastered with slogans and that statues be erected to revolutionary leaders. The latter in particular evoked the most conservative of tsarist and neoclassical cultural habits. The avant-garde was appalled. But this conservatism or regression was of a piece with other kinds of turnings-back. For the Commissar of the Enlightenment, Anatolii Luncharsky, as for Lenin, the classics were national property and thus to be tampered with at peril. Lunacharsky's slogan, 'new content in old forms' – must have given the modernists pause in their belief in a new order, as must have the critic Turkel'taub's slogan, 'Backwards in art and culture'.

In the 1920s, the rhetoric of morality – modernism was wrong and destructive (Kurbas called it 'cheap demagoguery' [1925c: 244]) – soon drowned out intellectual debate. The unpredictability of modernism and its apparently cyclical view of history could hardly coexist for long within a new, official master narrative: the story of 'scientific', inexorable progress toward a new paradise on earth. In such a narrative, in which the answers were already known, what point could experimentation possibly serve? Among the first to welcome the Revolution, the avant-garde had few allies. Dismissive of the old ethnographic school, of the bourgeois and much of the intelligentsia, the Ukrainian avant-garde worked itself into a political corner from which, by the 1930s, there was little possibility of escape.

The 1920s debate concerning *Macbeth* usefully points out many of the broader difficulties with modernist Shakespeare and the modernist project – at least in Ukraine. While modernism provides freedom in opening up space and, especially, time, and attempts simultaneously to distance and to draw in, often only its discontinuities and ruptures are immediately evident. By contrast, the mimetic approach to the theatre, although only a convention and without objective validity is, as Benjamin Bennett astutely pointed out, a 'communal initiative': 'if the realistic begins by being discredited, if it is recognized from the outset as mere convention, then the conscious decision to accept that convention *is* undoubtedly communicative, shared with others, a communal process.' What is crucial, then, continues Bennett, 'is not meaning, but *style* as the token of an ethical decision repeatedly taken in the theater' (1990: 26–7).

Conservative, academic or commercial theatre with its apparently easy acceptance of 'ordinary reality' thus functions in a seemingly harmonious manner; it provides a readily identifiable common ground for actor and audience. Such a desire for clearly-defined and understood concepts of communion were most obviously found in the first years of the Revolution. Thus, Nikolai Evreinov's staging of *The Storming of the Winter Palace* on the third anniversary of the October Revolution with at least 8,000 participants and 100,000 spectators (whose participation, observes Lars Kleberg, 'was merely a question of degree rather than kind' [1990: 64]) was both an expression of this conflation of life and art and a harbinger of things to come. Inspired by the artistic precedents created during the French Revolution and by the ideas of Richard Wagner and Romain Rolland, such huge spectacles, mass festivals and glorifications of revolutionary leaders, it is true, did not last very long. But that does not mean that the desire for such 'realism' and the communion which underlaid it disappeared; rather, it found a less obvious outlet in the theatre's return to 'realism' as the officially sanctioned approach to art in the Soviet Union.

Rather than foreground the audience–actor connection, Kurbas's modernist productions presumed that the audience wished to co-create a new ground for interpretation and communion while creating a semiotic earthquake where nothing remained stable or certain. Modernism optimistically endowed the audience with the desire to work while at play, to think critically and to question in an individual way in order to achieve a long-term project of a new community. Thus, for many Ukrainian modernists, it was commonplace to think of the theatre as the church of literature, the best expression of collective ceremonial thinking.[22] Here, we may see that the modernists themselves reverted to religious and, in other cases, to moral terms. For both camps, this emotion-laden terminology revealed the deeply-ingrained belief in the monumentality and potency of the classic for our culture.

Yet modernism was also deeply sceptical of its communicative tools and signifying practices, as the interrogations of Kurbas showed. Using rhetoric while also drawing attention to its manipulations, modernism had enormous political and subversive force (Eysteinsson 1990: 228) – a fact which goes some way to explaining both Hitler's and Stalin's detestation of it.

Modernism's idealistic conception of the audience and its occlusion of the psychology of viewing – the perhaps overwhelming need for harmony, what we really like in mimesis – doomed Ukrainian modernist productions to a specialized or special audience. It is perhaps not surprising, after all, that, in 1995, Ukrainian theatrical historians remained uncomfortable with what one critic called Kurbas's 'fireworks', his 'whimsies', his too intellectual, too contemporary production (Zabolotna 1992 53–4). Tired of political interpretations of plays and anxious to rejoin the European community, Ukrainian theatrical artists and critics seem, at the moment, happiest with a psychological realism.

Notes

1 Kurbas (1924) All translations are the author's.
2 I deal extensively with the topic of national revival and the first performance of Shakespeare in Ukraine in Makaryk 2000: 1–22.
3 See, for example, Ilnytzkyj (1997) and Shkandrij (1992).
4 Les' Kurbas, folio 42/24, p 9, M. Ryl'skyi Institute of Art History, Folklore, and Ethnography, Kyiv.
5 Kurbas (1925b: 256) Kurbas's extensive theoretical writings and his work on Shakespeare are a complex topic only briefly sketched here. They are the subject of a book-length study in which I am currently engaged.

6 Vasyl' Vasyl'ko, *Shchodennyk* [unpublished diary], 1 January 1923 to 14 May 1924, vol 5, MS 10369, State Museum of Theatrical Arts and Cinema, Kyiv.

7 Numerous reviews and memoirs attest to this view. A representative view is Savchenko (1924a: 6).

8 Although various scholars cite the opening of the play as 1 April 1924, in fact, according to Vasyl' Vasyl'ko's diary, it did not open until 2 April, because the costumes were not ready. On 2 April, even as the performance was proceeding, the costumes were still being completed.

9 Meller is the father of constructivism on the Ukrainian stage and was responsible for some of Kurbas's most inventive, original stage designs. He turned to stage design after his paintings were destroyed during the First World War; his theatrical *début* took place in 1918. See Kucherenko (1975) for a beautiful catalogue of his surviving works.

10 Virlana Tkacz (1990) argues that these may have been influenced by silent movies. Also see Iona Shevchenko (1929: 83), who argues that the notion of *peretvorennia* is linked to methods of cinematographic montage. He cites Eisenstein and his notion of 'an attraction' in this relation.

11 See Shmain's description (1969: 137–42).

12 Hirniak noted that the work of Viktor Shklovskyi was widely read by the members of *Berezil'* (interview with Hirniak 10 August 1982, New York, cited by Tkacz 1983: 65). Kurbas's practical use of 'estrangement' techniques occurs first in this production of *Macbeth*, and, as Tkacz notes, predates Brecht's use by almost ten years (68).

13 So, at least, my examination of the photos in the archival collection of the State Museum of Theatrical Art and Cinema seemed to me. In one, Hakkebush faces the viewer in a close-up which shows her heavily-made up eyes, and her whole face shrinking in terror from something. In the second photo, looking beautiful and innocent, she carries a light in front of her in her outstretched hand. This is the only photo extant which I have examined which shows her in an upright posture, her head back, her long hair streaming behind her. In other photos from the earlier parts of the play, she was always stylized in her movements, and usually hunched over, whether reading the letter from Macbeth, walking with him, or responding to his rage (probably after the murder of Duncan). In the sleepwalking photos, she is also shown sitting or, more accurately, reclining. Had I not known that these were photos taken of Lady Macbeth, I would certainly have thought that they were photos of Ophelia. The stage imagery of femininity – the white colour of her shift, the loose hair, the feminine and less stylized gestures – suggest this.

14 On the three Lady Macbeths of the Soviet Ukrainian stage, all played by Liubov Hakkebush, see Smolych (1977: 155–66) and Kuziakina (1969).

15 So, according to Valentyna Zabolotna, a theatrical historian and great-grand-daughter of Ambrosii Buchma, who played the Fool in

this production (1992: 53). Also, similar views were voiced in an interview with me in Kyiv on 12 September 1995.

16 The description of the intermedia, and of all of Kurbas's productions described here, is a composite derived from many sources including Hirniak (1982: 103); Kryha (1969: 190–3); Kuziakina (1969 and 1978: 50-66); and Savchenko (1924a), each of whom recalls or writes about different elements of the production. The fact that both celebrators and detractors mention the final sequence, the crowning scene, is a good indication of its potency.

17 Valerian Revutsky, in correspondence with me, letter dated 3 December 1992. The interpretation of the production as scandal is best indicated by Savchenko's review (1924a).

18 For attacks on Kurbas, see the printed speeches from the Theatrical Discussions of 1927 and 1929 (Revutsky 1989, especially 606). In one of the many defenses of Kurbas, Mykhailo Mohylians'kyi makes the sensible point that every production, including that of Shakespeare's company, in some way modifies the original play. Mohylians'kyi argues that it is pointless to stand on principle; rather, the attackers should simply respond to the 'spring delight' of this 'great artistic achievement' (1924: 6).

19 'Avanti' is a pseudonym, possibly for Mykola Bazhan, although this is not certain.

20 Hnat Iura (1934). This vicious attack appeared the same month in which Kurbas was arrested; however, it may have been written by someone else but conveniently attributed to Iura, who had often been unfavourably compared with Kurbas in the 1920s.

21 This is a point many scholars of Slavic drama have made; most recently, Lars Kleberg (1990: 4).

22 See Bennett (1990: 60-83) for a discussion of ceremony. The notion of theatre as church occurs frequently in the writings of Kurbas.

8

'Lice in fur'

The aesthetics of cheek and Shakespearean production strategy

MAARTEN VAN DIJK

> Went into the Cottesloe late to see the preview of *The Hunchback of Notre Dame* and found Dave Rappaport leading the audience in community singing to the words of 'Bums and Tits, Bums and Tits, Having it Away . . .' Christ, I thought, here is the National Theatre's family Christmas Show . . . Michael Bogdanov's production has vigour and vitality and is a romp. But it is simply not my kind of show.
>
> Sir Peter Hall's *Diaries*, December 1977 (1983: 326)

When the Three Tenors romp through 'Nessun Dorma' from *Turandot* in some football stadium it is probably safe to assume that neither they nor the majority of their audience are aware they are testifying to how intricately the commedia dell'arte has been embedded in modernist culture.[1] But by way of Puccini through Carlo Gozzi, Busoni (who wrote an opera with the same title, and was Kurt Weill's teacher), the director Yevgeni Vakhtanghov (whose famous 'grotesque' production of Gozzi's *Turandot* was seen by Bertolt Brecht in Moscow in 1932), and Brecht himself, who finally finished a play of the same name in 1953 inspired by this 'marionette-like' production, that is exactly what they are doing.[2] At the same time, they are also testifying to postmodernism by reprocessing high-cultural forms into the contexts of rock concerts, videos, and especially sports competitions like the World Cup. The rather unpleasant hero from the opera, Calaf, is triangulated by them into a jolly three-man team, which shares the wild ride of the demanding music and engages in some vigorous macho competition: whose high B – sung on that ultimate sportsmanly word, '*vincerò*', 'I'll win' – will be the best? Depending on one's point of view, this is either depressing (the Culture Industry at its most kitschy, vulgar, and crass), or exhilarating (élite forms opened up to a huge popular audience, a new public for opera in a carnivalesque situation). Either way, it encapsulates how the spirit of commedia has functioned as a strategy for producing the classics in the contemporary theatre.

It is important to stress 'spirit', since a generalization is thematically more productive than the surface characteristics of commedia, which tend to reduce it to a set of sentimental and aestheticizing decorative elements (the sad Pierrot, the mysterious mask, stylized balletic gestures, naïve slapstick). In relation to modernism, the commedia dell'arte is rather 'a collection of images with many meanings' (Green and Swan 1986: xiii). One of its centrally productive meanings since Jarry's *Ubu Roi*, has been its cheeky resistance to authority. It has served consistently as a multifaceted, irreverent, oppositional utopia, where ebullient artifice could interrogate entrenched structures of power, genre, taste, and tradition.

Cheek

That cheek of this kind need not necessarily be simple-minded schoolboy transgression has been elaborately demonstrated by the German philosopher Peter Sloterdijk in his *Critique of Cynical Reason* (1987), which in a sense applies the spirit of commedia to philosophy. A pastiche of Enlightenment thought, this work is an attempt to theorize a strategy that might counter cynicism, the dominant mode of modern culture, according to Sloterdijk. The result of a post-1968 (and 1989?) disillusionment with the 'rigged game of discourse', cynicism needs an antidote of 'low theory' to subvert 'high theory' from Plato on. This consists of the counter-tradition of *kynicism* (literally 'dog philosophy'), embodied originally by Diogenes, who 'smells the swindle of idealistic abstractions and the schizoid staleness of a thinking limited to the head'. In a spirit of satirical resistance to all dominant modes of discourse, he starts a 'non-Platonic dialogue'.

Painfully aware, through fascism, of the consequences of intuitional philosophies of power and blood, however, Sloterdijk shows another face for Apollo, one that escaped Nietzsche, of 'a thinking satyr, oppressor, comedian'. Through the principle of *Frechheit*, or cheek, 'low theory' forms an alliance with poverty and satire to expose the lies 'which lull themselves into security behind authorities' (1987: 102). His method of wishing to preserve habits of thought that history has exposed as sham, while appropriating them at the same time in a different guise, is similar to the contortions undergone by most modern directors of the classics who wish to appear relevant. *Frechheit* necessarily becomes a fundamental attitude or stance (the basis of Brecht's gestus) for dealing with seemingly entrenched traditions; it is not a position, but a strategy. Sloterdijk points out that the word 'cheeky' (*frech*) has gained a negative connotation only over the last two hundred years:

> Initially, as for example in Old High German, it meant a productive aggressivity, letting fly at the enemy: 'brave, bold, lively, plucky, untamed, ardent.' The devitalization of a culture is mirrored in the history of this word. Those who are still cheeky today were not affected by the cooling off of the materialist heat as much as those who are inconvenienced by brazen people would like. The prototype of the cheeky is the Jewish David, who teases Goliath, 'Come here, so I can hit you better.' He shows that the head has not only ears to hear and obey but also a brow with which to menacingly defy the stronger: rebellion, affront, effrontery.
>
> (1987: 102–3)

Productive aggressiveness and effrontery become weapons against a vapidly consensual dominant discourse. According to this definition, cheek has been particularly useful for dealing with another familiar three-man tandem that has created challenges for modern producers of the classics, especially Shakespeare. We could call them the Three C's: containment, canonicity, and consistency.

Consistency was the nineteenth-century progeny of neoclassical decorum, and of historicism. With implications for acting, directing, and design in all areas of interpretation and style, the concept matured in revivals of the classics. The European tours of *Julius*

Caesar by the Meiningen players, for example, combined an almost fetishistic historical accuracy, with a development of the blocking and grouping principles with which Goethe had first experimented. These productions especially interested Stanislavski, who absorbed their practical influence with the theoretical one of Tolstoy, which held that art should aim to be 'transparent' (Benedetti 1988: 46). Thus the organic consistency of naturalism, combined with the formal unity of historicism to produce the 'Super-Objective' of the Stanislavski system, integrating all elements of production, including the subconscious, inner life of the actor-characters. The director emerged as the indispensable figure whose vision coordinated, orchestrated, and most of all, originated this organic interpretation of play texts.

William Poel made a decisive break with this nineteenth-century teleological tradition of historical literalism by staging Shakespeare in Elizabethan costume and theatre space. His break paved the way not only for a new, non-proscenium relationship of performers and spectators, but also for productions in modern dress, or in the costume of an historical period that would allow Shakespeare to be 'read' differently. So we have had, to take several random recent examples, *Coriolanus* set in the Napoleonic era, a Wild-West *Taming of the Shrew*, a Voyageur *As You Like It*. This tradition, which is still very much with us, has sometimes lived up to the modernist agenda of provocation. But such 'concept' productions are inevitably locked into a naïve consistency through the premise of 'resitings' which can be seen as 'essentialist strategies that tend to remask a . . . set of binary opposites' (Salter 1996: 127). In all the instances of resiting, however, time and place are fixed, and through the director's super-objective concept, also fixed in meaning. It was not until the staging of Shakespeare in post-Second-World-War Germany that this inherently decorative tradition was structurally challenged through the influence of Brecht.

Canonicity has had seriously delimiting implications for the theatre. Through the ideology of the global market, a culture-industry, festival Shakespeare has been commodified into a valuable 'centre of excellence'. Like a Trojan horse, he has the potential to evade this thuggish instrumentalism because of his classical status, but only at the cost of becoming a museum artefact marketed by university-trained specialists in cultural management. As first encountered by many students, this is an élitist bard, inaccessible because of his language, resented for his status as set text, and treated with hostility for his irrelevance to popular culture. At Stratford, Ontario, it has become necessary for a stage manager to make a short address before school performances, pleading for respect for the actors, to prevent a transgressive hail of pennies or catcalls. Management has tried unsuccessfully to develop strategies for dealing with a systemic problem, because the style of performance (and the audience behaviour thought appropriate to it), projects not the plays, but their status as old masterpieces. Consequently, 'mainstream' criteria must operate on both production values (eye-catching costumes or settings), and interpretation (Shakespeare's transhistorically great, 'timeless' masterpieces). Since 'timelessness' is still one of the favourite words in publicity material, it is used not just to convince audiences they are getting a top-quality product for their money, but also to reassure them that the product will not be *timely*, that is, having urgent, perhaps uncomfortably relevant things to teach them about their own situation that might require thought.[3]

These advances from the right have been reinforced by sorties from the left. Alan Sinfield attacked what he called 'culturism' – the liberal enlightenment belief that a wider distribution of high culture through society is desirable and can be achieved through government spending. He showed how the Royal Shakespeare Company, founded under the expectation that its large subsidy would free it from the pressures of commercial conformity, and that its artistic director's policy would lead to radical and 'relevant' readings, ended up catering to a largely middle-class audience whose ideology was both reflected and reinforced by RSC productions (Sinfield 1985: 184).[4] Even attempts to produce Marxist readings have been vulnerable to the ultra-left allegation that these are in fact a form of class-collaboration (Said 1983: 158–9).

In the 1980s another constraint on productions emerged expressed by the term 'containment'. The legacy of Althusser and Foucault seemed to have created the now familiar, pessimistic entrapment model according to which any demystifying, sub-versive, critical, or dissident potential of Shakespeare – the Shakespeare read by Brecht, for example (Heinemann 1985) – is always already contained by a dominant ideology, since any classic is a hegemonic instrument, part of an ideological state apparatus, both shaping and instilling the dominant culture. Given all the critical, cultural and ideological restrictions, Terry Eagleton asked whether it was possible for any interpretations or productions, even radical ones, to have a future. Instead of concentrating on new productions, he suggested we redirect our energies to the replacement of the study of Shakespeare with the study of 'Shakespeare' and 'to find a genuine new range of use-values for the texts' by 'challenging and dismantling their present exchange values' (Eagleton 1988: 207–8). In other words, no more cakes and ale, only the lenten fare of theory, for the moment.

The resulting Shakespeare would seem to be, confusingly, both good and bad news for those who still enjoy the thought of going to performances, or like producing them. On the one hand critical theory promises the theatre director a greater freedom: since all interpretations are appropriations, there is no unitary text, and there is no such thing as an unpolitical staging (Bate 1989: 210). On the other hand, Shakespeare's classical cultural status seems to place him squarely in the camp of the dominant authority and thus ensures that all politically progressive, subversive, or radical readings are already contained (Greenblatt 1985).

A central question is therefore raised for directors and actors: what specific strategies, given the cultural composition of Shakespeare, are available for mounting accessible productions uncontaminated by classical status? Such questions, according to Andreas Huyssen, are central to postmodern culture: 'how can the search for alternative traditions, whether emergent or residual, be made culturally productive without yielding to the pressures of conservatism which, with its vise-like grip, lays claim to the very concept of tradition?'[5] Indeed, the answer to such questions has been sought in the theatre so consistently since the beginnings of modernism that it must be seen as a tradition.

Carnival, the grotesque, cabotinage

Mikhail Bakhtin's concept of the carnivalesque has been much probed as a promising strategy for countering such fixed and impermeable hierarchies, especially in connection with Shakespeare (e.g. Knowles 1998b; Pfister 1992). The carnival-grotesque form, he thought, had the function to consecrate freedom, to permit the combination of a variety of different elements and their rapprochement, to liberate from the prevailing point of view of the world, from conventions and established truths, from clichés, from all that is humdrum and universally accepted. This carnival spirit offers the chance to have a new outlook on the world, to realize the relative nature of all that exists, and to enter a completely new order of things.

(Bakhtin 1984: 34)

This anti-formalistic approach to cultural traditions provides a way for linking the motifs of popular folk, or 'low' culture by means of the grotesque, to 'high' culture figures such as Rabelais, Cervantes, Shakespeare, and through the 'realist grotesque', with writers like Dickens, Balzac, and even Brecht.[6] Bakhtin was primarily concerned with Rabelais, with the novel, and not with the theatre. Yet it is significant that one of his key examples for illustrating his concept of the grotesque was drawn from the theatre, precisely at the moment in eighteenth-century Germany where a clear split occurred between high and low forms during the attempt by Gottsched and others to banish the popular Hanswurst characters from the respectable stage. Bakhtin cited Justus Möser's essay, 'Harlequin, or the Defence of the Grotesque-Comic', and saw the commedia dell'arte as the form connecting carnival with literary genres. For Bakhtin any move away from this bridging tradition transformed grotesque realism into the limiting consistencies of 'naturalist empiricism' (1984: 52). Although his analyses are theoretically inspiring, they have a restricted potential with regard to theatrical method. Moreover, there are several problems with Bakhtin's carnival which seem to place him in the containment camp: the paradox of the authorized transgression of norms (Hutcheon 1989: 99), and his 'failure to see the degree to which popular culture is permeated or circumscribed by elements of the dominant culture or ideology' (Gardiner 1992: 187). Others have seen 'more than a hint of appropriation' and containment in the Bakhtin vogue because it can be centred on a 'very generalized notion of "the people" with the carnival constituted as *essentially* subversive through the "radical" ironies played over "high" . . . culture' (Longhurst 1988: 73).

The most important exploration of how carnival cheek, in its commedia incarnation, could be specifically useful as a theatrical strategy had already been made in 1912 by the director Vsevolod Meyerhold, in a brilliant essay which summed up the ideas he had begun to formulate in 1906 during his production of Alexander Blok's play *The Fairground Booth*, where he appropriated the commedia dell'arte to break down the conventions of the heroic Shakespearean theatre. Significantly, the epigraph to Blok's work was taken from Dumas' play on Edmund Kean: 'Well, old nag, let's go smash our Shakespeare' (Jones 1993: 193).

Meyerhold's essay attacks the aesthetic principles of the Moscow Art Theatre, specifically Nemirovitch-Danchenko's production of *The Brothers Karamazov*, which the director Alexander Benois had seen positively as a new type of mystery play. In an analysis surprisingly similar to that of Bakhtin, Meyerhold concludes that the two forms of public performance, the mystery and the theatrical entertainment, have become totally divorced from each other since the strolling players moved from the medieval church into the market place. Truly popular theatre has become impossible because modern dramatists have turned 'literature for reading into literature for the theatre'. As a result 'the same deathly hush prevails in the auditorium as in the reading-room of a library and it sends the public to sleep'.[7]

Benois praised the Moscow Art Theatre's devotion to naturalistic 'truth', while he attacked Meyerhold for 'deception' and '*cabotinage*', a French term used derogatively for strolling players. Meyerhold turns this argument around, and having proved the historical connection between the *cabotin* – the highly skilled mimes relied on by the mystery plays to perform the more technically demanding tasks – with the actors of the improvisational commedia, and ultimately with the art of genuine folk theatre, he states that a theatre without cabotinage is not possible, because it will have become text and not performance-based. On the same grounds of untheatricality he dismisses the performer who in the Moscow Art style tries to 'live', his part through unconscious creativity, as an 'inspirational actor'. The true actor is the technical one who has mastered the art of gesture and movement. The term 'mystery play' itself he uses in a metaphoric sense for all forms of theatre which indulge in mystification by raising drama into a high literary art for initiates and which reject the cabotin.

He calls for a revival of the cult of cabotinage, and the fairground-booth theatre 'where entertainment always precedes instruction and where movement is prized more highly than words' (Meyerhold 1969: 127). Accessibility is the goal; therefore all forms of physical gesture and visual expression become central. He cites commedia masks and routines, and the metonymic gestures of puppet theatre where, 'when the puppet weeps, the hand holds the handkerchief away from the eyes', as productive examples. These schematized choreographic gestures, however, may too easily be understood as 'stylization', which 'reduces empirical abundance to typical unity' (138). Obviously he was thinking of Oriental theatre here, the methods of which Meyerhold found inspiring. But he also understood the limitations of a strictly codified language of gesture; it had the tendency to turn performances into museum pieces. While searching for a more fluid definition of anti-naturalistic theatricality Meyerhold then made his most significant move. The favourite techniques of the fairground booth needed to be described by his complex concept of the grotesque which took no account of unities of any kind:

> The grotesque does not recognize the *purely* debased or the *purely* exalted. The grotesque mixes opposites, consciously creating harsh incongruity and *relying solely on its own originality*. . . . [T]he grotesque parades ugliness in order to prevent beauty from lapsing into sentimentality. . . . The grotesque deepens life's outward appearance to the point where it ceases to appear merely natural . . . the grotesque synthesizes opposites . . . forces the spectator to adopt an ambivalent attitude towards the stage action . . . by switching the course of the action with strokes of contrast. The basis of the grotesque is the artist's constant desire to switch the spectator from the plane he has just reached to another which is totally unforeseen. . . . The art of the grotesque is based on the conflict between form and content . . . *joie de vivre* will be discovered in the tragic as well as in the comic.
>
> (Meyerhold 1969: 137–42)

In other words, the grotesque is at once positive and negative: it hybridizes creatively, while it transgresses both the established modes of received discourse, and the formalistic codes authorized by high culture. It is a device that demands stylistic discontinuity from actors and directors. Since it works to create an unstable synthesis of different elements, one of its main targets is any kind of theatre relying for its effect on consistency, completeness of form, or unity of tone. In scenographic terms Meyerhold's grotesque requires a radically eclectic approach.

As in Bakhtin's definition, the goal of this grotesque is the renewal of life; it celebrates *joie de vivre* in all genres, whether comic or tragic, so that 'old age is pregnant' and 'death is gestation' (Bakhtin 1984: 52–3). Its function is remarkably like Brecht's alienation effect – it renders the familiar strange and requires the audience to have a critical attitude by drawing attention to the means of expression. By extension, it assumes that the theatre itself is always the location of the action. The elements of contradiction and surprise also become part of performance technique. The technically adept *cabotin* is not interested in presenting lived emotions, but in telling stories with the same ease as the juggler or magician, relishing the act of showing off his skill, but always within the unpretentious, 'poor theatre' limits of the fairground booth, which itself refers to an approach rather than to a specific place and structure. For Meyerhold rediscovery and reapplication of the principles of the commedia dell'arte was the way to break down the élitist interests of the literary theatre, especially those founded on the deadly serious elaborations of a character's subconscious.

The role of the grotesque, he thought, was to 'subordinate psychologism to a decorative task' (Meyerhold 1969: 141). Yet it is precisely this overcompensating stress on the decorative task that reveals the tendency of Meyerhold's '*balagan*' (fairground booth) to drift towards an anti-populist, art-for-art's sake preciosity by placing a stylistic restriction on technique. His interpretation of the grotesque, at this particular stage of his career, tended to emphasize his interest in dazzling virtuoso effects and theatricality for their own sake. The grotesque conceptions had to be 'subordinated' to a decorative task by means of dance (141). In a letter he stressed that the *balagan* would still be 'artistic' and would 'be able to flourish in an atmosphere unpolluted by the belches (pardon my vulgarity) of clubmen. Wait and see – our group will create a haven of rest for the cultured Petersburg theatregoer.'[8] In spite of the irony, this exhibits a certain fastidious anxiety of contamination concerning the coarser material aspects of popular culture. As Bakhtin saw, the sharp difference between Shakespeare's Renaissance grotesque and the Romantic and

Modernist version was 'first of all its materialistic concept of being, most adequately defined as realistic'. It was the realism, 'fearless, sober (yet not cynical)', of Shakespeare (Bakhtin 1984: 52; 275). The mode of understanding Bakhtin called 'the material bodily lower stratum' is required for avoiding the containment of the grotesque.

Brecht versus classical status

Brecht's reputation as a serious, tendentious political writer has tended to obscure the subversive, cheeky (in Sloterdijk's sense), commedia side of his work as a playwright and director. His love of clowns like Valentin and Charlie Chaplin is well known, however, and many of the external characteristics of commedia informed his work from first to last.[9] A large number of his productions employed masks or stylized make-up.[10] The fairground *Bänkellied*, or street ballad, was a recurring element. And the famous white half-curtain incorporated the 'poor theatre' devices of the fairground into the plush velvet of the bourgeois performance site, while his bright, white lighting replicated the demystifying conditions of the daylight public performance. In *Galileo*'s marketplace scene carnival actually turns into revolution. A case could even be made that Brecht thought of performance as a series of routines rather like the *lazzi* of commedia (van Dijk 1990: 129). He did not unfortunately develop further a plan he sketched for the fourth night of *The Messingkauf Dialogues*, where we find 'Chaplin/comedy/*die Jahrmarktshistorie* (fairground story-telling).' But the connection with Meyerhold's *balagan* is made explicit.

The surrealistic, grotesque element of commedia is already evident in his 1923 film with Karl Valentin, *Die Mysterien eines Frisiersalons* (*The Mysteries of a Barber's Shop*), where the central gag consists of a customer having his head cut off by mistake (it is later reattached).[11] Brecht's *Haltung* of cheek, however, was not simply part of a youthful pre-Marxist phase. In his 1953 production of Strittmatter's *Katzgraben* for the Berliner Ensemble, which was a calculated attempt to meet the current official artistic policy of anti-formalist Socialist Realism, he could not help introducing some provocative comic routines which subverted the wishful thinking of the text. One wonders what party functionaries made of the scene where Ekkehard Schall with the butter churn between his legs, energetically and obscenely churns, while his mother, Frau Großmann, acted by Helene Weigel with great relish, plays the harmonium to drown out the noise.[12] Brecht's *kynical* defiance was often expressed through the lower bodily stratum. It was not the external characteristics of commedia that mattered most, however, but the underlying stance, which then informed the practice, especially with regard to the classics.

That clowns and classics were hybridized very early on in his practice was evident with his first production. During his work on Marlowe's *Edward II* in Munich, the great comedian Karl Valentin and his partner, Liesl Karlstadt, happened to be sharing the theatre with him and were encouraged to comment on rehearsals. Brecht later acknowledged that he had learned blocking from Valentin (1964a: 224). At the age of 22 he wrote enthusiastically in his diary about a clown who 'banged himself on the head, developed a large bump, sawed it off and ate it'. He concluded that 'there's more wit and style in that than in the entire contemporary theatre', then immediately made a connection with the classical drama that represented his aesthetic attitude for the rest of his life:

> Once I get my hooks on a theatre I shall hire 2 clowns. They will perform in the interval and pretend to be spectators. They will bandy opinions about the play and about the members of the audience. Make bets on the outcome. . . . The hit of the week will be parodied. (Up to and including *Hamlet, Faust.*) For tragedies the scene-changes will take place with the curtain up. . . . The clown will laugh about any hero as about a private individual.
>
> (Brecht 1979: 32–3)

As a young man he had clearly already rejected both the transcendent author and theatrical illusionism.

His attitude to the great heroic characters, often with tongue in cheek, was as undeferential as it was unorthodox, with a strong emphasis on the corporeal. He insisted on taking 'thou art fat and scant of breath' literally because the Hamlet at the Globe had been played by a short-winded, fat character actor (Brecht 1965: 59; *GBFA* 22.2: 749). The notorious difficulty for the actor of Gloucester to make his seduction of Lady Anne convincing can be easily solved: Richard succeeds in winning her with very coarse flattery because she is ugly and is not used to compliments. His 'triumph' is therefore made to look small.[13] Brecht parodied this wooing scene in *The Resistible Rise of Arturo Ui*, where Richard becomes the Hitler figure. He suggests King Lear literally tear up a map when he divides his kingdom among his daughters (1964a: 143; 1965: 63; *GBFA* 22.2: 807). Macbeth's castle does not have a 'pleasant seat', but in contrast to the dialogue, is a 'semi-dilapidated grey keep of striking poverty', to show that the Macbeths were only petty nobility and thus 'neurotically ambitious', like any suburban couple trying to keep up with the Joneses (1964a: 231). Romeo is already in love before he has seen Juliet because he has a bad case of '*gefüllte Samenstränge*' (lover's balls) (*GBFA* 22.2: 820; 1965: 61). Brecht was explicit about his connection of the fairground-booth tradition with the classics in a 1922 note on *Antony and Cleopatra* (a play he loved), which he envisaged could be staged in a Berlin pub if advertised like a nineteenth-century sideshow:

> 'Antony and Cleopatra' with piano accordion
>
> The downfall of the Roman general in Egypt. Cleopatra, the Ethiopian snake! A naval battle in Act 3!
> >   (Brecht *GBFA* 21: 134, and 643, n. 134, 29)

That he felt this stance to be a fundamental part of his theatrical gestus as a director, is demonstrated by the conclusion of a long dramaturgical discussion with his assistants about the production of *Coriolanus* he was preparing but did not live to realize. Peter Palitzsch asked him if they were doing the play to bring out the serious political issues they had been discussing:

> B. Not only. We want to have and to communicate the fun of dealing with a slice of illuminated history. And to have first-hand experience of dialectics.
> P. Isn't the second point a considerable refinement, reserved for a handful of connoisseurs?
> B. No. Even with popular ballads or the peepshows at fairs the simple people (who are so far from simple) love stories of the rise and fall of great men, of eternal change, of the

ingenuity of the oppressed, of the potentialities of mankind. And they hunt for the truth that is 'behind it all.'

(Brecht 1964a: 264–5; *GBFA* 23: 402)

Truth was obviously not to be separated from fun, nor dialectics from peephows. As he had stated in an early discussion of *Macbeth*, Shakespeare was '*absoluter Stoff*', 'pure raw material' (*GBFA* 24: 55). In a 1929 essay provoked by the critical reaction to Leopold Jessner's mounting of classical works, he wrote that the Vandals had a 'brash' ('*schnoddrig*') attitude towards old Roman cultural products, treating them simply as useful material because they saw not intricate carving, just firewood (*GBFA* 21: 288–9). Only through such an attitude of brashness (or cheekiness) was it possible to learn the material value of 'the old things'.[14] 'Old junk', like a partially destroyed hackney cab that had been disassembled, was attractive to him because it provided the basic 'stuff'. At the same time he took care to point out that the raw material had to be good in the first place. Quite apart from its status as a museum artefact, Schiller's *Wallenstein*, had a not inconsiderable material value because of certain of its qualities – that is, they were 'usable'. Cheeky vandalism had to be seen in a positive sense, as a counter to the inhibiting false piety and reverence of the public towards the classics, which made both of them inert. This attitude, termed 'creative vandalism' by Jonathan Dollimore, has recently been employed as a directorial strategy with 'a deliberately antagonistic relationship to [the] source text(s) as well as to the operations under which that source is generally produced and/or received' (S. Bennett 1996: 1–2). The difference between this stance and that of Brecht is that the former emphasizes the negative aspects of the 'vandalism', while the latter was concerned to employ traditions positively and productively for his own purposes. In 'The Art of Reading Shakespeare', a draft for a foreword to a projected edition, Brecht was careful to distance himself from the mindless forms of iconoclastic vandalism:

> I can understand that many people get angry when they hear that reading Shakespeare is an art. Doesn't that raise a barrier? Doesn't it mean, 'Keep away, don't have the cheek to approach this genius!' Is it an artistic temple you can only enter after taking off your shoes? Do you first have to pore over thick

books, take lessons, pass an exam? How can it be difficult
reading plays that are among the most beautiful of world
literature?
    Of course I don't mean that. But when someone tells me: 'To
read Shakespeare, you need nothing', I can only say: 'Try it!'
                                                (*GBFA* 23: 252)

Brecht was forced to elaborate his views about the 'Three C's'
in East Germany. In the important essay 'Classical Status as an
Inhibiting Factor', he attempted both to justify the Berliner
Ensemble's demystifying production of Goethe's *Urfaust* (directed
by Egon Monk) to the authorities (it had been called 'a denial of
the national cultural heritage', full of 'fatalism and pessimism'),
and to come up with some practical theatrical answers (1964a:
272–4). Old masterpieces, he felt, tended to be subject to a
traditional style of performance which tried to project not the
work so much as its status as an old masterpiece. As the classics get
more dusty with neglect, the 'copyists more or less conscientiously
include the dust in their replica'. Thus what has got lost is their
original ability to surprise us with their newness, most of all their
'productive stimulus'. Instead we end up with performances that
produce two, frequently connected, attitudes which neutralize
the text: a cozy, institutionalized familiarity, and a reverential
idealization. Brecht shows how a superficial attitude of 'greatness'
is generated in theatrical performances, a false sublime, which is
expressed by actors through ingratiating hamming and 'pompous
olympian strutting'. To combat this he encouraged his actors
to use their local dialects when speaking verse (1964a: 234; 244).
Canonical status reproduces a stultifyingly reverential (and de-
politicized) conservative approach to performances, as if they took
place in an autonomous, hermetically sealed realm, and come
freighted with a fear of humour, of genuine accessibility and
of contamination by popular culture. Debunking the cliché of
'timelessness', Brecht wryly noted in 1951 that Shakespeare's
'greatness' is the result of insignificant historical periods being
overawed by his themes, his language, and his fame; consequently,
these insignificant epochs feel that productions must be mounted
according to their own conception of greatness, but because they
are insignificant, they fail pathetically.[15]
    That such problems are still with us is made clear by the chapter
heading, 'Does Shakespeare's Verse Still Send You to Sleep?' in a

book on contemporary production (Elsom 1989: 99). Of course we think we have come a long way from the kind of acting Brecht was attacking, but what was more important for him than the physical style, is the reverential *Haltung* or attitude of the actor towards his material which leads to the sleeping. In words remarkably similar to those of Meyerhold, Brecht shows that the result is an inevitable 'ghastly boredom', which actors and directors attempt to counter by thinking up formalistic strategies, 'sensationally new effects', as if, he says vividly, 'a piece of meat had gone off and were only made palatable by saucing and spicing it up'.[16] The rotten meat was for him the 'unchanging reactionary content' of the bourgeois theatre. 'Wild changes of fashion in external form' represented the spicing agent – in other words, the endless and ever more desperate efforts at exotic or 'relevant' resitings, that still characterize many contemporary productions (1964a: 251).

The only answer was to look at the classics in a fresh way that would in the first instance derive from a basic gestus of demystifying irreverence and contradiction, by understanding the historical situation of the work in relation to its own time and to ours. How was this to be done aesthetically? The answer required an awareness of the linkage between ideology and theatrical praxis. This was not a question of style, but of the basic attitude on the part of the actor and the director: 'The choice of viewpoint is also a major element of the actor's art, and it has to be decided outside the theatre' (1964a: 196). Only a thorough, probing dramaturgical analysis of a classical play's significance in relation to its own time and ours would result in a meaningful production. As Brecht's work on *Coriolanus* demonstrates, this methodology made an extremely significant contribution to contemporary performance practice.[17] Yet in spite of the elaborate and time-consuming effort this was not a process fetishizing a 'great' text, but one of cutting it down to the size of raw material.

Brecht addressed the problem of consistency by attacking the uniform tone demanded by classical status, so that a hero, for example, cannot behave unheroically in a classical play and that sections presenting him as unsympathetic would have to be cut. This analysis uncovered the tendency of bourgeois realist and romantic drama to impose a stylistically 'correct' smoothness, homogeneity, and uniformity as part of the freight of dust. Actors themselves wished to erase contradiction for the sake of consistency: 'I can't play it that way, the character wouldn't do it' (*GBFA* 23: 316). His answer, as has been seen, was to alienate the characters through humour. The strategy is vividly demonstrated by Syberberg's extraordinary clips of the Berliner Ensemble *Urfaust* production which he filmed (without sound) in 1953. Recent studies on Bakhtin and Shakespeare have also shown how traditions of performance from Garrick to Franco Zeffirelli, (of *Romeo and Juliet*, for example), cut most of the comedy in order to emphasize romance and pathos.[18] Brecht's cheek was a way of making humour an essential function of learning for the performer. The most powerful demonstration of how he used Shakespeare is found in *The Resistible Rise of Arturo Ui*, where the gangster, Hitler-Ui, is given acting lessons by a superannuated old ham using 'Friends, Romans, countrymen', as an example for study. The scene as a whole is almost slapstick comedy until the end, when Ui is left alone to demonstrate his command of the speech. As the lights fade, with not a word of Shakespeare changed, the audience has the chilling experience of seeing Hitler's Nuremberg-rally gestus appropriating Shakespeare with devastating effect.

In his foreword to Sloterdijk's *Critique of Cynical Reason*, Andreas Huyssen explicitly recognizes the relevance of Brecht's positive, productive *Frechheit* strategy to postmodern culture:

> Sloterdijk's pastiche is endowed, from the very beginning, with a combative impulse, and his text asserts a notion of embodied subjectivity. . . . It is a philosophical pastiche that remains self-consciously satirical and never denied its substantive ties to the tradition of literary modernism and the historical avant-garde. Rather than postmodern in Jameson's sense, suspended as it were, in the gap between signifier and signified, Sloterdijk's relationship to the discourses of various disciplines and media is Brechtian, even though without Brecht's Leninist politics, in that it has definite purposes, makes contingent arguments, and uses traditions critically to its own advantage. In this sense, Sloterdijk's work could be claimed for a critical and adversarial postmodernism, a postmodernism of resistance. . . .
>
> (Sloterdijk 1987: xv–xvi)

As Fredric Jameson has recently argued, the 'doctrine' in Brecht is 'simply the method itself' (1998: 99). Shakespeare was one of many raw materials to be used strategically for learning how people live together in society. In Germany Brecht's *kynical* approach has worked itself out in the Shakespearean productions of directors who first collaborated with him, like Benno Besson and Peter Palitzsch, as well as of those directors like Peter Zadek and the young Leander Haußmann, who shrug off his influence, and even the anarchic versions of Frank Castorf, where cheek becomes an instrument of brutal vandalism.[19] In Michael Bogdanov and Michael Pennington's production of the *Wars of the Roses* cycle for the English Shakespeare Company, which barnstormed its way around the world, all Meyerhold and Brecht's aesthetics of cheek were employed to mount a devastating attack on Thatcher's Britain.

Bogdanov made Falstaff's piss a cheeky running gag through-out the *Henry* plays, almost as if he were citing the 'torrents of Gargantua's urine' in Bakhtin's discussion of the grotesque body.[20] In *2 Henry IV*, all the Eastcheap characters stopped to listen to a long splashing of water off stage, after which June Watson as Mistress Quickly said, with delighted recognition, 'Lo, here comes Sir John'. Falstaff then entered, preceded by a servant carrying a steaming bucket like some holy relic. In the spirit of Bakhtinian 'prandial libertinism' Falstaff even mistakenly drank his own urine while dining in a posh restaurant (*2 Henry IV*, I.iii), and the drunken Bardolph did the same, with evident enjoyment. The grotesque body of Falstaff was established by a food *lazzo* straight out of the commedia which Bogdanov introduced to John Woodvine's brilliantly seedy Falstaff: he broke six eggs one after another into a 'pint of gin', stirred it with his sword stick and then swallowed the concoction with relish, to the delighted horror of the audience. In the ludic spirit of carnival, Bogdanov spoke of the joy they took in comic invention: 'He and I were rather like naughty schoolchildren pretending to be grown up' (Bogdanov and Pennington 1990: 44–5). The carnivalesque, it has been pointed out 'was marked out as an intensely powerful semiotic realm precisely because bourgeois culture constructed its self-identity by rejecting it' (Stallybrass and White 1986: 202). Pennington summarized the ESC strategy: 'A certain cheek sus-tains us . . . a certain devilry. . . . Cheek and intellect are not a very English combination' (Bogdanov and Pennington 1990: 246).

Conclusion: 'A good wit will make use of any thing. I will turn diseases to commodity.'

A tendency to take a victimological stance towards cultural productions and to see them mainly as structures of oppression and
exploitation has become fashionable in some recent discussions
of Shakespeare, even those employing it as an alienation effect
(e.g. Knowles 1996: 107–8). There has also been a certain anxiety
about how performance criticism itself tends to use '"Shakespeare"
to regulate potential signification, and to cast the stage as an
interpretive institution for the recuperation of Shakespearean
authority' (Worthen 1997: 163). But among the post-colonial
or gender abjects, or Terry Eagleton's 'mangled members,
tormented torsos, bodies emblazoned or incarcerated', it is as well
to place Sloterdijk's Diogenes, publicly flaunting his bodily
functions in the marketplace and telling Alexander the Great
to 'get out of his sun' (Eagleton 1996: 69; Sloterdijk 1987: 104,
106). Not that the process we have examined – what has been
called 'the endless "rediscovery" of the carnivalesque' – is a
sufficient stratagem without a social function (Stallybrass and
White 1986: 202). As Brecht wrote in Los Angeles in 1942:

> eisler quite rightly recalls how dangerous it was when we were
> putting purely technical innovations into circulation, un-
> connected to any social function. the postulate then was
> rousing music. you can hear rousing music on the radio here
> 100 times a day, jingles encouraging the purchase of coca cola.
> it's enough to make you call for *l'art pour l'art* in desperation.
>
> (1993: 229)

It is a great irony that Brecht has now himself achieved classical
status and badly needs a dose of his own medicine; yet he proved
that appropriation need not be a one-way street. The marathon
runs of the ESC demanded stamina and commitment from both
actors and audiences, and so demonstrated that the fairground-
booth theatre could create, globally, however briefly, what
Raymond Williams called 'subcultural communities'. Emblematic
'poor' theatre of this kind also encourages the audience (and
performer) equivalent of what Jonathan Bate termed a 'strong
reader'. Such readers, he says, expand the range of meaning of a
classic by bringing it into our own world. At the same time they are

also required to surrender themselves to the demands of this classic (Bate 1989: 210). Learning was for Brecht the central purpose of his theatre. It is utopian to suggest that the aesthetics of cheek can evade hegemonic containment, classical status, and economic exploitation all at the same time, not to mention the marginality of live theatre. But they are something to get on with, '*brauchbar*' (usable), as he would say – Shakespeare as opportunity. Or in the words of his Mother Courage which have always sustained barnstorming actors in hard times: 'We're prisoners. But so are lice in fur.'

Notes

1 The influence of commedia on modernism is discussed at length in Green and Swan (1986).

2 The first production of Busoni's opera was directed by Max Reinhardt, who was himself deeply interested in commedia Brecht worked on his *Turandot, or the Congress of Whitewashers* off and on from the early 1930s to 1953. The director Benno Besson is given as the source for the Vakhtanghov influence: see Bertolt Brecht, *Werke* (1988–99), further cited as *GBFA*; here vol. 9 (*Stücke* 9): 398.

3 'A timeless romantic comedy to be enjoyed and savoured', promised the publicity of Michael Hoffman's 1999 film of *A Midsummer Night's Dream*.

4 The implications of Sinfield's attack on public subsidy have been challenged by Isabel Armstrong: 'What is required is another kind of debate, a more radical exploration and redefinition of the function and politics of public finance for "cultural" activity. A vapid consensual culturism has created the possibility for a Thatcherite attack through its own élitism and exclusiveness. But need public subsidy always be appropriated?' (1989: 3).

5 Huyssen (1986: 184). Hugh Grady comes to similar conclusions in an essay arguing that 'the containment-and-subversion debate has outlived its usefulness'. He poses the question: 'How to create an emancipatory stance from within the changed situation of culture under conditions of Postmodernism' (1993: 33). See also 'Subversion and Containment' in Bristol (1990: 189–211).

6 Bakhtin (1984: 52, 46); the grotesque is always seen as positive by Bakhtin.

7 'The Fairground Booth', in Meyerhold (1969: 121–3). See also Clayton (1994).

8 To the critic Gurevitch (Meyerhold 1969: 111).

9 Green and Swan link Brecht to commedia by citing his 'cabaret aesthetic, vaudeville turns, the jaunty doggerel, the quick changes', but Brecht's 'overriding concern for social and political meaning

took him some distance from the commedic impulse' since they feel commedia does not have these qualities (1986: 114).

10   For example: *Edward II, Man equals Man, The Roundheads and the Pointed Heads, Puntila, The Good Person of Szechwan,* and the *Caucasian Chalk Circle.*

11   Silent film (24 mins) with intertitles made by Brecht and Erich Engel. Other members of the cast were Liesl Karlstad, Blandine Ebinger, and Erwin Farber.

12   The scene is a highlight in the 1957 film of this performance by the DEFA Studio, directed by Max Japp and Manfred Wekwerth.

13   'Shakespeare auf dem epischen Theater', *GBFA* 22.2: 610.

14   Brecht uses the term '*Schnoddrigkeit*' literally 'brashness', with overtones of rudeness and insolence.

15   '[Grösse bei Shakespeare]', *GBFA* 23: 190.

16   The substantial influence of Meyerhold on Brecht is examined by Katherine Bliss Eaton (1985).

17   See Rouse (1989: 1–5 and 25–50).

18   Knowles (1998a: 43) See also Bristol (1996), where *Othello* is read as charivari.

19   For further discussion of these directors see Hortman (1998). For the rich tradition of Shakespeare performance in the GDR see also Gunter and McLean (1998).

20   Bakhtin (1984: 312, 334) The Bakhtin connection with *The Wars of the Roses* is also made by Crowl (1992: 149).

Bibliography

The 110th Report of the Council, 1985/86 (1986) Royal Shakespeare Company Executive Council, Geoffrey Cass, chair, 4 November.

Adorno, T. W. (1992) 'Theses upon Art and Religion Today', in *Notes to Literature*, vol. 2, ed. R. Tiedemann, New York: Columbia University Press.

—— (1997) *Aesthetic Theory*, trans. R. Hullot-Kentor, Minneapolis, MN: University of Minnesota Press.

Agnew, J.-C. (1986) *Worlds Apart: The Market and the Theater in Anglo-American Thought, 1550–1750*, Cambridge: Cambridge University Press.

Arac, J. (ed.) (1986) *Postmodernism and Politics*, Minneapolis, MN: University of Minnesota Press.

Armstrong, I. (1989) 'Thatcher's Shakespeare', *Textual Practice* 3, 1.

Aston, E. (1995) 'Daniels in the Lions' Den: Sarah Daniels and the British Backlash', *Theatre Journal* 47, 3: 393–403.

Atwood, M. (1992) *Good Bones*, Toronto: Coach House Press.

Austin, J. L. (1975) *How to Do Things with Words*, ed. J. O. Urmson and M. Sbisà, Cambridge, MA: Harvard University Press.

Avanti *sic*. (1924) 'Shakespir dybom' [Shakespeare Upside Down] *Bil'shovyk* [Kyiv] 76 (974), 4 April.

Avdieva, I. (1969) 'Pro naikrashchu liudyny, iaku ia znala v iunats'ki roky' [About the best person, whom I knew in my youth], in V. Vasyl'ko (ed.) *Les' Kurbas: spohady suchasnykiv* [Les' Kurbas: Memoirs of his Contemporaries], Kyiv: Mystetstvo.

Bakhtin, M. M. (1981) 'Discourse in the Novel', in *The Dialogic Imagination: Four Essays*, ed. M. Holquist, trans. C. Emerson and M. Holquist, Austin: University of Texas Press.

—— (1984) *Rabelais and His World*, trans. Hélène Iswolsky, Bloomington, IN: Indiana University Press.

—— (1986) 'Response to a Question from *Novy Mir*', in *Speech Genres and Other Late Essays*, trans. V. W. McGee, eds C. Emerson and M. Holquist, Austin, TX: University of Texas Press.

Banu, G. (1977) 'L'écriture spatiale de la mise en scène', *Les voies de la création théâtrale*, vol. 5, Paris: CNRS.

—— (1987) *Mémoires du théâtre*, Arles: Actes Sud.

Barker, F. (1984) *The Tremulous Private Body: Essays on Subjection*, London: Methuen.

Bate, J. (1989) *Shakespearean Constitutions: Politics, Theatre, Criticism 1730–1830*, Oxford: Clarendon Press.

Baudrillard, J. (1981) *For a Critique of the Political Economy of the Sign*, St. Louis, MO: Telos Press.

—— (1988) *Selected Writings*, ed. M. Poster, Stanford, CA: Stanford University Press.

Benedetti, J. (1988) *Stanislavski*, London: Routledge.

Benjamin, W. (1968) 'Theses on the Philosophy of History', in *Illuminations*, ed. H. Arendt, trans. H. Zohn, New York: Schocken.

Bennett, B. (1990) *Theatre as Problem: Modern Drama and Its Place in Literature*, Ithaca, NY: Cornell University Press.

Bennett, S. (1996) *Performing Nostalgia: Shifting Shakespeare and the Contemporary Past*, London: Routledge.

Bensman, J. (1983) 'Introduction: The Phenomenology and Sociology of the Performing Arts', in J. Kamerman (ed.) *Performers and Performances; The Social Organization of Artistic Work*, New York: Praeger.

Berman, A. (1985) *Les Tours de Babel: essais sur la traduction*, Mauvezin: Trans-Europ-Repress.

Berry, R. (1989) *On Directing Shakespeare: Interviews with Contemporary Directors*, London: Hamish Hamilton.

Blayney, P. W. M. (1997) 'The Publication of Playbooks', in J. D. Cox and D. S. Kastan (eds) *A New History of Early English Drama*, New York: Columbia University Press.

Bloom, H. (1998) *Shakespeare: The Invention of the Human*, New York: Riverhead.

Bogdanov, M. and Pennington, M. (1990) *The English Shakespeare*

Company: The Story of 'The Wars of the Roses' 1986–1989, London: Nick Hern Books.

Bonnefoy, Y. (1988) 'Un acte de poésie', *La Croix/L'Evénement*, 10–11 July.

Borgmann, A. (1984) *Technology and the Character of Contemporary Life*, Chicago: University of Chicago Press.

Bourdieu, P. (1972) *Esquisse d'une théorie de la pratique*, Genève: Droz.

—— (1993) 'The Field of Cultural Production, or: The Economic World Reversed', in R. Johnson (ed.) *The Field of Cultural Production: Essays on Art and Literature*, Cambridge: Polity Press.

Branswell, H. (1990) 'Witty, Bawdy Play Takes Some License With Shakespeare', *The Chronicle-Herald*, 7 February.

Brecht, B. (1964a) *Brecht on Theatre*, ed. and trans. J. Willett, New York: Hill and Wang.

—— (1964b) 'Study of the First Scene of Shakespeare's "Coriolanus"', in J. Willett (ed. and trans.) *Brecht on Theatre*, New York: Hill and Wang.

—— (1965) *The Messingkauf Dialogues*, trans. J. Willett, London: Methuen.

—— (1979) *Diaries 1920–1922*, ed. H. Ramthun, trans. and annotated by J. Willett, London: Eyre Methuen.

—— (1988–99) *Werke. Große kommentierte Berliner und Frankfurter Ausgabe* (*GBFA*), 30 vols, ed. W. Hecht, J. Knopf, W. Mittenzwei, and K.-D. Müller, Berlin and Weimar: Aufbau; Frankfurt: Suhrkamp.

—— (1993) *Bertolt Brecht: Journals 1934–1955*, trans. H. Rorrison, ed. J. Willett, London: Methuen.

Bristol, M. D. (1990) *Shakespeare's America, America's Shakespeare*, London: Routledge.

—— (1996) *Big-Time Shakespeare*, London: Routledge.

Brook, P. (1974) 'Interview with Peter Brook', *Timon d'Athènes*, trans. J.-C. Carrière, notes by J.-P. Vincent, Paris: C.I.C.T.

—— (1974–1975) Interview for *Shakespeare et Peter Brook*, broadcast prepared by Isidoro Romero, Richard Merienstras, and Peter Brook for the National Audiovisual Institute.

Brydon, D. (1993) 'Sister Letters: Miranda's *Tempest* in Canada', in M. Novy (ed.) *Cross-Cultural Performances: Differences in Women's Re-Visions of Shakespeare*, Urbana, IL: University of Illinois Press.

Bürger, P. (1984) *Theory of the Avant-Garde*, Minneapolis, MN: University of Minneapolis Press.

Burke, K. (1969) *A Grammar of Motives*, Berkeley, CA: University of California Press.

Butler, J. (1997) *Excitable Speech: A Politics of the Performative*, New York: Routledge.

Carlson, M. (1993) *Theories of the Theatre: A Historical and Critical Survey, from the Greeks to the Present*, expanded edn, Ithaca, NY: Cornell University Press.

Carlson, S. (1991) *Women and Comedy: Rewriting the British Theatrical Tradition*, Ann Arbor, MI: University of Michigan Press.

Carrière, J.-C. (trans.) (1974) *Timon d'Athènes*, notes by J.-P. Vincent, Paris: C.I.C.T.

—— (1982) 'Naviguer au plus près', Interview with Georges Banu, *théâtre/public* 44, March–April.

—— (1985) 'De la traduction au jeu', *Les voies de la création théâtral*, vol. 13, Paris: CNRS.

Chambers, C. (1980) *Other Spaces: New Theatre and the RSC*, London: Eyre Methuen and TQ Publications..

Charitou, I. (1993) 'Questions of Survival: Towards a Postmodern Feminist Theatre: Interview with Deborah Levy', *New Theatre Quarterly* 39, 35: 225–30.

Cima, G. G. (1983) 'Discovering Signs: The Emergence of the Critical Actress in Ibsen', *Theatre Journal* 35: 5–22.

Clark, T. J. (1985) *The Painting of Modern Life*, London: Thames and Hudson.

Clayton, J. D. (1994) *Pierrot in Petrograd: the Commedia dell'arte/Balagan in Twentieth-Century Russian Theatre and Drama*, Montreal: McGill-Queen's University Press.

Coveney, M. (1986) review of *Heresies*, *Financial Times*, 17 December.

Cox, J. D. and Kastan, D. S. (eds) (1997) *A New History of Early English Drama*, New York: Columbia University Press.

Crowl, S. (1992) *Shakespeare Observed: Studies in Performance on Stage and Screen*, Athens, OH: Ohio University Press.

Crowther, P. (1993) 'Postmodernism in the Visual Arts: A Question of Ends', in T. Docherty (ed.) *Postmodernism: A Reader*, New York: Columbia University Press.

Davis, T. C. (1991) *Actresses As Working Women: Their Social Identity In Victorian Culture*, London: Routledge.

de Grazia, M. (1995) 'Soliloquies and Wages in the Age of Emergent Consciousness', *Textual Practice* 9, 1: 67–92.

Delay, F. (1982) 'Le traducteur de verre', interview with Georges Banu, *théâtre/public* 44, March–April: 25–9.

Derrida, J. (1982) 'Signature Event Context', in *Margins of Philosophy*, trans. A. Bass, Chicago: University of Chicago Press.

Desniak, V. (1925) 'Berezil' ', *Hlobus* [Kyiv] 5: 116–19.

Docherty, T. (1993) 'Postmodernism: An Introduction', in T. Docherty (ed.) *Postmodernism: A Reader*, New York: Columbia University Press.

Dunderdale, S. (1984) 'The Status of Women in British Theatre Survey', *Drama* 152: 9–11.

Eagleton, T. (1988) 'Afterword', in G. Holderness (ed.) *The Shakespeare Myth*, Manchester: Manchester University Press.

—— (1996) *The Illusions of Postmodernism*, Oxford: Blackwell.

Eaton, K. B. (1985) *The Theatre of Meyerhold and Brecht*, London: Greenwood Press.

Eliot, T. S. (1932) 'Hamlet and his Problems', in T. S. Eliot, *Selected Essays: 1917–32*, New York: Harcourt.

—— (1949) Introduction to G. W. Knight, *The Wheel of Fire: Interpretation of Shakespeare's Tragedy*, 4th edn, London: Methuen.

—— (1922) 'London Letter', *The Dial* 73, 6: 659–62.

Elsom, J. (ed.) (1989) *Is Shakespeare Still Our Contemporary*, London: Routledge.

Evans, G. B. (textual edn) (1974) *The Riverside Shakespeare*, Boston, MA: Houghton Mifflin.

Evans, G. B. and J. J. M. Tobin (eds) (1997) *The Riverside Shakespeare*, 2nd edn, Boston, MA: Houghton Mifflin.

Eysteinsson, A. (1990) *The Concept of Modernism*, Ithaca, NY: Cornell University Press.

Fairchilds, C. (1993) 'The Production and Marketing of Populuxe Goods in Eighteenth-Century Paris', in J. Brewer and R. Porter (eds) *Consumption and the World of Goods*, London: Routledge.

Felperin, H. (1972) *Shakespearean Romance*, Princeton, NJ: Princeton University Press.

Fish, S. (1995) *Professional Correctness: Literary Studies and Political Change*, Oxford: Clarendon Press.

Flannery, J. W. (1976) *W. B. Yeats and the Idea of a Theatre: The Early Abbey Theatre in Theory and Practice*, New Haven, CT: Yale University Press.

Foucault, M. (1983) 'Structuralism and Post-structuralism: An Interview With Michel Foucault', by G. Raulet, *Telos* 55: 195–211.

Foster, H. (ed.) (1983) *The Anti-Aesthetic: Essays on Postmodern Culture*, Port Townsend, WA: Bay Press.

Frank, J. (1945) 'Spatial Form in Modern Literature', *The Sewanee Review* 53: 221–40, 433–56, and 643–53.

G-tov, A. (1924) 'Kul'tura i iskusstvo *Makbeta* u Kurbasa', *Khar'kovskii proletarii* [Kharkiv] 37, 30 May: 6.

Gardiner, M. (1992) *The Dialogics of Critique: M.M. Bakhtin and the Theory of Ideology*, London: Routledge.

Gardner, H. (1982) *In Defence of the Imagination*, Cambridge, MA: Harvard University Press.

Gilder, R. (1965) *John Gielgud's Hamlet; A Record of Performance*, Freeport, NY: Books for Libraries.

Goodman, L. (1993) *Contemporary Feminist Theatres: To Each Her Own*, London: Routledge.

Goodman, L. and Wandor, M. (1986) *Carry On, Understudies: Theatre and Sexual Politics*, rev. edn, London: Routledge.

Grady, H. (1991) *The Modernist Shakespeare: Critical Texts in a Material World*, Oxford: Clarendon Press.

—— (1993) 'Containment, Subversion – and Postmodernism', *Textual Practice* 7, 1.

—— (1996) *Shakespeare's Universal Wolf: Studies in Early Modern Reification*, Oxford: Clarendon Press.

Green, M. and Swan, J. (1986) *The Triumph of Pierrot: The Commedia dell'arte and the Modern Imagination*, New York: Macmillan.

Greenblatt, S. (1980) *Renaissance Self-Fashioning: From More to Shakespeare*, Chicago: University of Chicago Press.

—— (1985) 'Invisible Bullets: Renaissance Authority and its Subversion', in J. Dollimore and A. Sinfield (eds) *Political Shakespeare: New Essays in Cultural Materialism*, Ithaca, NY: Cornell University Press.

—— (1988) *Shakespearean Negotiations: The Circulation of Social Energy in Renaissance England*, Berkeley, CA: University of California Press.

Greenfield, J. (1997) 'Timber Framing, The Two Bays and After', in J. R. Mulryne and M. Shewring (eds) *Shakespeare's Globe Rebuilt*, Cambridge: Cambridge University Press, in Association with Mulryne and Shewring, Ltd.

Greg, W. W. (1955) *The Shakespeare First Folio*, Oxford: Clarendon Press.

Grumberg, J.-C. (trans.) (1988) *Three Sisters*, Paris: Actes Sud, Papiers.

Gunter, J. L. and McLean, A. W. (eds) (1998) *Redefining Shakespeare: Literary Theory and Theatre Practice in the German Democratic Republic*, Newark, DE: University of Delaware Press; London: Associated University Presses.

Gurr, A. (1997) 'Shakespeare's Globe: A History of Reconstructions and Some Reasons for Trying', in J. R. Mulryne and M. Shewring (eds) *Shakespeare's Globe Rebuilt*, Cambridge: Cambridge University Press, in Association with Mulryne and Shewring, Ltd.

Habermas, J. (1979) *Knowledge and Human Interests*, trans. J. Shapiro, Boston, MA: Beacon.

—— (1983) 'Modernity – an Incomplete Project', in H. Foster (ed.) *The Anti-Aesthetic: Essays on Postmodern Culture*, Port Townsend, WA: Bay Press.

Hall, P. (1983) *Peter Hall's Diaries: The Story of a Dramatic Battle*, ed. J. Goodwin, London: Hamish Hamilton.

Halpern, R. (1997) *Shakespeare Among the Moderns*, Ithaca, NY: Cornell University Press.

Harbage, A. (ed.) (1969) *William Shakespeare: The Complete Works*, Baltimore, MD, Penguin.

Hassan, I. (1993) 'Toward a Concept of Postmodernism', in T. Docherty (ed.) *Postmodernism: A Reader*, New York: Columbia University Press.

Havel, V. (1992) 'The End of the Modern Era', *The New York Times*, 1 March, 1992, International Edition, sec. 4, p.15.

Hawkes, T. (1973) *Shakespeare's Talking Animals: Language and Drama in Society*, London: Arnold.

Heinemann, M. (1985) 'How Brecht Read Shakespeare', in J. Dollimore and A. Sinfield (eds) *Political Shakespeare: New Essays in Cultural Materialism*, Ithaca, NY: Cornell University Press.

Hine, T. (1986) *Populuxe*, New York: Knopf.

Hirniak, Y. (1982) *Spomyny*, New York: Suchasnist'.

Hobson, H., Howell, J., Wardle, I. and Calder, J (1970) 'A Discussion with Edward Bond', *Gambit* 17, 5: 5–37.

Horkheimer, M. and Adorno, T. (1977) *Dialectic of Enlightenment*, trans. J. Cumming, New York: Seabury.

Hortman, W. (1998) *Shakespeare on the German Stage: the Twentieth Century*, Cambridge: Cambridge University Press.

Horwitz, T. (1998) *Confederates in the Attic: Dispatches from the Unfinished Civil War*, New York: Pantheon.

Hutcheon, L. (1989) 'Modern Parody and Bakhtin', in G. S. Morson and C. Emerson (eds) *Rethinking Bakhtin: Extensions and Challenges*, Evanston, IL: Northwestern University Press.

Huyssen, A. (1986) *After the Great Divide: Modernism, Mass Culture, Postmodernism*, Bloomington, IN: Indiana University Press.

I., I. (1924) 'Beseda s rukovoditelem *Berezilia* L. Kurbasom'

188 Bibliography

[A Conversation with the Leader of Berezil', L. Kurbas] *Teatral'naia gazeta* [Kharkiv] 18, 20–26 May: n.p.

Ilnytzkyj, O. S. (1983) 'Ukranian Futurism, 1914–1930: History, Theory and Practice', unpublished Ph.D. dissertation, Harvard University.

—— (1997) *Ukranian Futurism, 1919–1930: History, Theory, and Practice*, Cambridge, MA: Harvard University Press for the Ukranian Research Institute.

Ingram, W. (1992) *The Business of Playing: The Beginnings of the Adult Professional Theater in Elizabethan London*, Ithaca, NY: Cornell University Press.

Iura, H. (1934) 'Natsionalistychna estetyka Kurbasa' [The Nationalistic Aesthetic of Kurbas], *Za markso-lenins'ku krytyku* [For a Marxist-Leninist Criticism], [Kyiv] 12, December: 48–61.

Jameson, F. (1991) *Postmodernism, or, The Cultural Logic of Late Capitalism*, Durham, NC: Duke University Press.

—— (1998) *Brecht and Method*, London: Verso.

Jenkins, H. (ed.) (1982) *Hamlet*, The Arden Shakespeare, London: Methuen.

Jones, W. G. (1993) 'Blok and Meyerhold, 1905–1917', in D. J. George and C. J. Gossip (eds) Studies in the Commedia dell'Arte, Cardiff: University of Wales Press.

Jonson, B. (1960) *Bartholomew Fair*, ed. E. A. Horsman, Revels Plays, London: Methuen.

Jourdheuil (1982) 'De quoi parlions-nous?', interview with Georges Banu *théâtre/public* 44, March–April: 35.

Kastan, D. S. (1999) *Shakespeare after Theory*, New York: Routledge.

Kennedy, D. (1993) *Looking at Shakespeare: A Visual History of Twentieth-Century Performance*, Cambridge: Cambridge University Press.

—— (1998) 'Shakespeare and Cultural Tourism', *Theatre Journal* 50: 175–88.

Kermode, F. (1999) 'Writing About Shakespeare', *London Review of Books* 21, 24.

Kirshenblatt-Gimblett, B. (1977) 'Afterlives', *Performance Research* 2, 2: 1–9.

Kleberg, L. (1990) *Theatre as Action: Soviet Russian Avant-Garde Aesthetics*, trans. C. Rougle, Houndsmill, Basingstoke: Macmillan.

Knowles, R. (1996) 'Shakespeare, Voice, and Ideology: Interrogating the Natural Voice', in J. C. Bulman (ed.) *Shakespeare, Theory, and Performance*, London: Routledge.

—— (1998a) 'Carnival and Death in *Romeo and Juliet*', in R. Knowles (ed.) *Shakespeare and Carnival After Bakhtin*, Houndsmill, Basingstoke: Macmillan.

—— (1998b) *Shakespeare and Carnival After Bakhtin*, Houndsmill, Basingstoke: Macmillan.

Koltès, B.-M. (trans.) (1988) *Le conte d'hiver*, Paris: Editions de Minuit.

Kosach, I. (1973) *Dushi liuds'koi charodii* [The Magician of the Soul], Kyiv: Veselka.

Kott, J. (1964) *Shakespeare Our Contemporary*, ed. B. Taborski, London, Methuen.

Kryha, I. (1969) 'Samobutnii pedahoh' [The Original Pedagogue], in V. Vasyl'ko (ed.) *Les' Kurbas: spohady suchasnykiv* [Les' Kurbas: Memoirs of his Contemporaries], Kyiv: Mystetstvo.

Kucherenko, V. (1975) *Vadym Meller, 1884–1962*, Kyiv: Mystetstvo.

Kuhn, T. S. (1962) *The Structure of Scientific Revolutions*, Chicago: University of Chicago Press.

Kurbas, L. (1923) '*Berezil*'', rpt. in M. Labins'kyi (ed.) *Berezil': Les' Kurbas, iz tvorchoi spadshchyny* [Berezil: Les' Kurbas from his Creative Legacy], Kyiv: Dnipro, 1988.

—— (1924) 'Do postanovky "Makbeta" v 4 maisterni M.O.B. (rozmova z Kurbasom)' [About the Production of *Macbeth* in the Berezil Artistic Association Fourth Studio (A Conversation with Kurbas)], *Bil'shovyk* [Kyiv] 1 April: n.p.

—— (1925a) '*Berezil*' i teperishni ioho dosiahnennia shcho do teatral'noi formy', [The Berezil' Artistic Association and Its Current Achievements in the Theatrical Form], *Hlobus* [Kyiv] 5: 118–20.

—— (1925b) 'Shliakhy i zavdannia *Berezolia*' [The Aims and Directions of Berezil'], rpt. in M. Labins'kyi (ed.) *Berezil': Les' Kurbas, iz tvorchoi spadshchyny* [Berezil: Les' Kurbas from his Creative Legacy], Kyiv: Dnipro, 1988.

—— (1925c) 'Z pryvodu symptomiv reaktsii' [Apropos the Symptoms of a Reaction], rpt. in M. Labins'kyi (ed.) *Berezil': Les' Kurbas, iz tvorchoi spadshchyny* [Berezil: Les' Kurbas from his Creative Legacy], Kyiv: Dnipro, 1988.

—— (1927) 'U teatral'ni spravi' [In a Theatrical Matter], rpt. in M. Labins'kyi (ed.) *Berezil': Les' Kurbas, iz tvorchoi spadshchyny* [Berezil: Les' Kurbas from his Creative Legacy], Kyiv: Dnipro, 1988.

Kuziakina, N. (1969) 'Ledi Makbet ta inshi' [Lady Macbeth and Others], *Vitchyzna* [Kyiv] 3: 190–8.

—— (1978) '*Makbet* Shekspira v postanovkakh Lesia Kurbasa'

[Shakespeare's *Macbeth* in the Productions of Les' Kurbas], in A. Z. Iufit (ed.) *P'esa i spektakľ* [The Play and the Spectacle], Leningrad: Gosudarstvennyi Institut teatra, muzyky i kinematografii.

Lassalle, J. (1982) 'Du bon usage de la jeste', interview with Georges Banu, *théâtre/public* 44, March–April: 11–13.

Lavaudant, G. (1984) Interview with J. P. A. Bernard and J. P. Saez, *Silex* 27–8.

Lenz, C., Greene, G., and Neely, C. (eds) (1980) *The Woman's Part: Feminist Criticism of Shakespeare*, Urbana, IL: University of Illinois Press.

Levine, L. (1988) *Highbrow/Lowbrow: The Emergence of Cultural Hierarchy in America*. Cambridge, MA: Harvard University Press.

Lichtenfels, P (1999) personal letter (email), 28 January.

Longhurst, D. (1988) '"You Base Football-player": Shakespeare in Contemporary Popular Culture', in G. Holderness (ed.) *The Shakespeare Myth*, Manchester: Manchester University Press.

Lyons, D. (1994) *Postmodernity*, Minneapolis, MN: University of Minnesota Press.

Lyotard, F. (1984) *The Postmodern Condition: A Report on Knowledge*, Minneapolis, MN: University of Minnesota Press.

MacDonald, A.-M. (1990) *Goodnight Desdemona (Good Morning Juliet)*, Toronto: Playwrights Canada Press.

Maher, M. Z. (1992) *Modern Hamlets and Their Soliloquies*, Iowa City, IA: University of Iowa Press.

Makaryk, I. R. (2000) '*Macbeth* and the Birth of a Nation', in A. L. Magnusson and T. E. McGee (eds) *Elizabethan Theatre XVI*, Waterloo: P. D. Meany.

Marienstras, R. (1977) 'La représentation et l'interprétation du texte', [*Timon of Athens* by Shakespeare and its production by Peter Brook], *Les voies de la création théâtrale*, vol. 5, Paris: CNRS.

Marowitz, C. (1975) *The Shrew*, London: Calder and Boyars.

—— (1991) *Recycling Shakespeare*, London: Macmillan.

Marx, K. and Engels, F. (1974) *The Manifesto of the Communist Party*, in K. Marx, *Political Writings*, vol. 1, *The Revolutions of 1848*, ed. D. Fernbach. New York: Vintage.

Maus, K. E. (1995) *Inwardness and Theater in the English Renaissance*, Chicago: University of Chicago Press.

Mazer, C. M. (1981) *Shakespeare Refashioned: Elizabethan Plays on Edwardian Stages*, Ann Arbor, MI: UMI Research Press.

McCullough, C. (1988) interview with Terry Hands, in G. Holderness (ed.) *The Shakespeare Myth*, Manchester: Manchester University Press.

Mesguich, D. and Vittoz, M. (1977) Interview with Daniel Bougnoux, Gilles Liporetsky and André Targe, *Silex* 3: 13–35.

Meyerhold, V. (1969) 'The Fairground Booth', in E. Braun (trans. and ed.) *Meyerhold on Theatre*, London: Eyre Methuen.

Millon, M. (1975) 'Entretien avec Peter Brook', *Travail théâtral* 18–19, January–June.

—— (1985) '*Mesure pour mesure*: les options de la traduction', *Les voies de la création théâtrale*, vol. 13, Paris: CNRS.

Mohylians'kyi, M. (1924) '*Macbeth* u Berezoli' [*Macbeth* at Berezil], *Chervonyi shliakh* [Kharkiv] 4–5, April–May: 282–3.

Morand, E. and Schwob, M. (trans.) (1986) *Hamlet*, Paris: Gérard Lebovici Editions.

Muir, K. (ed.) (1960) *Macbeth*, The Arden Shakespeare, London, Methuen.

Mulryne, J. R., and Shewring, M. (eds) (1997) *Shakespeare's Globe Rebuilt*, Cambridge: Cambridge University Press, in Association with Mulryne and Shewring, Ltd.

Oliver, H. J. (ed.) (1963) *Timon of Athens*, The Arden Shakespeare, London: Methuen.

Olivier, L. (1948) 'Foreword', in A. Dent (ed.) *Hamlet, The Film and the Play*, London: World Film Publications.

—— (1986) *On Acting*, London: Weidenfeld and Nicolson.

Orrell, J. (1997) 'Designing the Globe', in J. R. Mulryne and M. Shewring (eds) *Shakespeare's Globe Rebuilt*, Cambridge: Cambridge University Press, in Association with Mulryne and Shewring, Ltd.

Owens, C. (1983) 'The Discourse of Others: Feminists and Postmodernism', in H. Foster (ed.) *The Anti-Aesthetic: Essays on Postmodern Culture*, Port Townsend, WA: Bay Press.

Pafford, J. H. P. (ed.) (1966) *The Winter's Tale*, The Arden Shakespeare, London, Methuen.

Pannwitz, R. (1947) *Die Krisis der europäischen Kultur*, Nüremberg.

Parker, A, and Sedgwick, E. K. (1995) Introduction, in A. Parker and E. K. Sedgwick (eds) *Performativity and Performance*, New York: Routledge.

Parks, S.-L. (1995) *The America Play and Other Works*, New York: Theatre Communications Group.

—— (1997) *Venus*, New York: Theatre Communications Group.

Parrish, S. (1984) 'The Status of Women in the British Theatre,

1982–1983', report presented at the Conference of Women Directors and Administrators, London, January.

Pascal, J. (1985) *City Limits*, 25–31 October.

Peak, C. (1999) personal letter (email), 25 January.

Peter, J. (1986) 'Dancing to the Music of Drama', review of *Heresies*, *The Sunday Times*, 21 December.

Pézard, A. (trans. and ed.) (1965) *The Inferno*, in Dante, *Oeuvres complètes*, Pléiade 182, Paris: Gallimard.

Pfister, M. (1992) 'Carnival and History: *Henry IV*', in G. Holderness (ed.) *Shakespeare Recycled: The Making of Historical Drama*, London: Harvester Wheatsheaf.

—— 'Comic Subversion: A Bakhtinian View of the Comic in Shakespeare', *The Shakespeare Yearbook* 27–43.

Planchon, R. (1977) Interview with Jean-François Halté and Charles Tordjman, *Pratiques* 15–16, July 1977.

Pylypenko, N. (1968) *Zhyttia v teatri*, New York: n.p.

Quigley, A. E. (1985) *The Modern Stage and Other Worlds*, London: Methuen.

Quinones, R. J. (1985) *Mapping Literary Modernism: Time and Development*, Princeton, NJ: University of Princeton Press.

Revutsky, V. (ed.) (1989) *Les' Kurbas u teatral'nii dial'nosti, v otsinkakh suchasnykiv* [Les' Kurbas's Theatrical Activities, in the Valuation of his Contemporaries], Baltimore, MD: Smoloskyp.

Risset, J. (trans.) (1985) *L'Enfer*, Paris: Flammarion.

Roach, J. (1992) 'Mardi Gras Indians and Others: Genealogies of American Performance', *Theatre Journal* 44: 461–83.

—— (1996) *Cities of the Dead: Circum-Atlantic Performance*, New York: Columbia University Press.

Rokem, F. (1998) discussion session: Shakespeare's Globe Theatre, Performance Analysis Working Group and Historiography Working Group Joint Session, International Federation for Theatre Research/Fédération Internationale pour Recherches Théâtrales World Congress, Canterbury, 6 July.

Romeo and Juliet (1998) dir. Peter Lichtenfels, Department of Theatre and Dance, University of California, Davis, 5 December.

Rouse, J. (1989) *Brecht and the West German Theatre: The Practice and Politics of Interpretation*, Ann Arbor, MI: U.M.I. Research Press.

—— (1992) 'Textuality and Authority in Theater and Drama: Some Contemporary Possibilities', in J. G. Reinelt and J. R. Roach (eds) *Critical Theory and Performance*, Ann Arbor, MI: University of Michigan Press.

Rudnitsky, K. (1988) *Russian and Soviet Theatre: Tradition and the Avant-Garde*, trans. R. Permar, New York: Thames and Hudson.

Said, E. W. (1983) 'Opponents, Audiences, Constituencies and Community', in H. Foster (ed.) *The Anti-Aesthetic: Essays on Postmodern Culture*, Port Townsend, WA: Bay Press.

Salter, D. (1996) 'Acting Shakespeare in Postcolonial Space', in J. C. Bulman (ed.) *Shakespeare, Theory, and Performance*, London: Routledge.

Samiilenko, P. (1970) *Nezabutni dni horin'* [Unforgettable Shining Days], Kyiv: Mystetstvo.

—— (1924) 'Vid "Molodoho teatru" do "Berezolia"' [From the Young Theatre to Berezil'], *Literatura i mystetstvo, Visti VUTSVK* [Kharkiv], 16 May.

Schapiro, M. (1937) 'The Nature of Abstract Art', *Marxist Quarterly* 1, 1: 77–98.

Schechner, R. (1982) 'Collective Reflexivity: Restoration of Behavior', in J. Ruby (ed.) *A Crack in the Mirror: Reflexive Perspectives in Anthropology*, Philadelphia, PA: University of Pennsylvania Press.

Schoch, R. W. (1998) *Shakespeare's Victorian Stage: Performing History in the Theatre of Charles Kean*, Cambridge: Cambridge University Press.

Semenko, M. (1924) 'Mystetstvo iak kult' [Art as a Cult], *Chervonyi shliakh* 3: 222–9.

Shakespeare, W. (1998) *The First Quarto of Hamlet*, ed. K. O. Irace, Cambridge: Cambridge University Press.

Shaw, G. B. (1961) *Shaw on Shakespeare: An Anthology of Bernard Shaw's Writings on the Plays and Production of Shakespeare*, ed. E. Wilson, New York: Dutton.

Sheren, P. (1971) 'Three Experimental Macbeths', *NTQ* 1.3: 45.

Shevchenko, I. (1929) *Suchasnyi ukrains'kyi teatr* [The Contemporary Ukranian Theatre], Kharkiv: Derzhavne vydavnytstvo Ukrainy.

Shkandrij, M. (1992) *Modernists, Marxists and the Nation: The Ukranian Literary Discussion of the 1920s*, Edmonton: CIUS.

Shmain, K. (1969) 'Rezhyser, pedahoh, uchenyi' [Director, Pedagogue, Scholar], in V. Vasyl'ko (ed.) *Les' Kurbas: spohady suchasnykiv* [Les' Kurbas: Memoirs of his Contemporaries], Kyiv: Mystetstvo.

Shulman, M. (1986) 'Naïve Feminist Notions', review of *Heresies, Evening Standard*, 17 December.

Sinfield, A. (1985) 'Royal Shakespeare: Theatre and the Making of Ideology', in J. Dollimore and A. Sinfield (eds) *Political Shakespeare:*

New Essays in Cultural Materialism, Ithaca, NY: Cornell University Press.

—— (1992) *Faultlines: Cultural Materialism and the Practice of Dissident Reading*, Berkeley, CA: University of California Press.

Sloterdijk, P. (1987) *Critique of Cynical Reason*, trans. M. Eldred, foreword A. Huyssen, Minneapolis, MN: University of Minnesota Press.

Smith, D. E. (1990) *Conceptual Practices of Power*, Toronto: University of Toronto Press.

Smolych, I. (1977) *Pro teatr* [About Theatre], Kyiv: Mystetstvo.

Stallybrass, P. and White, A. (1986) *The Politics and Poetics of Transgression*, London: Methuen.

Stead, P. (1991) *Richard Burton: So Much, So Little*, Bridgend: Poetry Wales Press Ltd.

Steshenko, I. (1969) 'Pro navchytelia moho i druha', in V. Vasyl'ko (ed.) *Les' Kurbas: spohady suchasnykiv* [Les' Kurbas: Memoirs of his Contemporaries], Kyiv: Mystetstvo.

Stowell, S. (1992) 'Rehabilitating Realism', *Journal of Dramatic Theory and Criticism* 6, 2: 81–8.

Styan, J. L. (1977) *The Shakespeare Revolution: Criticism and Performance in the Twentieth Century*, Cambridge: Cambridge University Press.

Taylor, C. (1994) *Multiculturalism: Examining the Politics of Recognition*, ed. and intro. A. Gutman, Princeton, NJ: Princeton University Press.

Taylor, G. (1991) *Reinventing Shakespeare A Cultural History from the Restoration to the Present*, New York: Oxford University Press.

Thomas, A. (1986) 'Hand [*sic*] up in Arms at RSC Women's Attack', *Stage and Television Today*, 10 April.

Thomas, M. W. (1992) 'Kemp's Nine Daies Wonder: Dancing Carnival into Market', *PMLA* 107: 511–23.

Thomson, P. (1997) 'Rogues and Rhetoricians: Acting Styles in Early English Drama', in J. D. Cox and D. S. Kastan (eds) *A New History of Early English Drama*, New York: Columbia University Press.

Tkacz, V. (1983) 'Les [sic] Kurbas and the Creation of a Ukranian Avant-Garde Theatre', unpublished M.A. thesis, Columbia University.

—— (1990) 'Les [sic] Kurbas's Use of Film Language in his Stage Productions of *Jimmie Higgins* and *Macbeth*', *Canadian Slavonic Papers* 36, 1: 59–76.

Tokar, K. (1933) 'Desiat' let "Bereziliia"' [Ten Years of Berezil'], *Teatr i dramaturgiia* [Moscow] 4: 59–66.

Turkel'taub, I. (1924) 'Hastroli M. "Berezil" Ledi Makbet', *Kul'tura i mystetstvo, Visti VUTsVK* [Kharkiv] 121, 30 May.

van Dijk, M. (1990) 'Blocking Brecht', in P. Kleber and C. Visser (eds) *Re-interpreting Brecht: His Influence on Contemporary Drama and Film*, Cambridge: Cambridge University Press.

Vincent, J.-P. (1974) *Timon d'Athènes*, Paris: C.I.C.T.

Vitez, A. (1976), *Dialectiques* 14.

—— (1982) 'Le devoir de traduire', interview with Georges Banu, *théâtre/public* 44, March–April: 6–9.

—— (1988), *Libération* 2249, August 13 and August 14.

Vittoz, M. (trans.) (1977), *Silex* 3 [First Quarter].

—— (trans.) (1986) *Hamlet*, Paris: Papiers.

Vynnychenko, V. (1920) *Vidrodzhennia natsii* [The Renaissance of a Nation], vol. 1.

Warner, M. (1986) 'The Tragedy of Mrs Leah', review of *Heresies*, *Independent*, 18 December.

Weimann, R. (2000) *Author's Pen and Actor's Voice: Playing and Writing in Shakespeare's Theatre*, Cambridge: Cambridge University Press.

Werner, S. (1996) 'Performing Shakespeare: Voice Training and the Feminist Actor', *New Theatre Quarterly* 47: 249–58.

Weschler, L. (1999) *Boggs: A Comedy of Values*, Chicago: University of Chicago Press.

Wiles, D. (1987) *Shakespeare's Clown: Actor and Text in the Elizabethan Playhouse*, Cambridge: Cambridge University Press.

Williams, D. (1988) *Peter Brook: A Theatrical Casebook*, London: Methuen.

Williams, R. (1989) *The Politics of Modernism: Against the New Conformists*, London: Verso.

Wise, J. (1998) *Dionysus Writes: The Invention of Theatre in Ancient Greece*, Ithaca, NY: Cornell University Press.

Woddis, C. (1987) 'A Woman's Role', *Plays and Players* 409, October: 14–16.

Worthen, W. B. (1992) *Modern Drama and the Rhetoric of Theater*, Berkeley, CA: University of California Press.

—— (1997) *Shakespeare and the Authority of Performance*, Cambridge: Cambridge University Press.

—— (1998) 'Drama, Performativity, and Performance', *PMLA* 113: 1093–107.

—— (forthcoming) 'Reconstructing the Globe, Constructing Ourselves', *Shakespeare Survey*.

Yachnin, P. (forthcoming) 'The Populuxe Theatre', in A. Dawson and
    P. Yachnin (eds) *The Culture of Playgoing in Shakespeare's London.*
Zabolotna, V. (1992) *Aktors'ke mystetstvo Ukrainy (1922–1927)* [The
    Actor's Art in Ukraine, 1922–1927], Kyiv: Institut teatral'noho
    mystetstva im. K. Karoho.

Index